Starting Your Own
Online Business

Other titles in the Startups series

Bright Marketing for Small Business
How to Start a Successful Business
Starting Your Own Online Business
Starting Your Own Shop
Starting Your Own Restaurant
Start Your Own Coffee or Tea Shop
Start Your Own eBay or Amazon Business
Online Marketing for Small Business
Going Freelance
Taking on Staff
Business Plans for Small Businesses
Free Publicity for Small Businesses
Accounting for Small Business
Start Your Own Business 2011

Starting Your Own Online Business

Kim Benjamin

2nd edition

crimson

This second edition first published in Great Britain 2011 by
Crimson Publishing, a division of Crimson Business Ltd
Westminster House, Kew Road
Richmond
Surrey
TW9 2ND

First edition by Kim Benjamin published in 2009

A catalogue record for this book is available from the British Library.

ISBN 978 1 85458 554 7

Typeset by RefineCatch Limited, Bungay, Suffolk
Printed and bound by in the UK by Ashford Colour Press, Gosport, Hants

Contents

Contents

Profit and loss
VAT

VAT
Price changes
Accountants
Paying your staff

Introduction

D
o you want to be part of an industry with a potential customer base of 38 million with £5bn to spend? Starting an online business will give you access to this and more. Consumer habits have changed rapidly in recent years, with a greater number of people turning to the internet to shop for goods and services than ever before.

While traditional high street stores are still struggling to return to pre-recession levels, the online industry continues to defy such downward trends. Online sales figures in the UK reached a three-year high in July 2010, with the average consumer spending £81 on internet shopping.* This represents an 18% increase on the same month last year, the fastest rate of growth since before the recession. Meanwhile the size of the UK's online audience grew from 36.9 million people in May 2009 to 38.8 million just one year later.

The growth of social media, led by the likes of Facebook and Twitter, and the recent economic recession, have prompted an even greater number of people to go online, eager to spot a bargain or wanting to save time by accessing services online. With online sales now accounting for more than 15% of UK retail spending, there is no better time to start an online business. By 2020, some experts predict that 90% of transactions will take place online or be internet-influenced.

While this may seem like quite some time away, the pace at which the internet has matured and the development of technology means that the sooner you can get started, the more chance you have of taking advantage of new technologies and services. A greater number of businesses and individuals have turned to the internet to successfully launch and grow their products and services, following in the footsteps of internet behemoths Amazon, Play and Lastminute.

New business ideas can be hard to come by and even harder to execute, but the internet has provided a host of opportunities to help you kick-start and grow your business. If you are looking for new ideas for starting your own business, then modelling your business after an existing one online can help. Providing a product or service of a higher quality or for less money than a competitor is a great way to get ahead. Online businesses that cater specifically to a particular area can also make the best of their website by providing enhanced customer

---

* Figures from IMRG/CapGemini

service to customers in that area. You can even create a website and take in revenue from on site advertisements, and draw in users with entertainment media or helpful information.

While the future for e-commerce appears bright, you will not be the only one trying to make money online and the competition you will encounter will be far bigger and fiercer than in your local market. The greater visibility e-commerce offers will mean that many businesses can expand far beyond the limits of a physical store, but this has also created a market at risk of becoming saturated – your potential customer base could run into the millions and you will need to keep one step ahead of your rivals to ensure you attract and retain customers.

Online businesses, however, aren't just confined to the e-commerce model – there are opportunities and money to be made from web-based subscriptions and services, and more and more companies are recognising the potential of advertising on the web.

Whatever your motivation for starting your own online business, whether it be to simply achieve a better work–life balance or taking the first step towards rivalling the likes of Amazon and eBay, we've packed this book with practical hands-on advice for you to not just read, but act on. The book is structured to take you through the journey of starting an online business from concept to planning, from launching your website, raising finance, to finding suppliers and generating interest for your brand.

Case Studies

From the experts

- Reid Hoffman, LinkedIn
- Nick Robertson, ASOS
- Simon Nixon, moneysupermarket.com

These experts have been there and done it, and turned their online businesses into a sensation. Reid Hoffman launched LinkedIn in 2003 and has grown the online professional network into a massively profitable website with more than 80 million members in over 200 countries. Nick Robertson launched AsSeenOnScreen in 2000 (renamed ASOS in 2003), in an attempt to cash in on the public's desire for clothes and accessories worn by celebrities. Price comparison website moneysupermarket.com, founded in 1999 by Simon Nixon, has established itself as a leading online service enabling consumers to compare a wide range of products. Read about their experiences here, and benefit from their expert advice throughout the book.

In my experience

- Jamie Murray Wells, Glasses Direct
- Rowan Gormley, Naked Wines
- Lopo Champalimaud and Salim Mitha, Wahanda
- Mark Leather, Country Products

These businesses may not be national phenomena, but they are certainly well positioned to give their advice on starting an online business. Most have launched in the past five years, and are now well established within their communities. These are companies you should aspire to be like within a year of opening, and they've got some great advice to help you on the way.

From the experts

Company: **LinkedIn**
Owner-manager: **Reid Hoffman**
Type: **Social network**
Start year: **2003**

There's an old saying in business: it's not what you know but who you know. LinkedIn set out to make this a reality online, creating a site to help professionals connect to other like-minded individuals.

The site is the brainchild of Reid Hoffman, who grew up in Berkeley, California and had an interest in technology from an early age. Studying artificial intelligence and cognitive science at Stanford university. In the early 1990s, he gained a scholarship to Oxford University to study philosophy, but soon realised that he was more suited to technology rather than academia, prompting him to take jobs at technology companies, including Apple in 1994 and Fujitsu two years later.

This gave him a real taste for all things technology and in 1997 he quit his job at Fujitsu to set up Socialnet, one of the earliest versions of a social networking site. The aim was to build on the particular kinds of relationships that people have, from people they'd like to date to roommates, even meeting up with potential tennis and golf partners. The idea was to put users near the people they'd be interested in, but in an online environment. Just over two years later, however, Reid resigned from the company after a difference of opinion with the board on the direction in which the business was going.

But this didn't dent his ambitions to start another business, a desire he shared with his friend, Peter Thiel, who had studied with him at Stanford and who at the time was the chief executive and founder of internet payment system PayPal. Peter, however, persuaded him to join PayPal (Reid had been one of its board members since launch) as executive vice-president in charge of business development.

While at PayPal, Reid continued to be fascinated by how the internet accelerated the rate at which people did business and he wanted to explore how professional people could establish their profiles online so that other people could find them, effectively creating a network to enhance and further their careers.

It was to be a few years later, however, before Reid could capitalise on this idea, as he believed that it wasn't possible to perfect his business plan while he was still in another job. In 2002, PayPal was acquired by internet auction site eBay for $1.5bn and Reid received $10m for his share in the business. He now had the funds and the time to make his idea a reality. The economic climate was less than favourable, but Reid reasoned that there would be less competition and therefore more of a chance that his venture would stand out.

Reid recruited a team of people he had previously worked with and known from his college days, and whose experience and opinion he valued. Over several months, they met in Reid's living room and hatched the plan that was to become LinkedIn, with a business model based on a number of revenue streams, such as advertising and potentially subscriptions, and at its core, a valuable proposition for prospective members.

By May 2003, the founders felt confident enough to launch the site, which was unveiled on the 5th of that month. For a business network to be useful, though, it had to have business people registered for the service and using it.

Reid set himself the challenge of getting a million people to register for the site. The point of LinkedIn, where people could search for other members and share information meant the site had to have enough people signed up in order for it to be valuable. Right from the start, Reid planned to grow LinkedIn organically by word of mouth – it seemed the most cost-effective and efficient way to get members. The LinkedIn founders began by inviting 350 of their most important, well-connected and trusted contacts to join, encouraging them to get their friends and contacts to join, too.

This worked well. At the end of its first month in operation, LinkedIn had a total of 4,500 members in the network. Reid had also recruited staff members to work on the technical side, bringing the total number of employees to 13, and rented office space. The site encouraged members to connect with colleagues, clients and people they had worked with in the past. Connections were therefore based on the trust and experience of those individuals. Reid believed that this increased the value of people's network by focusing on existing connections in the real world, as opposed to the random connections that are common on some social networks.

Timing was also now on LinkedIn's side. When it launched, there were no other similar businesses in operation. Such was the nature of the internet, however, that it didn't take long for other professional networks to spring up, including the likes of Tribe and Friendster.

All of which was good news for LinkedIn as it was now looking to raise venture capital funds. Reid recalls how he was besieged by at least a dozen unsolicited knocks on his door from venture capitalists. At the end of October 2003, he ended up signing with Sequoia Capital, a leading venture capital firm whose support he'd targeted in the first place. LinkedIn secured $4.7m and by this time, the site was doubling in size every six weeks and had gained users in more than 80 countries and 120 industries.

As an increasing number of social networking sites emerged, many of them sought to introduce revenue models and LinkedIn was no different. In 2005, it introduced job listings and a subscription-based service, which offered users an enhanced search service, enabling people to connect to those they didn't know already. While advertising had not been part of the original business plan, Reid decided this would become the site's third revenue stream, as it had built up a demographic base that appealed strongly to advertisers. The self-selecting nature of LinkedIn's membership (it was targeting successful and ambitious professionals) would provide an opportunity for certain brands to reach their target audience in an efficient way. Just a year later LinkedIn announced it had turned a profit, with the lion's share of its money estimated to have come from its premium services, such as job listings.

LinkedIn may be one of the few businesses that has benefited and thrived in the recent recession. Rising levels of unemployment worldwide and a global, sagging economy caused by the credit crunch, have resulted in more and more people on the hunt for jobs, and for LinkedIn, this can only be good news. Today, the site has more than 80 million members in over 200 countries.

From the experts

Company: ASOS
Owner-manager: Nick Robertson
Type: Online fashion
Start year: 2000

Fashion and advertising are often viewed as two of the most glamorous industries to be involved in and Nick Robertson has had the good fortune to have worked in both. He began his career in the advertising industry, before moving on to the position of associate director for media planning business Carat UK in 1991.

In 2000, Nick co-founded Entertainment Marketing, which provided product placement within television and film for clients including Samsung, Honda, Sky and Tropicana. A natural progression emerged to bring celebrity lifestyle to the consumer and the idea for ASOS (formerly known as AsSeenOnScreen) was hatched in June that year. The original business plan was based on selling products and brands online (everything but clothes) enabling consumers to purchase products endorsed by celebrities.

Robertson raised just over £2m from friends and family, with the condition that the business would float on AIM (the stock market for smaller, growing companies) in the near future. 'Our business plan was written on the back of a cigarette packet but the exit strategy for our investors was a little more defined,' says Nick. 'Everybody does something for something, so when we raised the money, we ensured we had an exit plan for investors in place.'

He believes that two areas were significant to the business' growth. Uptake of broadband was on the increase and soon after launch, Robertson hired Lorri Penn, a fashion buyer who had worked at leading high street fashion retailer Topshop and who had an eye for spotting the latest celebrity trends. Penn approached suppliers to source clothes similar to those seen on celebrities, and according to Nick, this helped to move the business firmly into fashion, prompting the name change to ASOS. The site began to sell clothes that allowed consumers to emulate the style of celebrities like Victoria Beckham and Jennifer Aniston, but for a fraction of the cost.

'The key to our business plan was to be flexible and understanding – don't get into a market unless you understand it thoroughly,' says Nick. 'This was particularly true when we launched the business as the internet was evolving so quickly – we were changing our business model on a day-by-day, week-by-week basis.'

Getting the technology right was crucial too. 'We launched back in the days when technology could very often let you down. We spent a lot of money on the website and it took a long time for sales to catch up. I wasn't tech-savvy but I was fortunate enough to employ people who were.'

By 2003, the business had gone from strength to strength and broken even, with a turnover nudging £8m. Demand for the site's products continued to soar. But in December 2005, an explosion at the fuel depot next door to ASOS' warehouse dealt the business a serious blow, as the warehouse went up in flames, crippling the business over the crucial Christmas period. Nearly £4m worth of stock was destroyed and 19,000 orders had to be cancelled as they could not be fulfilled.

'Having our warehouse next to a fuel depot was probably not the smartest move. We closed the business for six weeks and had a holding page in place of the website, announcing a clearance sale,' recalls Nick. 'Having insurance and our customers' details was crucial – we emailed all our customers who were affected and gave them refunds – it's important to be transparent and keep in touch with customers when anything affects the business.'

The clearance sale attracted hordes of shoppers and ASOS has doubled its revenues every year since the fire. Nick believes the success of ASOS has been down to focusing on the brand and its products, as well as keeping issues such as logistics top of the agenda.

'Logistics is such an important part of an internet business – you simply can't fail in this area,' he says. 'If you know an order is not going to make it, you have to let the customer know. There is no point in driving traffic to a website if you are going to disappoint your customers.'

Surprisingly for an online brand, ASOS invests heavily in offline advertising, with press ads in women's weeklies targeted at its core market. This has certainly paid off as the site has 6.9 million unique visitors a month and 2.9 million registered users. In 2006, ASOS launched a monthly women's magazine, which now boasts a circulation of nearly 430,000. The business now offers more than 19,400 branded and own label product lines across womenswear, menswear, footwear, accessories, jewellery and beauty, with around 1,150 new product lines being introduced every week. Last year, it invested in social media with the launch of ASOS Life, a community site enabling its customers to talk about fashion, create profiles and make friends online.

'When it comes to managing the growth of an online retailer, fundamentally we have not done anything different to how traditional retailers would approach it,' believes Nick. 'The internet is still evolving and the key to a successful online business is to keep moving forward. Customers are fickle – if you evolve, customers will go with you. If you stagnate, they will go elsewhere.'

 From the experts

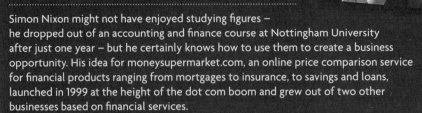

Company: **moneysupermarket.com**
Owner-manager: **Simon Nixon**
Type: **Price comparison**
Start year: **1999**

Simon Nixon might not have enjoyed studying figures –
he dropped out of an accounting and finance course at Nottingham University after just one year – but he certainly knows how to use them to create a business opportunity. His idea for moneysupermarket.com, an online price comparison service for financial products ranging from mortgages to insurance, to savings and loans, launched in 1999 at the height of the dot com boom and grew out of two other businesses based on financial services.

After taking the decision to leave university, Simon had the option of selling pensions and life insurance, but was not inspired by this prospect. Instead, he decided to specialise in mortgages and came up with the idea of teaming up with a local sales office, in order to get sales representatives to contact him directly to set up mortgages for their clients. While working on mortgage enquiries, he spotted a gap in the market – there was no easy way for mortgage brokers to compare deals that were available. He subsequently launched a fortnightly trade magazine, *Brokers Update*, in 1990, listing the best deals and products for reference. The magazine turned out to be a success, and a few months later, Simon was making more money from magazine subscriptions than from arranging mortgages. He decided to devote himself full time to the business, but within two years, subscriptions had started to dwindle as mortgage brokers were increasingly turning to technology as a source of finance information – it provided more immediate data than that contained in the magazine.

Quick to spot the next opportunity, Simon used funds generated by the magazine to write a software program that was updated daily over the internet, allowing brokers to enter criteria and find the most competitive mortgage. Software programmer and business partner Duncan Cameron came on board and the pair launched Mortgage 2000 in 1994.

Towards the end of the 1990s, internet access was increasing and broadband too was achieving higher levels of penetration. This led Simon to believe that the real money lay in offering the same kind of service to people who actually wanted mortgages rather than those selling them. Moneysupermarket.com was launched in 1999, and makes its money every time a consumer clicks on a link to a financial services provider. The business has never needed any external funding, as it grew from Simon's existing ventures, so many of the administrative and legal structures were already in place.

'The business evolved from the start, from small, to medium to big and we've never bitten off more than we can chew,' says Simon. 'It's been an evolution rather than a revolution and we've never sought external funding. If we'd had a big injection of cash, it would have meant taking a bigger risk. I never liked the idea of taking on venture capital as it would mean less control over the business.'

As the business grew, Simon took on researchers who specialised in personal finance to boost content and recruited internet developers to manage the technical side of the business. In the early years, moneysupermarket.com did not invest in any advertising, relying instead on press coverage, which Simon says was crucial to business growth. 'It's critical to have media coverage and PR. It can be a cost-effective way to drive traffic to your site as well as helping you with issues such as branding,' he says.

Technology also played an important part in business growth. In 2002, moneysupermarket. com developed technology that made the site faster and more efficient. When a consumer keyed in their details, the technology used enabled hundreds of sites to be searched, with the results being shown on one page. By 2003, the business had expanded into new markets, with insuresupermarket.com offering consumers the ability to compare insurance quotes in real time using technology that was also developed in-house. Travelsupermarket.com followed a year later, enabling consumers to search for and compare online flights and related travel products.

'Diversification has been critical to the business' growth and success,' believes Simon. 'We wanted to become the number one price comparison site, not just for money but for other areas too. We launched insurance first as it was related to money, followed by travel, home services and most recently shopping.'

Moneysupermarket.com floated on the stock market in 2007 at 170p a share, valuing the group at £843m and making Simon £102m in the process. Most recently, the site has been making use of web 2.0 technologies, such as blogs and forums. 'We invite comments from our customers and encourage them to visit forums,' says Simon.

The onset of the credit crunch in 2008, however, resulted in the company experiencing some tough times, and it suffered a drop in share price as well as increased competition from the likes of Tesco. In February 2009, Simon stepped down as chief executive of the business, to take on the role of executive deputy chairman. He retains 54% of the business and works one day a week at moneysupermarket.com, focusing on strategic innovation and development. This has enabled him to focus on other online interests and in June last year, he launched Simonseeks.com, a travel website that allows internet users to write about their holidays and get paid for it.

In my experience

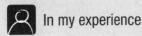

Company: Glasses Direct
Owner-manager: Jamie Murray Wells
Type: Online prescription glasses retailer
Start year: 2004

Glasses Direct was conceived with the aim of providing cut-price prescription glasses over the internet, allowing people to afford several pairs. The idea came to its founder, Jamie Murray Wells, while he was at university, when he found he needed a pair of reading glasses and was shocked at the price he would have to pay – £150. 'I chose a market that was getting to grips with the web,' says Jamie. 'The optical industry was one of the few sectors that had not yet made the move online, there was the precedent to build on this and do something different.'

His idea was simple. Instead of walking into a high street opticians and paying through the nose, simply enter your prescription on the internet, choose your frames, and Glasses Direct will supply you with your glasses, within a week, for just £19. 'I chose an online business model as it was the quickest way to reach as wide an audience as possible,' says Jamie. While the idea came to him fairly quickly, doing the research was another matter altogether. Jamie was met with a wall of silence from everyone across the optical industry when he tried to research the actual cost of making glasses. Each laboratory he called would not disclose any information on prices or supply.

On the brink of giving up on the idea, he called one more laboratory and got the information he needed. But that was just the start. Suppliers were equally reticent, and even when one was secured it withdrew its services only a matter of weeks after he launched Glasses Direct. This could have driven the company into the ground, but Jamie recognised that the industry opposition was based entirely on its price protectionism, and he was spurred to take them on.

The business was launched in the front room of his parents' house in 2004 and has gone from strength to strength, securing angel funding and a multimillion investment deal through venture capitalists in 2007. The business has recognised the importance of putting customers first and has strived to make the web experience as interactive as possible. 'We had a customer-oriented approach right from the beginning, which is important as the web can be quite anonymous,' says Jamie. 'We needed to make it more transparent and we're always looking at ways of making the website increasingly interactive.' An example of this includes a virtual mirror, which enables customers to upload photos and try glasses remotely.

Today Glasses Direct is the largest direct-seller of glasses in the world, selling a pair every three minutes around the clock and has achieved a multimillion pound turnover. The company estimates that it has saved the UK public in excess of £25m on their glasses.

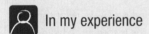

In my experience

Company: Naked Wines
Owner-manager: Rowan Gormley
Type: Online retailer
Start year: 2008

Originally from South Africa, Rowan Gormley spent seven years working in private equity in London before a chance meeting with Richard Branson led to him joining the Virgin Group in the mid-nineties. Branson put him in charge of his new financial services business Virgin Direct (now Virgin Money) which Rowan headed up from Norwich.

He then launched other brands for the Branson empire, including the Virgin One Account and then Virgin Wines, set up in 2000, a business he had launched separately a year previously under the name Orgasmic Wines. Branson was convinced that the venture could be a financial success and it was subsequently rebranded as part of Virgin.

'I'm a failed accountant – although I couldn't count, I eventually realised that I was quite good at starting new companies,' says Rowan.

Virgin Wines was eventually sold to competitor Laithwaites, prompting Rowan to set up his own wine business, together with 12 ex-employees of Virgin Wines. The business – Naked Wines – aims to champion independent winegrowers. Rowan launched the business in November 2008, with an undisclosed investment from German wine group WIV AG, which bought a majority stake. Every employee is a shareholder.

Rowan describes the company as a 'wine venture capital business', which sources talented winemakers who want to set up on their own but who need a helping hand financially.

Rowan had long thought that some of the most expensive famous wines available were mediocre, while some unknown winemakers were producing solid wines that few people had ever heard of, let alone tasted.

Potential customers are given the opportunity to become business angels for wine, and are known as Naked Angels. They pay a monthly subscription fee of £20, in return for discounts later on (33% cashback) which helps fund new small winegrowers.

'Instead of taking shares, we get their wine at cost price,' explains Rowan. 'Our dream is to build a business where wine drinkers get better wine for less money, and winemakers can focus on what they do best – making great wines.'

The website has also been designed with social networking in mind. Naked Wines was the first wine retailer to include user reviews and ratings of wine, in the same way that Amazon users rate books and other products. Rowan was determined to establish an active community for users and winegrowers to exchange ideas, enabling them to connect with other like-minded people. Customers can speak directly to the winemakers, and to other customers, so they can see if the wine is really as good as Naked Wines claims it is.

'We only charge our customers for the actual wine in the bottle and that means we have very slender margins, but it also means our customers are very loyal,' says Rowan. 'Our volumes are great and we end up making more money by charging customers the lowest possible price.'

Two years on from launch, the business has gone from strength to strength and has recruited in excess of 100,000 new customers, set up 22 winemakers in business and helped to create 55 new wines, exclusive to the business. Affiliate marketing has been key to gaining new customers. By offering customers who signed up to credit cards and broadband offers a free Naked trial, the business quickly gained traction and word of mouth momentum.

Rowan is now focusing on profitability and the possibility of shipping in Europe but is as passionate now as he was two years ago to improve the quality of wine and seek out the best independent winemakers.

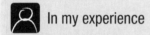
In my experience

Company: Wahanda.com
Owner-manager: Lopo Champalimaud and Salim Mitha
Type: Online health and beauty
Start year: 2008

The concept of spas – the practice of bathing in hot springs and minerals – dates back at least as far as the Babylonians and Greeks but two internet entrepreneurs have made it a far more modern proposition, with the creation of Wahanda.com in 2008. It is an online resource and social networking site for health, beauty and wellness, enabling users to create content, post reviews and buy vouchers for all things health-related.

The online business is the brainchild of Lopo Champalimaud and Salim Mitha. Lopo was an early adopter of the internet, co-founding Cyber Dialogue in 1994, the world's first online market research firm. He then progressed to senior roles at travel firms Lastminute.com and Travelocity, leaving to start Wahanda with business partner Salim Mitha. He had previously worked at Yahoo! Search as senior European director, at Merrill Lynch as an investment banker and was a management consultant at McKinsey.

Having worked at a variety of online businesses, the pair spotted a gap in the market for a site providing worldwide listings of health resources, such as spas, salons and gyms. Lopo and Salim came up with the name Wahanda – which means 'great spirit and creator' in Native American – as they wanted a term that was related to the business and which could be easily identified across global markets.

'Wellness is a massive industry, bigger than the film or music markets, and yet largely under-represented online,' says Lopo. 'There are thousands of spas and treatments out there and so finding and choosing the right one could be intimidating.'

The company was founded in February 2008 and officially launched in April, with initial investment from the founders. A few months later, they raised further investment of £1.5m from a group of backers including Brent Hoberman, the founder of Lastminute.com. In October 2008, six months after launch, an e-commerce element was added to the site, enabling users to buy vouchers from hundreds of spas across the UK.

To increase the business' profile, the founders ensured it was active on social networking sites such as Facebook and Twitter, in order to generate word of mouth.

'We felt that satisfied customers, great service and a great product generate fantastic word of mouth. It was our best and most effective form of marketing and advertising in the early days, and continues to be so,' says Lopo.

By 2009, the recession was starting to bite, presenting tough challenges for both start-ups and established businesses. It may not have been the best time to develop a business, but both Lopo and Salim were confident that the economic situation would be to their advantage. They believed that health and beauty was an area that consumers would continue to spend money on.

The site generates revenue through transaction and listing fees and Lopo says they are constantly on the lookout for ways of improving the community aspect of the site.

In October 2009, Lopo and Salim launched the Wahanda concept in the US. Innovation online continues to be an integral part of the business, and in January 2010, Wahanda introduced the 'MobDeal'. These are special volume discounts, whereby consumers can benefit from the power of group buying to access the best daily deal on offers such as massages, facials, spa days, haircuts, manicures, yoga and Pilates classes.

Wahanda was named number 38 in the 2010 Startups 100 list. Published by Startups. co.uk, the list showcases the UK's best new businesses. With a range of online credentials between them, it's not surprising that Lopo and Salim have set themselves an ambitious target, with the aim of doing for well-being what Amazon did for retailing.

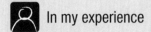
In my experience

Company: Country Products
Owner-manager: Mark Leather
Type: Health food store
Start year: 1983

In the early 1970s, Mark Leather saw a niche in the market for high-quality, ready-packed goods for the health food, delicatessen and grocery trade. At the time these foods, such as pulses and seeds, were sold loose, but Mark saw the opportunity to package the food for the customer, and therefore increase impulse sales, and solve problems of cross-contamination and stock rotation in one fell swoop. He initially funded the business with only £50, buying stock, selling it on, and repeating this process. The business grew organically, serving a wide variety of customers – from health food shops and pharmacies, to offices and cinemas.

The company had a web presence from 1994, when they set up a simple website, but in 2004, they launched the e-commerce side of the site and the business took the leap online. Mark remembers he took a while to be convinced an online business would work, 'I couldn't believe that customers would purchase say a kilo of brown rice online instead of at the local health store – boy was I wrong!' He was eventually convinced by his web designer, who pointed out they had the stock, an invoicing system in place, order pickers and a delivery system set up – so the transition to online retailing could be achieved for a very small additional outlay.

It hasn't necessarily been from the volume of online sales that Country Products has seen the impact, but from the amount of wholesale customers that see the online shop and then choose to buy from it, and establish a relationship. Mark sees the business' online presence as an essential 'shop window', and says that 'an online business is one of the easiest and most economic ways of expanding your business.' He believes that it's now imperative for businesses to have an online presence.

With little technical knowledge pre-launch, Mark believes a 'common sense approach and sensible business practice are all that is required'. He advises others moving online to use local, small firms that you can build a relationship with, and to use 'someone who doesn't talk too much jargon, someone you can meet and speak with face to face'.

Mark believes one of their best business moves ever was moving payment providers to Sage Pay (formerly Protx), which was recommended to them by their web designer. The system provided a simpler, easier and speedier process, which benefits themselves and their customers. They have also benefited from lower costs and charges, an important factor in the current climate.

Mark's advice to anyone starting a business online is first and foremost to listen to advice from others who have been there, done it, and made the mistakes so you don't have to.

 **CHAPTER 1**

Idea to reality

If you're determined to make your dream of starting an online business come true, in this chapter we take you through the first steps to turning your idea into reality. From getting the right experience and finding out the best support networks, to the different types of online business available, to targeting the right customers and evaluating a website, we'll cover the essential steps. After this chapter, you should have a pretty good idea of your concept and the steps you can take to make it work.

In this chapter we'll cover:

- → Is an online business right for you?
- → The experience you need
- → Support networks
- → Market conditions: Is now a good time?
- → Your idea and USPs
- → The different types of online business
- → Identifying your target market
- → Standing out from the competition
- → Evaluating a website.

Is an online business right for you?

The beauty of an online business is that it's suited to just about anyone. You don't need to have a particular set of qualifications or industry experience and nor do you need to be based in a specific location. You can operate an online business from anywhere, as long as you've got access to an internet connection and a bit of business know-how. Ask yourself why people buy products and services on the internet. They do so because it's easy, efficient and they can instantly see what is available. There's no reason why anyone, from any background and any walk of life, can't successfully start and run their own business. So be assured, whatever your concerns and anxieties: you can do it.

Motivation

What exactly is it that prompts people to set up an online business? For surprisingly few, money is the main motivation and as the dot com boom and bust at the turn of the millennium proved, online millionaires are not made overnight. For others, being their own boss is the decision maker. For most it's to realise a dream, idea or desire to live a life that's more fulfilling.

An online business is one of the most popular businesses you can start from home so it's ideal for those couples and families looking to spend more time together, and one of the most flexible businesses to set up and run. The web lets you test out business models cheaply. You can start small, see what works and build on that.

Others, such as those who have been made redundant or those who, for whatever reason, struggle to find employment, turn to running their own businesses because they feel there's little alternative to get ahead. But they still 'do it' instead of giving up. People start their own business for individual and deeply personal reasons and as such what's perceived as 'success' is almost always related to personal challenges.

What it takes

Enthusiasm and motivation aren't all it takes of course, as proved by the number of super-keen people who put every last drop of energy into starting online businesses only to see them fail within the first year. It's important not to be put off by statistics. Yes, people fail but many succeed as well, and remember, it's a personal measure. Lots of first-time business people don't succeed in others' eyes but use the experience positively to either start another business or return to employment with a greater sense of fulfilment.

In my experience

Be passionate about what you do. No business, big or small, can succeed without that passion and your employees, customers and partners will feed off it.

Company: Wahanda.com
Owner–manager: Lopo Champalimaud

But you also have to consider risk – business is all about balancing risk and reward and unless you are fully aware of the implications of running a business and what impact this will have on your life and relationships, then you are increasing your risk.

Becoming your own boss and setting up a small business is one of the most rewarding, exciting and fulfilling things you can do in life, but it's also one of the most stressful, testing and demanding experiences you are likely to undertake.

For at least the first two to three years, put the holidays on hold and expect to work longer and harder than you are now. Expect to make sacrifices with family and friends.

For online business owners, the longer hours and isolation can make it hard to meet new contacts. You effectively have a sales outlet that is open 24 hours a day, 365 days of the year and a global customer base. Sure you'll be mixing with the public, but the fact that you can operate your business at all hours of the day means your opportunity to get out and meet other business owners will need to be carefully planned.

Analysing your skills

While passion and determination are vital assets for any entrepreneur, in excess they can be dangerous. Critical skills are important and none more so than when looking at yourself.

Startups Tips
If you have read all this and are undaunted by the prospect of setting up your own online business, then you probably relish a challenge and are ready to take the plunge and start now.

Here are a few skills you need to start an online business:

- An aptitude for selling
- Negotiation skills
- A basic understanding of technology
- Decisiveness
- Initiative
- The ability to multitask
- Experience of customer service
- Leadership.

This is by no means an exhaustive list but there are hundreds of multimillion pound industries, making decisions that affect hundreds of thousands of people, who will happily admit that their skills don't encompass the range outlined above. They are able to compensate for this though, as they are surrounded by consultants, advisers and experts in particular fields.

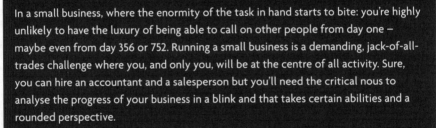

 From the experts

Company: **moneysupermarket.com**
Owner-manager: **Simon Nixon**

To succeed in an online environment today, an idea is only 20% of what is required. You also need marketing skills, both on and offline, and experience on the IT side too. Three people setting up a business in a bedroom sounds simple, but in reality there's more to an online business than that.

In a small business, where the enormity of the task in hand starts to bite: you're highly unlikely to have the luxury of being able to call on other people from day one – maybe even from day 356 or 752. Running a small business is a demanding, jack-of-all-trades challenge where you, and only you, will be at the centre of all activity. Sure, you can hire an accountant and a salesperson but you'll need the critical nous to analyse the progress of your business in a blink and that takes certain abilities and a rounded perspective.

It's these abilities that dictate who can run a business and who can't. The upside is that you can teach and equip yourself with the basics. If you want to succeed badly enough, you won't be embarrassed about admitting where you need help. You'll make mistakes, learn from them and move on. Remember, each time you do that and pick up something new the risk of failure decreases and the chances of success grow.

Experience needed

Statistically, there's no evidence that people are more likely to succeed if they've been in business before and the increasing numbers of 'teenpreneurs' making their fortunes fresh out of school proves a lack of experience certainly shouldn't be a barrier. It's also true you'll learn most from the mistakes you'll inevitably make.

In my experience

I chose a market that was getting to grips with the web – the optical industry was one of the few sectors that had not yet made the move online. There was the precedent to build on this and do something different, to bring a new take to the industry.

Company: Glasses Direct
Owner-manager: Jamie Murray Wells

It would be foolish to discard the value of experience, however. Banks and investors operate on a purely risk against reward policy and the fact that they'd prefer a proven track record in business or industry over almost any other factor in an investment proposition should tell you everything you need to know about the importance of experience.

 ## In my experience

A common sense approach and sensible business practice are all that is required – I see an online business as an easy way to 'dip your toes' into business – you can run it in the evening or weekends until it's up and running.

Company: Country Products
Owner-manager: Mark Leather

It might not be backed up statistically, but it's instinctive to trust someone with the experience to do something well more than someone just starting out. It's also a fair assumption that the more experience you have, the better informed your decisions are. The more of the pitfalls you know about, the earlier you'll see them and the easier it'll be to avoid them. Founder of easyJet and the numerous easyGroup brands, Sir Stelios Haji-Ioannou, is known as a risk taker, and while a supporter of young entrepreneurs, he believes 28 is a better age to start a business than straight from school or university because by then you'll have had time to understand how companies operate and, crucially, have made mistakes at someone else's expense.

Relevant experience

Possibly you've worked in retail and you may feel fairly confident you understand the everyday operations of selling stock. If you've management level experience of ordering and maintaining stock, negotiating with suppliers, excelling at customer service and dealing with remote orders, then all the better.

Having experience related to the type of online business you are planning is not always necessary. It might be that you've got skills honed in other businesses.

From the experts

Company: ASOS
Owner-manager: Nick Robertson

One of the benefits in starting ASOS was not having a retail background. I approached the business with a clean sheet of paper, without any baggage.

You may be an expert user of the internet or an online shopping addict, but just because you've had experience of this environment does not mean you will have an idea how to run a business in this area.

Startups Tips

If you are looking to break into an industry you are not familiar with, consider getting experience to see if it is an area you are interested in pursuing further. Your friends and family may already be involved in that industry, so see if you can shadow them for a day to get a flavour of what lies ahead.

It's always different on the other side of the screen – all you see is the finished product, with little appreciation of the blood, sweat and tears that have gone into the back end of the site. No matter how much you think you already know, there will be more, and still more to learn.

A site specialising in fashion items differs greatly to one that sells widgets – the fashion site will concentrate on imagery and presentation and will need to be constantly updated to reflect industry trends, while a site selling widgets is likely to be less focused on the look and feel, containing essential product information and enabling users to find products quickly and easily.

Online travel sites need to offer some form of customer contact outside of normal office hours to cater for those people who experience problems travelling at weekends or in the evening, for example, and therefore are more staff intensive than other types of online business. Some online businesses can be remotely maintained and therefore need minimum staff levels. It can make sense to try to get experience in an environment that is similar to the one you are looking to start in.

Online businesses differ according to whether they are retail or whether they offer services, for example, and so too do their revenue models. Social networking and dating sites use ad placements and affiliate programmes to create revenues; retail sites make money from product sales and subscriptions; and business-to-business sites rely on a mixture of sales, services fees and contracts to generate cash.

You shouldn't necessarily be put off from starting an online business if you've never worked in an online environment before. No matter what it says in the business manuals, if you've set your heart on starting up and got as far as buying this book, you're highly unlikely now to put your grand plans on hold for a year or two while you sign up for some online training courses. Likewise you might have worked in retail all your life so how on earth do you go and land a job that teaches you how the business side of an operation works?

Startups Tips
You don't need to be tech-savvy to start an online business, but making the wrong IT decisions can cost you extra money and time as your business grows. So it's a good idea to keep up to date with the latest internet technology trends, think about what functions you want your website to perform and then explore the technology options.

If you are in the online game you can do the necessary research in the evenings at home so you can fit around family commitments – all you need is an internet connection to explore the world wide web. You can even tinker with basic website design, by designing some mock-ups of what you envisage the site should look like.

You could consider contacting established online businesses and ask if you can shadow someone for the day. Or contact your nearest Local Enterprise Partnership or Chamber of Commerce to see if there are any guest speaker events focusing on online business.

Support networks

The first support network you'll need is your family and friends, regardless of whether they are involved in the business or not. It doesn't matter how much you attempt to separate your business from your personal life – in the early days of starting up, your business will impact on your family so it's vital that both you and they are prepared for what lies ahead. If your family

To make sure your family doesn't suffer due to your own ambitions, before you pursue your dream business, sit down with them and discuss the following:

- Will the business venture take away from quality time spent with family members? If so, how much is acceptable to all involved?
- Will the new business be initially funded or supported using family monies? If so, will this put a financial strain on the family?
- Do all family members agree this is a potentially successful business idea?
- Do all family members realise that most new businesses do not succeed?
- If the business is not showing signs of becoming successful, what operational time period will the family tolerate before the business is considered a failure and should be sold or closed down?
- If the new business fails, what is the alternative plan for income?

(spouse, partner, children, parents) aren't on board with you 100%, at some point, you, your business and/or your family will bear the consequences.

New businesses require a tremendous amount of time and nurturing to develop and become successful; time that is taken from elsewhere, often from the family. Unless you're starting a 'family' business where all members are participants, someone will inevitably feel left out, or neglected.

This is particularly important in the world of online businesses – the majority of them are started from home and remain there for quite some time until you decide to source premises. Your family are likely to be immersed in the business from day one but from an observer's point of view – while they can see what is going on, they may not always understand why it's happening.

How other entrepreneurs can help you

The reason we asked some of the leading names in online business to contribute to this book is that there's simply no better place to get advice than from those that have, as the saying goes, 'been there, done it and got the t-shirt'. Entrepreneurs trust other entrepreneurs more than anyone else and naturally form support networks that might at first appear cliquey but are almost always born simply out of a shared understanding of each other's fairly unique lives.

Like all relationships you'll find that with support networks you'll get out what you put in. Networking comes naturally to some people; it fills others with dread. If you're the first sort of person, you're probably already aware of the value of getting out and meeting others. If you're the second type of person, you're going to have to be brave and bite the bullet. Get yourself to a business networking event, have a glass of wine and simply chat to people about what you're doing. It can be daunting, but once you've taken the plunge at one event, chances are you'll be raring to go to others.

From the experts

Company: **ASOS**
Owner-manager: **Nick Robertson**

Finding support networks was quite hard as not many people had done online retail before, there was no one there! But the principles of high-street retail still applied to the online world and I've met people over the years who have given me some advice.

The online world is certainly an industry where it pays to have contacts – the environment develops at a faster pace than other sectors so advice from peers can be invaluable. Networking is also a great way of picking up recommendations. Most people recommend people they use – whether good or bad – so don't swallow their advice blindly, but knowing an accountant or lawyer who's experienced in your sector or knowledgeable of the area is a far more valuable lead than your standard Google search – and will save you time.

Don't confine your networking to physical events. Social networking is growing beyond the fun and games of Facebook and MySpace into a serious business tool and with sites such as LinkedIn, BT Tradespace and Startups.co.uk you can easily interact with other entrepreneurs and business advisers.

Check out business bodies and lobby groups available both for small business and online ventures. The Federation of Small Businesses, Forum of Private Businesses, British Chambers of Commerce and Business Network International aim to represent, champion and advise small businesses, while you should also contact organisations such as e-commerce trade body Interactive Media in Retail Group.

 In my experience

Listen to recommendations, never be afraid to take advice – let other people make the hard or costly mistakes. After all 'not everyone has to invent the wheel'.

Company: Country Products
Owner-manager: Mark Leather

Business mentoring

Finally, think about getting a mentor – this could be someone you know or you could contact several companies who provide matching services.

You don't have to follow this route, though. You also don't need a high profile celebrity entrepreneur mentor. Someone who's done what you wish to do should be your number one criterion. An experienced entrepreneur who you can turn to once every month or so to test out ideas on and gauge advice from will prove just as, if not more, valuable.

From the experts

Company: **moneysupermarket.com**
Owner-manager: **Simon Nixon**

I never had a business mentor but I was inspired by Richard Branson and read many business books about him. If you can find a mentor for yourself and your business, it's definitely a good idea.

Don't be scared to approach someone you don't know. Many entrepreneurs feel a responsibility to encourage and help others and will be only too willing to help. If they're not it'll almost certainly be because they're simply too busy. If that's the case, ask someone else. You'll soon get used to moving on quickly and without a grudge when met with the word 'no'!

Going into business with partners/friends

Online businesses are one of the most popular couple-run businesses or ventures run by friends; as many can be started from someone's home, it's an ideal way to combine work with family and friend commitments.

What's more, it can work brilliantly. The attributes for a healthy relationship – trust, honesty, the ability to listen, understanding, the unity of or tolerance of shared or different interests – translate well into business. Google was started by two university undergraduates who went on to study computer science, and they shared a common skill – they both just happened to be geniuses with computers.

It's essential to be sure that, aside from your personal relationships, there's a business case for working together. Ideally your skill sets should complement each other so the business benefits from supporting two people.

If your decision to work together does make business sense, there's no reason you shouldn't continue: just be aware of the consequences. If the business doesn't work out then relationships could turn sour and the trauma of losing a business could be doubled by also losing an otherwise lifelong friend or partner. If your business partner is more of an associate than a friend, you need to be clear in your mind that you trust and like this person sufficiently to share such an epic journey with them. Aside from having the skills you don't have and vice versa, look for a partner with whom you have a natural business chemistry; someone who can enthuse you and whom you can inspire. You'll need to balance reward, responsibility and risk. Make sure you're clear what your goals are for the business on a shared and personal level, what you want in the short, medium and long term and what your respective roles are. Ensure you're each staking the same degree of risk.

However, with all partnerships, expect the unexpected and get legally binding shareholder agreements drawn up. These should cover what happens to the business and shares if any combination of unthinkable outcomes occur including, as morbid as it might seem, either of your deaths.

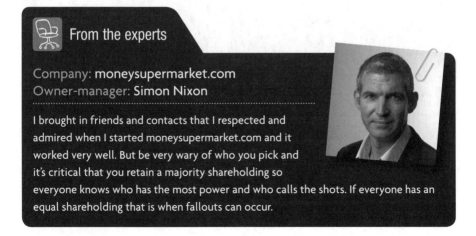

From the experts

Company: **moneysupermarket.com**
Owner-manager: **Simon Nixon**

I brought in friends and contacts that I respected and admired when I started moneysupermarket.com and it worked very well. But be very wary of who you pick and it's critical that you retain a majority shareholding so everyone knows who has the most power and who calls the shots. If everyone has an equal shareholding that is when fallouts can occur.

Market conditions: Is now a good time?

It's likely that the recent economic downturn has made you think twice about whether now is a good time to start your own online business. You may have felt the impact on your mortgage repayments, shopping bills or at the petrol station.

According to business information provider Equifax, the number of businesses that went bust in the UK in 2009 increased by 18%, but from the middle of 2009 onwards, the rate of business failures started to slow down compared with 2008 and early 2009. It says that every business sector, with the exception of wholesale, saw a downturn in businesses going bust in Q4 2009 compared with 2008.

There's no denying that economically, despite the signs of recovery in the last year, it's still a difficult time, and there is much uncertainty over what impact policies from the new coalition government, and its spending cuts, will have. What is more certain is that banks have cut lending options and it's certainly a tougher climate in which to raise funds for a business than, say, two years ago. This, of course, also impacts on what consumers have to spend.

 From the experts

Company: moneysupermarket.com
Owner-manager: Simon Nixon

An online business has lower overheads than other forms of business and can offer you national reach. If you are aspiring to be a national player, online is the most cost-effective route to choose. In current market conditions, online opportunities are probably 20%–30% lower than they were 12 months ago, but there are always opportunities when you can find a niche.

If there is one positive sign that online businesses should take from the current environment, particularly those specialising in retail, it should be that internet retail has outpaced sales on the high street this year, a trend that is set to continue in 2011. The reason for this could be explained by the fact that online shopping tends to be more cost-effective but industry figures show that on average people are still spending a lot more online.

According to IMRG, the membership community for the e-retail industry, total online sales will increase this year by 16% to make the online market worth £57.8bn. Clothing is a popular sector, with IMRG figures showing that during 2008, footwear recorded a growth of 25%, and in 2009, sales grew by 28%. Sales of electricals were also strong and grew by 22% in 2009, up from 14% in 2008. The health and beauty sector, meanwhile, grew by just 4% during 2008, but in 2009 yearly growth moved into double digits, increasing 21%. According to IMRG, in 2009 lingerie was the only sector to show negative annual growth, declining 8% year on year.

Online businesses also require virtually no overheads and offer you the ability to work at any time you like from virtually any location, so there is flexibility as well as potential cost savings to be made.

 In my experience

Our biggest benefit to our business comes not from the revenue received online but the volume of wholesale customers that see our online shop and want to purchase from us. After all who picks up a telephone directory these days? If you want something you look on the internet so get your 'shop window' out there.

Company: Country Products
Owner-manager: Mark Leather

If you can establish yourself on limited resources and build a loyal customer base when times are tight, you'll flourish in more affluent climates. There's never a bad time to start a good business, so don't let market conditions put you off: just make sure you plan even harder to get your offering spot on.

Your big idea: USPs

You've got an idea. Do some research, check out a few websites that seem similar to what you want to achieve and analyse them. What do you like about their approach and how does it relate to what you are trying to do? Are there any functions missing from these websites that you think yours could benefit from?

In my experience

Glasses Direct was third time lucky; I'd already looked at two other ideas, gambling online and property online. Regulations were too heavy for gambling and property was not as disruptive as we wanted. We wanted to shake up an industry.

Company: Glasses Direct
Owner-manager: Jamie Murray Wells

Types of online business

You'll probably already know what type of online business you'd like to start and run. Picking a type of online business is only half the challenge, though. Next you'll need to explore the specifics of that type of business to start sculpting exactly what your offering to the market will be.

> **Startups Tips**
> Start by making a list of what will make your online venture unique. Your USPs (unique selling points) will define how your business is different from the competition and will slowly build its identity and brand. Your USPs will be your sales story to convince people they should buy from your company instead of elsewhere.

There are three basic online business models you can follow.

E-commerce: The most closely aligned to the traditional business model of selling. With an e-commerce site you sell a product or service. Customers buy directly from your site, and the products are then either delivered to them or downloaded. Examples of e-commerce sites include Amazon, eBay, Play.com and Lastminute.com.

Advertising: The aim is to get as many visitors as possible, increasing the number of customers your advertisers reach. Content on this kind of site is usually free for the site user, providing them with information or entertainment. Examples of such sites include social networking operations such as Facebook, Bebo and MySpace.

Subscription: Similar to the advertising model, subscription sites generally provide information or entertainment, but the difference is the user pays to access all or part of that content. This type of site is particularly common in the business-to-business world.

You can of course base your site around a combination of one, two or all of these internet models.

The good news is, as a small business, you've far more flexibility and opportunity to find unique routes to appeal to customers. Carve out a niche or focus on a specialist category and gauge demand. In the competitive environment of online retail, selling something that is niche and desirable will get you noticed. Your USP could be that you offer substantial savings over high street prices.

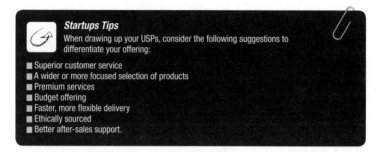

Startups Tips

When drawing up your USPs, consider the following suggestions to differentiate your offering:

■ Superior customer service
■ A wider or more focused selection of products
■ Premium services
■ Budget offering
■ Faster, more flexible delivery
■ Ethically sourced
■ Better after-sales support.

Who are your customers?

To assess if your business could work you'll need to prove there is enough demand for the product or services you're selling for the price you're charging. For some online businesses reliant on seasonal peaks and troughs this can be a complicated process and will involve investing in areas such as search engine optimisation and web design, in order to build interest well before these seasonal peaks occur to maximise sales.

In my experience

The business has developed brilliantly since launch. We have recruited 100,000 new customers, who are investing over £500,000 a month.

Company: Naked Wines
Owner-manager: Rowan Gormley

Don't fall for the mistake of convincing yourself that just because you love the idea, then others will. Unfortunately there are plenty of great-sounding 'ideas' that simply aren't viable. Banks will expect to see evidence of an existing customer base and so should you if you want the business to have a chance of working.

Research the market

Researching the market isn't a guessing game. Check out online statistics and demographics, particularly those that refer to your target audience. Too many people invest in all the right internet marketing strategies, only to find out that they don't really know who their market is. Those people that are increasing their search activities, for example are likely to appeal to younger and faster adopters of technology. If your target audience is likely to be older, you'll need to think of ways to draw them to your site.

Homemade surveys

Carry out your own research with the public as well. Take to the streets and carry out surveys and questionnaires exploring anything that can prove your case that a market for your online business exists. Ask respondents how much they'd spend a month on the products you're planning to sell and ask them to tick if your USPs would make them choose you over a competitor site.

DIY market research: Questions to ask members of the public

- How often do you go online?
  Hardly ever, once or twice a month, once or twice a week, more than twice a week
- How old are you?
  Under 18, 18–24, 25–34, 35–50, 50+
- What's your wage bracket?
  £5–£7k, £7k–£15k, £15k–£25k, £25–£35k, £35k–£50k, £50k+
- Would you welcome an online shop selling [enter your product(s) here]?

Startups Tips

Try the *Research Buyers Guide* when looking for reputable sources for market research, www. rbg.org.uk has a fully searchable directory of market research providers.

Research companies

There are professional research companies that you can hire to carry out feasibility studies. Their services will be out of the price range for most of you, and be wary of companies who claim to do this for comparatively low rates as it's likely they'll merely accumulate information already in the public domain that you could do yourself.

Competition and differentiation

Competition tends to come in two forms: directly from other sites selling the same or similar products, and indirectly from other ways those customers can spend money they'd otherwise spend with you.

Direct competition is relatively simple to research and observe, but indirect competition is subject to constant change, market forces and trends. For instance, mobile phones have changed the spending priorities of teenage girls. Where once, their pocket money would be spent on cosmetics and clothing, a significant percentage now goes on top-up cards.

DVD rental shops don't just compete with other shops selling DVDs but also cinemas and online film websites, as another example. So it's not just rival online businesses and bricks-and-mortar shops you need to consider when looking at competition, but anything competing for a slice of your target customer's disposable income.

Competition isn't always a negative, however, and is increasingly seen as collaborative. In the online environment, affiliate marketing uses one website to drive to another, and while the websites aren't in direct competition, they offer similar sorts of items, target similar audiences or offer related products.

Researching and learning from competitors

It rarely makes sense, however, to launch an online business in a saturated market. Too many 'me-too' businesses have come and gone to the dot com graveyard. Remember, you're proving the market as much as your online business.

As frustrating as it might seem, people don't always surf the internet with their heads and even if you present a better product for a superior price, some shoppers simply won't break habit or misplaced loyalty, so it's unlikely you'd ever take 100% of another business' customer base.

You should cross-reference the number of competitors in your area and their USPs with your demographics in order to establish if there's room for another business. It could be that on reflection you identify a new USP that would give you a better chance of securing market share. Don't be scared to tweak the concept where sensible.

From the experts

Company: **moneysupermarket.com**
Owner-manager: **Simon Nixon**

It's critical to check out the competition and see how they compare against your potential products.

Startups checklist

- It's too much hard work to start an online business if you're not fully committed to seeing it through. Know what you're getting into before you start.
- If you don't have enough experience, get some before you launch.
- Talk it through with friends and family: They may still offer support even if they're not convinced by the idea.
- If you can't do it alone, think long and hard about the type of person you want as a partner.
- Identify a USP from the very beginning.
- Do your research, and make it thorough.
- Know your competition inside out.
- The online world moves at a rapid pace, so keep up to date with the latest developments.

2

BUSINESS PLANNING AND FINANCE

CHAPTER 2.1

How to write a business plan

A business plan is a must-have for any serious start-up. It aims to capture your company's financial aim, its operations and its present and future direction. Without a business plan, you can wave goodbye to raising any finance, as it's the first thing any potential backer, be they friends, family, bank or private investor, will want to see. You won't be able to actually write it yet, though. For that, you'll need to compile all the data that the rest of this section covers.

In this chapter we'll cover:

→ How to write a business plan
→ The different types of business plan and the many uses you can put yours to
→ Budgeting for the year
→ Forecasts
→ Trading projections
→ Deciding your prices.

Why you need a business plan

Don't be overly daunted by writing a business plan – it's not difficult and if you do it, it probably won't be tedious either. In fact, if anything, it will help to reaffirm why you are doing what you are doing by giving the reasons for the business being established, including your goals, aspirations, prospects for future growth and what features will set it apart from the competition.

Tim Waterstone, founder of bookseller Waterstone's, did not have the most auspicious of starts when it came to writing a business plan. He visited his local bank, where the bank manager asked for 16 copies. Tim later found out that the plan was used on an internal training course to illustrate the type of business no self-respecting bank should invest in. But the rest, as they say, is history.

Certainly, there's no avoiding writing a business plan; and the more you embrace it the more you're likely to actually find it a meaningful and useful process, rather than merely a way of appeasing the bank. A good business plan will give you something to constantly refer back to when making tough decisions and strategy calls, and should be a working document you update as the business progresses.

 In my experience

When it comes to business planning, you've got to find a way of making your business unique and boil it down to something people can get in an instant. The test of the idea is, if you can walk into a bar, explain it to a bunch of piss heads and have them go 'ooh, that's nice, I would use that' it's a winner. If it requires PowerPoint, don't bother.

Company: Naked Wines
Owner-manager: Rowan Gormley

Doing a business plan isn't as hard as you might think. You don't have to write a doctoral thesis or a novel. And the good news is that there are plenty of business plan templates available that you can research to guide you in the process – you can download them from the internet or even consider asking your bank what sort of document it expects to see. You can also carry out a SWOT analysis, a method for describing your business proposition in terms of the factors that have the most impact. Essentially you nominate the strengths and weaknesses, and then identify threats and opportunities (see the Appendix for an example).

Don't worry too much about the design and layout of a business plan at this stage, though. Much like CVs, people often obsess unnecessarily about the supposed best format, structure, length and lay-out when what's far more important is that the document contains all the necessary information and is easy to understand. In the heady days of the dot com boom, many entrepreneurs' business plans were scrawled on the back of cigarette packets, but these days you'll need to come up with something more substantial.

From the experts

Company: ASOS
Owner-manager: Nick Robertson

Our business plan was written on the back of a cigarette packet but the exit strategy for our investors was a little more defined.

What to include in your business plan

Ask yourself the following questions. How are you going to develop your business? What timescales are you looking at? Who is going to be involved, and in what capacity? How are you intending to manage the money?

A standard business plan outlines the following:

→ What your business and your website will do

→ Who your customers will be

→ Why people will buy your products

→ Evidence this market exists and its potential

→ Evidence of why your business will survive when others don't; that is, an analysis of the competition

→ Who you are and why you're going into business

--> Why you believe you've got the skills and expertise to run an online business; your qualifications and experience

--> Details of any other directors or key management

--> How you will fund the setting up of the business

--> How you will repay any money you borrow

--> What your ongoing costs and overheads will be

--> Sales and revenue forecasts for the first 12 months of business

--> Details of suppliers and contracts

--> Your goals for the first 12 months and then beyond that.

That might sound fairly exhaustive, but it should be. Your business plan should present a watertight argument as to why and how your online business will work. If it doesn't, then you should be asking yourself if the business is still such a great idea.

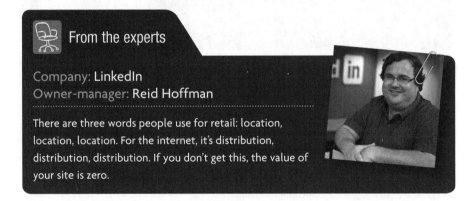

From the experts

Company: **LinkedIn**
Owner-manager: **Reid Hoffman**

There are three words people use for retail: location, location, location. For the internet, it's distribution, distribution, distribution. If you don't get this, the value of your site is zero.

How to get started

However unique your business idea, there will be companies elsewhere doing something similar, and undertaking some market research on these will help you understand your target market a little better. Companies have been classified into various categories by the UK government under the Standard Industrial Classification (SIC) system; start by identifying your particular class and identifying your SIC code. This will then help you search for data on your competitors and other industry participants. Then, seek some data from sources such as Cobweb (www.cobwebinfo.com), which produces various business profiles. This will enable you to obtain an external perspective on the characteristics of similar firms in your field.

Assess demand levels

One of the most difficult things to predict is the level of demand for your products or services. The general rule is to use conservative estimates on likely demand and to use proxies where data is hard to come by. One should also use proxies to help even when the idea is innovative or unique, rather than plucking figures from the air, or claiming there are no comparative figures available.

What to avoid

Cash not profits

How often have you heard small business owners saying they simply haven't got time to plan? The reality is, probably all too often, that many businesses draw up a business plan only when they need it for a specific reason, such as to raise finance. But the busier you are, the more you need to plan.

Most people think in terms of profits instead of cash. When you imagine a new business, you think of what it would cost to make the product, what you could sell it for, and what the profits per unit might be. We are trained to think of business as sales minus costs and expenses, which equal profits. Unfortunately, we don't spend the profits in a business. We spend cash. So understanding cashflow is critical. If you have only one table in your business plan, make it the cashflow table (see the Appendix).

Inflating your ideas

Don't overestimate the importance of the idea. You don't need a great idea to start a business; you need time, money, perseverance, and common sense. Few successful businesses are based entirely on new ideas. A new idea is harder to sell than an existing one, because people don't understand a new idea and they are often unsure if it will work. Plans don't sell new business ideas to investors, people do. Investors invest in people, not ideas. The plan, though necessary, is only a way to present information.

Leave out the vague and the meaningless babble of business phrases (such as 'being the best') because they are simply hype. Remember that the objective of a plan is to secure results, and for results, you need tracking and follow up. You need specific dates, management responsibilities, budgets, and milestones. Then you can follow up. No matter how well thought out or brilliantly presented, it means nothing unless it produces results.

Sales projections

Sales grow slowly at first, but then shoot up boldly with huge growth rates, as soon as 'something' happens. Have projections that are conservative so you can defend them. When in doubt, be less optimistic. Consequently, be honest. Don't exaggerate revenues and underplay overheads in order to make the plan work. Bank managers will have seen thousands of applications in their time and will see straight through it – and, of course, you'll be kidding yourself and invalidating your business plan as a useful document, as well as wasting your time. If anything, veer on the side of caution.

Many entrepreneurs say that, with the benefit of hindsight, when planning a business you should halve the income you anticipate and double the expenses you expect to pay – any discrepancy in your favour will be a bonus. Others insist they would never have secured the funding they needed without a few white lies and that whatever you ask for the bank will give you 20% less. Ultimately it's your call, but remember, your business plan should plot your progress and skewing it for any purpose limits how much it can help you.

Using your business plan

Tailor your plan to its real business purpose. Business plans can be different things: they are often just sales documents to sell an idea for a new business. They can also be detailed action plans, financial plans, marketing plans, and even personnel plans. They can be used to start a business, or just run a business better. In all these different varieties of business plan, the plan matches your specific situation. For example, if you're developing a plan for internal use only, not for sending out to banks or investors, you may not need to include all the background details that you already know. Description of the management team is very important for investors, while financial history is most important for banks.

Your business plan should cover several areas in detail, but you'll need to strike the right balance between being concise and being overly verbose – the latter will irritate more than it impresses. Potential investors will be far more concerned with being able to access key information than with whether you have a flair with words. Where appropriate use bullet points and break up the text; bite size chunks of information are far easier to absorb. Don't leave anything out but keep it brief; people can always contact you if they need to know more.

Startups Tips

Your business plan should plot your progress so be realistic about anticipated levels of profit – you need to strike a balance between what you know you can achieve and what will sway investors in your favour.

Startups Tips

Use your business plan to prove to yourself that your business can survive and prosper, not just as a tool for accessing finance.

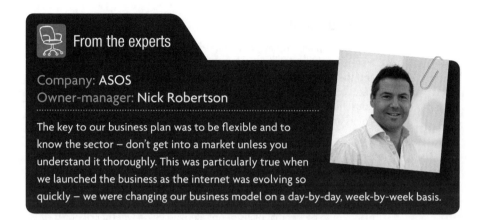

From the experts

Company: **ASOS**
Owner-manager: **Nick Robertson**

The key to our business plan was to be flexible and to know the sector – don't get into a market unless you understand it thoroughly. This was particularly true when we launched the business as the internet was evolving so quickly – we were changing our business model on a day-by-day, week-by-week basis.

Different types of business plan

Start-up plan

The most standard business plan is a start-up plan, which defines the steps for a new business. It covers standard topics including the company, product or service, market, forecasts, strategy, implementation milestones, management team, and financial analysis. The financial analysis includes projected sales, profit and loss, balance sheet, cashflow, and probably a few other tables. The plan starts with an executive summary and ends with appendices showing monthly projections for the first year.

Internal plans

These are not intended for outside investors, banks, or other third parties. They might not include detailed descriptions of the company or management team. They may or may not include detailed financial projections that become forecasts and budgets. They may cover main points as bullet points in slides (such as PowerPoint slides) rather than detailed texts.

Operations plan

An operations plan is normally an internal plan, and it might also be called an internal plan or an annual plan. It would normally be more detailed on specific implementation milestones, dates, deadlines, and responsibilities of teams and managers.

Strategic plan

A strategic plan is usually also an internal plan, but it focuses more on high-level options and setting main priorities than on the detailed dates and specific responsibilities. Like most internal plans, it wouldn't include descriptions of the company or the management team. It might also leave out some of the detailed financial projections. It might be more bullet points and slides than text.

Growth and expansion plans

A growth plan or expansion plan, or new product plan will sometimes focus on a specific area of business, or a subset of the business. These plans could be internal plans or not, depending on whether or not they are being linked to loan applications or new investment. For example, an expansion plan requiring new investment would include full company descriptions and background on the management team, as much as a start-up plan for investors. Loan applications will require this much detail as well. However, an internal plan, used to set the steps for growth or expansion funded internally, might skip these descriptions. It might not include detailed financial projections for the whole company, but it should at least include detailed forecasts of sales and expenses for the company.

Feasibility plan

A feasibility plan is a very simple start-up plan that includes a summary, mission statement, keys to success, basic market analysis, and preliminary analysis of costs, pricing, and probable expenses. This kind of plan is good for deciding whether or not to proceed with a plan, to tell if there is a business worth pursuing.

Budgeting for the year

Predicting figures for the first year of your business when you are just off the starting blocks might seem a little premature but when you're working out your costs, it's essential that you plan for the first 12 months – not just your start-up costs but overheads too. To make this more manageable, break these down into one month, six months and then first year budgets.

This will help you to plan your business finances, assessing areas such as how much money you have and how much revenue you need to generate your target profit. Budgeting will also be a good measure of whether your business plan is along the right path, or whether it needs adjusting.

For a full budget and to see how viable your business is you'll need to balance revenue forecasts against costs. It's just as crucial to work out and keep track of how much you're spending, not just the sales you hope to get through the site. Without expenses any forecasts or even sales prove very little as regards how profitable your online business can be. The good news is that it's far easier to work out reliable costings than revenues, especially if you veer on the side of caution.

Begin by looking at all your initial start-up costs. All the costs of getting your online business up and running go into the start-up expenses category. These expenses may include:

→ Domain name and hosting fees

→ Initial stock

→ Computer equipment

→ Online credit card sales

→ Website design costs.

This is just a sample list and you probably won't have trouble adding to it once you start listing your own costs.

Your operating costs are those expenses that your business will incur on an ongoing basis; essentially what you'll need to pay out each month. They may include:

→ Your salary

→ Staff salaries

→ Telecommunications

→ Website maintenance

→ Utilities

→ Stock

→ Storage

→ Distribution

→ Promotion

→ Loan payments

→ Office supplies

→ Maintenance

→ Professional services (ie accountancy fees).

Again, this isn't a complete list and outgoings will vary from month to month. However, once you've completed your own lists you should have a fairly good idea, even if they're ballpark figures, of what revenues and/ or funding you're going to need to support your business over a month, six month and yearly basis. These figures should go into a financial budget plan towards the end of your business plan which also takes into account, of course, how much money you can realistically make.

Making revenue forecasts

Sales forecasting is notoriously difficult and the point where many business plans fall down. This is because either the business owner is hopelessly optimistic or the plan only succeeds in proving the business isn't viable because of the number of sales needed to generate a profit. Similarly, the cost that goods would need to be priced at is unrealistic or the cost of sustaining the business until it breaks even is unsustainable.

The biggest challenge is that you don't have any previous sales history to guide you. This is hopefully where your market research can help with examples of sales figures for online businesses operating in a similar market. Also consider what stage your search engine optimisation (see Chapter 5.2 for more information on this) is at – how easy will it be and how long will it take for people to find your site online? However, this isn't entirely adequate as it's highly unlikely you'll perform at a similar level to your competitors for perhaps up to a year.

The simplest forecast is to start by working out what you hope to be selling within six months. Work this out per unit per day so you have a gross sales figure and multiply that by the number of 'opening' days in a month. Technically speaking, an online business is open 24 hours, 365 days of the year. Next, look to scale proportionately from month one, where you're unlikely to have many sales, upwards to month six. You can then extrapolate that scale over 12 months for an annual sales forecast.

In addition to that one forecast, carry out the process three times with a pessimistic, optimistic, and realistic outlook. Next try and put a real-time calendar next to your 'month one', 'month two' etc taking into account the peaks and troughs in trade you anticipate and are suggested from your research. Many online businesses see huge variations season-by-season, with many taking over half their annual profits during the build-up to Christmas.

Once you've worked out your financial outgoings (both initial start-up and ongoing costs) you can put the two together to produce a clearer analysis of the viability of your business on paper and when your business will break even.

Begin by compiling month by month expenses and sales forecasts. In the same way you accounted for peaks and troughs in sales, look at months where you expect expenses to be higher than others. For instance, if you cater for the Christmas rush you may buy far more stock in September, October and November than other months of the year.

Again, ensure you prepare three income/outgoings projections: pessimistic, optimistic, and realistic. Also try and account for the fact that the price you can purchase stock for will hopefully decrease as your sales levels increase. However, that's a calculation you probably want to reserve for your optimistic forecast unless you've already got such an agreement in place with your suppliers.

While your calculation will inevitably alter from month to month (something you'll need to be wary of when managing cashflow) the point where your sales equal your expenses is where you 'break even' and hopefully go on to generate profit.

There are some formulae used to demonstrate this:

Break-even Point (£) = Fixed Costs ÷ Gross Margin Percentage

For example: An online business buys portable fans for £10 each, marks them up and sells them for £20. Their monthly expenses (fixed costs) are £12,000. This means the break-even point would be £24,000 or 667 units.

£12,000 ÷ (10/20) = £24,000

This level of information should give you a much more powerful overview of not just how viable your business is, but what funding is required and when. It also enables you to pre-empt when you may need assistance with cashflow or credit.

Having this at your fingertips won't just impress investors and the banks but should also give you a much firmer grasp on your buying decisions when it comes to actually sourcing stock, for example.

Deciding your prices

If you are planning an online retail business, before you make any forecasts, plot any projections or arrive at a principal sum you'll need to borrow to start your online business, you need to think about roughly how much money you can make from the products or services you intend to sell. As it's difficult to tell exactly how much you'll sell, it's safer to start by looking at how much profit you can make per item sold, often referred to as 'per unit'. To do this, you'll need to start setting prices.

Exactly how much you intend to sell individual items for might seem like minutiae that can wait until later when you have 'big vision' considerations such as securing a bank loan, finding premises and creating a brand. However, it's actually a much bigger factor in deciding whether your business will work than any of those, and as such needs to be at the forefront of your planning. You can't possibly know how feasible a business is without being clear about the fundamentals of any operation involving sales: ie how much money you make per transaction.

The two key elements of deciding your prices will be:

--> **The costs of goods**

--> **Your operational expenses.**

The cost of goods should include any associated cost in the development or acquiring process such as packaging and delivery. Operational expense incorporates all your overheads such as staff wages, marketing and technology.

The sum of the two costs subtracted from the price you set will, in theory, be the profit you generate – although, of course, there are many outside influences that have the potential to impact on your bottom line.

You'll need to begin by ensuring you know exactly how much your product costs to the point it goes through the virtual till. You'll also need to establish the running costs of your business. You probably don't know all of them at the moment so make estimates and keep tweaking and adjusting the calculation when you know more.

If you don't have a thorough grasp of your figures, you'll be exposing your business to risk. For your online business to succeed, you'll need to know at all points what any item you sell costs you to buy and how much you make when you sell it.

At the end of the day, you need to make money from the business. It is profit that will pay your salaries and your mortgage and what the bank manager or investor needs to be confident about if they are to lend you money.

Developing a pricing strategy

Knowing what a product costs you and the percentage profit you'd like to make is rarely all it takes to make your online business proposition viable, unfortunately. The missing key consideration in this equation is, of course, a customer base that wants to buy at the figure you've set.

For some products, such as official sports merchandise or branded items like iPods, the manufacturer will have a suggested or minimum pricing policy to avoid price wars or heavy discounting which, while making things easier, will limit the ability to make the profits you've factored for.

Think carefully about setting up an e-commerce business selling such goods as it's likely you'll be competing against large retailers who have the advantage of buying in bulk and multimillion pound marketing budgets. If price was one of your USPs it's unlikely you'll compete here.

Check out the competitors

Do some research and find out what your competitors are charging – if you decide to undercut them, you'll need to work on keeping your overheads at a minimum. For example, if you decide to undercut a shop selling premium home electronics, you'll need to negotiate a superior supply rate with the manufacturer, which is highly unlikely. So you'll need to find another way of reducing your overheads, perhaps by offering a 'no frills' website design that requires little maintenance and which you can update yourself.

While budget or no frills online shops make some of the most profitable e-commerce operations, it's a strategy not without risk. Squeezing profits means there's little margin for error and you'll feel the impact of a drop in sales far quicker. Larger chains will know this and if they see you as a threat, could match your prices (even if it meant they'd be selling at cost value or even a loss) to force you out of business.

While the UK economy has emerged from recession, many analysts continue to warn that the recovery could easily be derailed, and as such, consumers are likely to be steered more by price than by anything else. On the plus side, the main resource many will be heading straight for will be internet comparison sites and providing you've invested in search engine optimisation (we'll cover more of this later in Chapter 5.2), your site has a good chance of being indexed and therefore noticed.

While people expect to find deals and bargains on the internet, being the cheapest isn't necessarily the best strategy to pursue. Many small internet businesses have managed to steal a march on the competition by providing value that is not price-based, and focusing on qualities such as luxury and service.

Other pricing strategies

Business manuals will talk about a few other strategies for pricing:

Keystone pricing

This refers to the practice of simply doubling the cost price of a product, but it's fairly academic now as there are few products which offer the chance to make such a mark up.

Multiple pricing

This is an increasingly popular strategy and a clever way to incentivise shoppers into buying more than they originally intended, or to shift poor selling stock. It involves offering multiple products grouped together for one superior price. For instance, buying two pairs of jeans, selling individually for £30, for £50, or one pair of the jeans and a £20 t-shirt for £40. It presents the illusive feeling of value for the shopper and if you've ensured you're still making your desired profit, can be a very effective pricing model. Buy one get one free food menus are another prime example, where the profit made on the cost of drinks for two people almost always generates enough to compensate for any profit sacrificed to entice people through the door.

Round down pricing

There's also a school of thought that shoppers round down a price instead of rounding it up, so it's better to price goods at £9.99 not £10. That's increasingly dismissed now though and some shops actually play on the notion of transparency and honesty of a rounded £10 price tag. In reality, other than all those missing pennies, it's unlikely to make a massive difference. If you're able to drop prices to, say, £9.49, then perhaps the argument becomes relevant again.

Discount pricing, sales and price reductions

These are also a crucial part of pricing strategy and certainly shouldn't be confined to traditional sales periods such as January. Neither should it be viewed as a way of shifting dead stock.

Loss leaders

The most effective and common discount pricing method in retail, and the one that causes the biggest challenge for online businesses competing with large chains and supermarkets, are loss leaders. The idea is that by pricing one in-demand item at cost price (or even below), you'll entice customers who will buy more than just that item. You'll have noticed supermarkets frequently competing for the lowest price for staple goods.

Cost-plus pricing or mark-up pricing

These are the terms commonly given to deciding your own profit amount or percentage to be added to its cost; it is likely to be where you'll start but it shouldn't be your only consideration. Most successful pricing strategies will include several of the pricing policies and almost always at the same time. This can be confusing, but always revert to the basic principle of knowing what you're paying and what you're making at the price you're selling at. Stick to that and you can't go wrong.

Pitching your plan

If you have a great business idea and the figures work on paper you're half way there. However, you'll never realise that potential of a great business plan unless it's presented in the correct way.

Before presenting your business plan double check to make sure that the document looks professional. No typing, grammar or spelling mistakes. Use graphs and charts where appropriate and titles and subtitles to divide different subject matters. While the aim is to make it look good, you should avoid expensive documentation, as this might suggest unnecessary waste and extravagance.

The length of a business plan depends on individual circumstances. It should be long enough to cover the subject adequately and short enough to maintain interest.

Practise your presentation in front of the mirror, family and friends and get them to critique you.

 In my experience

When it comes to presenting your business plan, keep it simple and short. If you can't explain your idea in a sentence then keep refining it.

Company: Wahanda.com
Owner-manager: Lopo Champalimaud

Startups checklist

- Don't just write your business plan for your investors: Use it as your main guide for the direction of the business.
- Include all the necessary detail but don't overload it: A good plan is thorough but succinct.
- Be realistic with your sales forecasts: It's better to underestimate than overestimate.
- Have three different trading forecasts: Pessimistic, optimistic and realistic.
- It makes sense to work on your budgeting, revenue forecasts and pricing strategies at this point to ensure that your business plan is as accurate as possible.

 CHAPTER 2.2
Raising finance

A decade ago, raising finance for a dot com business seemed almost like a no-brainer. When the bull run ended for hundreds of companies that used the internet to deliver products, goods and services, only a handful of dot coms emerged resilient. Today, raising funds for an online business is a very different story.

While the beauty of an online business means that the overheads are relatively low, expect your business plan to be scrutinised much like any other one when you are looking to raise finance. If you have a couple of thousand to spend and don't want to borrow anything, then an online model is perfectly do-able. But you'll still need funds to build your website and to invest in its growth, as well as meeting marketing costs and these can mount up. So if you're serious about having an online business for the long term, you might need to take on outside investors at a later stage, and perhaps sooner than you think.

In this chapter we'll cover:

–➢ Finance options
–➢ Friends and family loans
–➢ Equity finance
–➢ Banks
–➢ Applying for a loan
–➢ Pitching for finance
–➢ Paying yourself.

Finance options

It's likely you'll have three funding options for setting up an online business. The first is to fund it yourself, the second is to use a bank and the third is to seek equity investment from private investors. The route you choose may, to some extent, depend on the business model you have adopted. It may be a decade since the dot com boom and bust, but some online business models still tend to be regarded with a certain degree of caution when it comes to raising finance, and the economic climate is not making the search for funding any easier.

 In my experience

The low-risk way to go about raising initial finance is to do it in chunks over a couple of years. You need to allow six months to raise each stage of finance.

Company: Glasses Direct
Owner-manager: Jamie Murray Wells

There are also various grants specifically set aside for people looking to start an e-commerce or online venture. Of course, the current economic conditions mean that raising finance is a tougher proposition than ever before so it's even more important that you prepare cashflow projections in your business plan that adequately reflect what you need to borrow.

 From the experts

Company: moneysupermarket.com
Owner-manager: Simon Nixon

If you're looking to raise finance in the current economic climate, you've got to have a very compelling idea, a strong business case and a proven track record in the industry you are targeting.

Funding it yourself

Funding it yourself should be a fairly simple decision: either you can or you can't. There really is no such thing as free money so for pure efficiency nothing makes better financial sense than resisting borrowing altogether. On the downside, it's an option few are blessed with.

 In my experience

Our business is funded by the staff, all of whom are shareholders, and a German family company, WIV AG, which is in the wine business as well.

Company: Naked Wines
Owner-manager: Rowan Gormley

It's also an area some are distinctly uncomfortable with. Ask yourself if you really want to invest your life savings in a venture when it's possible to borrow from a bank. Possibly not. If that's the case, the first question to ask is: if you're not convinced why should any other investor be? The second is: how much can you comfortably put in? Banks are likely to expect you to match whatever they lend you and you'll do well to find an individual who'll give you their cash to play with while you keep your own in the bank.

 From the experts

Company: moneysupermarket.com
Owner-manager: Simon Nixon

As a business, we never had to raise external funding – we grew organically. We never bit off more than we could chew so the business evolved with gradual costs that we were in control of.

Friends and family

'Fools' is often jokingly tagged onto the end of this duo and not just for its alliterative appeal. Start-up businesses are risky investments, even when they're backed by the canniest of high yielding, wealthy business veterans. Yet strangely, people seem willing to part with princely sums for decisions based on little more than emotion, love and the conviction someone they believe in will look after their money. There is no shortage of successful internet businesses that started off with funding from friends

From the experts

Company: ASOS
Owner-manager: Nick Robertson

We raised just over £2m from friends and family, with the condition that the business would float on AIM (the stock market for smaller, growing companies) in the near future. Everybody does something for something, so when we raised the money, we ensured we had an exit plan for investors that was defined.

and family. ASOS is one and Steve Pankhurst and Jason Porter, founders of the phenomenally popular website, Friends Reunited, raised £50,000 from friends who received shares in the company in return.

As you're the one looking for the money, not blindly pumping it in, this might not concern you. Indeed, it's easy to turn the situation on its ear and let your determination to get your dream online business up and running convince you that you're actually doing them a favour by letting them share in your success. If all goes well, this could be true.

It's what happens if it doesn't that you need to consider. Many friendships and relationships have gone out of the window as the bailiffs have walked through the door, so think long and hard about raising funds from friends and family. Explain the risks, get any investment tied up in a legally binding contract that secures the rights of all those who have invested and ensure that those investing are aware that there is no guarantee that the business will succeed. Funding from friends and family, when it works, will leave you the freedom to save bank financing for a later stage when you're looking to expand and grow.

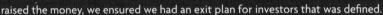

Startups Tips

It can actually be sensible to fund start-up costs with a loan and save a slice of your own cash for running costs and future investment; borrowing for a loan will be less expensive than an overdraft or credit cards. There could also be tax advantages to structuring how much you invest yourself and borrow. This is the point where you should get an accountant on board who'll advise you on the best way to proceed.

Equity finance

Equity finance involves giving away a percentage of your business in exchange for the money you require to start or grow your business.

Equity finance usually comes from one or more wealthy individuals commonly known as business angels who are often experienced entrepreneurs with money to invest in other up and coming companies. While the reality is far removed from the drama of the TV show, these are the kind of deals struck on the BBC hit series *Dragons' Den*.

It's also possible to raise equity finance through organised public or private funds which are usually run by either experienced entrepreneurs or investment companies. Private equity deals usually fill the gap between standard bank loans and venture capital deals, but can vary from anything from £10,000 to £250,000.

Venture capital (VC) works on the same principle but is run by large organisations and deals are usually in excess of £500,000, although this is rare for start-up businesses and the VC will usually expect to place someone on the board, so you'll need to be comfortable with this arrangement.

Private equity is certainly more common but not easy to find. However, if you've run an online business before or have a proven track record in your planned sector it might be that you'll find an investor willing to back you from day one.

From the experts

Company: moneysupermarket.com
Owner-manager: Simon Nixon

Venture capitalists are looking for a business that has already proven itself and that can be taken to the next stage. I didn't like the idea of raising venture capital, as it meant having venture capitalists on your board and less control.

The problem is that whatever you're giving away at the start won't be worth very much, so it's almost certain you'll lose a chunky slice of what in a few years' time might seem a meagre sum. It's far better to use debt finance and then refinance once you're in a better position to bargain from and can offer a greater chance of reward for the investor's risk.

Taking on an equity partner also provides a new sense of responsibility and pressure. With the money comes a need to create a substantial return in an agreed period of time and once you commit to that the decisions you make must become more focused on generating that return than what works for you in a lifestyle scenario. That can be a very healthy motivation and it's worth it if that's the type of business you want to run.

Regional venture capital funds

The Capital Fund: www.thecapitalfund.co.uk
South East Growth Fund: www.segrowthfund.co.uk
East of England Fund: www.createpartners.com
South West Regional Venture Capital Fund: www.southwestventuresfund.co.uk
Advantage Growth Fund: www.midven.co.uk
East Midlands Regional Venture Capital Fund: www.catapult-vm.co.uk
Yorkshire and Humber Fund: www.yfmventurefinance.co.uk
Capital North East: www.nel.co.uk
North West Fund: www.nwef.co.uk

Sources of business angel funding

Advantage Business Angels: www.advantagebusinessangels.com
Beer & Partners: www.beerandpartners.com
British Business Angels Association: www.bbaa.org.uk
Envestors: www.envestors.co.uk
Equus Capital: www.equuscapital.co.uk
Great Eastern Investment Forum: www.geif.co.uk
Hotbed: www.hotbed.uk.com
London Business Angels: www.lbangels.co.uk
Northwest Business Angels: www.nwbusinessangels.co.uk
Pi Capital: www.picapital.co.uk
SWAIN: www.swain.org.uk
Yorkshire Association of Business Angels: www.yaba.org.uk
Xenos: www.xenos.co.uk
NB: some sources only cover certain areas of the UK

Grants for websites

As well as exploring the opportunities above, as an online business start-up, you may qualify for certain grants to help launch your website. Contact your local authority in the first instance as the number of grants and amounts available varies between different councils. IT and e-commerce grants are normally available up to £1,000, to help you meet the costs of designing a website, purchasing a domain name and acquiring software. To qualify for these, your business will most likely need to be based in a specific region of the UK and will need to be operating in a certain sector, such as retail.

In my experience

I received £650,000 of angel funding and many millions of venture capital. You need to be very creative about how you raise money. We really looked at how we could leverage debt and how to talk to a lot of different investors. We thought about different finance options such as friends and family, angel networks and venture capitalists.

Company: Glasses Direct
Owner-manager: Jamie Murray Wells

Bank or debt finance

Unsurprisingly, the recent recession has had a severe impact on bank finance, meaning that small businesses will find it harder to secure loans from banks. UK lending to small businesses collapsed in 2009, as Britain's banks lent £900m to small businesses, less than a quarter of the average annual rate for the past five years, according to figures from the British Bankers Association. The statistics show that total lending to small business grew from £54.4bn to £55.3bn in 2009. In each of the previous five years, lending grew by roughly £4bn.

While the demand for credit is as strong as in previous years, the Federation of Small Businesses (FSB), the UK's largest campaigning pressure group promoting and protecting the interests of the self-employed and owners of small firms, says that the sector is 'losing faith in the banks' because of the rising cost of finance. According to the FSB, small businesses are increasingly turning towards friends and family as a source of finance.

On a more positive note, in 2009, the government unveiled details of business loan schemes designed to offer help to small businesses across the UK that are having problems accessing finance from their banks. The schemes are aimed at encouraging the banks to lend more and will help those businesses that are having cashflow difficulties and those that are looking for investment for future growth. There are three main packages available (listed below), and although not all of them apply to start-ups, they are worth noting as they are designed to help your business as it grows.

As banks are continuing to make finance available, they should be your first port of call when looking to finance your online business. Banks are vastly experienced in helping start-ups and should be able to offer a number of finance packages tailored to suit your needs as well as providing a fair degree of support. A good bank manager should be able to give you a clear explanation of your options and what is expected to meet any lending criteria.

Be warned though, that banks see thousands of business plans and will see through any overly optimistic forecasts, dressing up of figures or holes in your business plan, so you'll need to ensure your research is comprehensive.

Working capital scheme: Designed to help banks increase all types of lending, such as existing and new loans. The scheme is open to companies with a turnover of up to £500m.

Enterprise finance guarantee scheme: Open to businesses with a turnover of up to £25m, to enable them to secure loans of between £1,000 and £1m, repayable over 10 years. The recent Comprehensive Spending Review has guaranteed that this scheme will continue for a further four years, making around £2bn available to viable small companies without a credit history or collateral.

Capital for enterprise fund: This £75m fund will enable businesses to sell debt in exchange for equity.

Choosing a bank

It's natural that you'll probably turn to your current bank first – after all, you are already familiar with them. At least half of a successful banking relationship relies on the ability to work with the bank manager who has been assigned to your case, rather than the bank itself.

Different banks offer different incentives such as so many years' free banking to open a business bank account as well as pricing and organising their charging mechanisms differently. Some offer a greater level of service and usually offer lower interest rates or higher charges as a result, while other banks specialise in keeping basic costs low but offering little service.

Even if you're keen to stay with your main bank, do shop around and examine the start-up packages on offer, if only to check you're not missing out on something offered elsewhere. If you are, negotiate.

While there are savings it's likely you'll derive more long-term value from finding a bank you're comfortable with, which makes the effort to listen and understand your business and, ultimately, will lend you the money you need to start up.

Even if you've decided on a bank offering make sure you meet the bank manager you'll be dealing with. The relationship with your bank manager is absolutely fundamental to your success, especially in raising finance.

Managers will have a threshold of loans they can sign off and even though you'll be assessed by the bank's credit and decisions programmes, having your manager onside will make a massive difference.

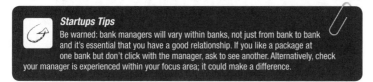

Startups Tips
Be warned: bank managers will vary within banks, not just from bank to bank and it's essential that you have a good relationship. If you like a package at one bank but don't click with the manager, ask to see another. Alternatively, check your manager is experienced within your focus area; it could make a difference.

Applying for a bank loan

Bank loans are one of the most common and preferred types of finance for start-ups, suitable for paying for assets such as computers and for start-up capital and other areas where the amount of money you need is not likely to change.

Banks, however, have very clear expectations of what they want to see from your business plan before they'll give you a penny and it's crucial you bear this in mind.

They'll want to see you've accounted for all eventualities, your own income and been realistic about your anticipated revenues. They will have clear criteria you'll be expected to meet for them to be convinced they'll see a return on their investment. If you're at all unsure about your forecasts or figures it's worth speaking to a bank manager before submitting any loan application to see if you're heading along the right lines or need to have a rethink. It's far better to spend time at the beginning refining your plan and application for a loan than to start the process and find there is still a considerable amount left to do.

Depending on how much you want to borrow, banks will usually expect to see that you're matching what you're borrowing with your own money and could also ask for security against your home. This is something that puts many people off and can seem understandably frightening. If you reach this point and are having second thoughts, you're possibly not ready to start a business after all. What you're about to do inevitably involves a high level of risk. However, providing it works it's also full of rewards. If you're not convinced that the balance is in your favour you have to ask why the bank should be.

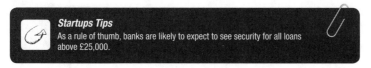

Startups Tips
As a rule of thumb, banks are likely to expect to see security for all loans above £25,000.

If you're reluctant or unable to offer security or match the bank's lending, the other option is to lower the amount you want to borrow. Providing you've a decent credit rating and can offer reasonable evidence you'll be able to afford the repayments, banks will often give sanctions to personal loans up to around £15,000 which can be used for start-up costs and repaid over a period of time, ranging from 36–84 months.

Banks will also offer you credit card and overdraft facilities, but will discourage you from using them for anything other than cashflow management and short-term borrowing. That's not to say you can't use them however you see fit but, especially in the current climate, be very careful about borrowing anything you couldn't afford to pay back at very short notice or you could find yourself in real trouble over a relatively small amount.

Pitching for finance

Before we get into the detail of what you should say, how you should dress, and what banks and investors expect when you pitch for finance, it's important to highlight one all significant, and too often overlooked fact about borrowing money: banks (and investors) want to lend it.

Regardless of how bad the economic climate gets, banks and investors will always lend money if they're confident they'll get a healthy return. After all, they are in the business of making money. Your challenge then isn't to beg and grovel for any scrap of money you can get your hands on, but to present a compelling opportunity for them.

It's on this premise you should base your pitch. Remember banks are investing other people's money so they need to, as closely as possible, guarantee a return. They're certainly not gamblers. You'll need to present a clear, low-risk proposition that demonstrates how the money will be

 In my experience

Getting the right investor can be crucial to your success. Focus on getting people that will not only provide you with funding but who also have the knowledge and experience to help, who share the passion for what you are doing and who you like – you will be spending a lot of time with them.

Company: Wahanda.com
Owner–manager: Lopo Champalimaud

spent and, crucially, how it'll be repaid and when. While investors might be entailing a slightly higher degree of risk and possibly expect to, bankers won't entertain anything but a sensible punt.

Preparation

Make sure you're 100% prepared. If you're actually making a presentation, be clear about all your facts and figures and know them off by heart. It's likely that a bank will have already read your business plan by the time you get to pitch or talk through your proposition so you should be prepared for questions that delve beyond the facts and figures.

If you are making a presentation, view this as good news that the bank wants to talk further. However, think what else they might want to ask you. Critique your own business plan or ask others to do it for you with a view to pre-empting any questions that stand out. Practising a pitch in front of family and friends can help prepare you and offer you tips on areas for improvement.

A clear concise answer will reassure the bank you're clear about what you're doing and that this matters to you sufficiently to have put the effort in. Don't attempt to try and answer a question if you can't; this only sends a message that you'll try and fudge. All investors prefer honesty so be upfront and admit you don't know, but suggest you could certainly find out. Perhaps even flatter them by thanking them for bringing it to your attention.

From the experts

Company: **LinkedIn**
Owner-manager: **Reid Hoffman**

Part of the reason we took a round of funding and part of what we did with it is focus on building our team and the features available on our website.

Appearance

Dress smart. If you are not in the habit of wearing a suit, put on a smart shirt and trousers/skirt. The fact that how you dress not how talented you are or how great your business idea is might determine if you get a bank loan or not is a contentious issue for many people. For others, wearing a suit demonstrates a sense of professionalism and desire to be taken seriously. Whatever your personal view, it's probably best to err on the side of caution and assume that the majority of bank managers will still expect you to dress smart. Neglecting to do so is risky and can put you on the back foot from the start. If you're someone who simply couldn't bear to change their appearance then by all means dress as you see fit, but be aware one of the most important attributes of a small business owner needs to be flexibility and your reluctance to adapt could be viewed as representative of your personality.

If you go into the room feeling confident you've put your homework in, have belief in your idea and are looking smart there's every chance the bank will believe you're the type of individual they're looking for. There are, however, no guarantees in business.

Dealing with a no

Rejection is something you should get used to quickly. There's every chance several banks will say no before one says yes. See each rejection as a learning experience or rehearsal for the one that says yes.

Find out why they've said no, as the feedback might be useful. Don't let it dampen your spirits though, there's always more money out there. And don't argue with the decision either. Disputing a bank's decision to say no is as futile as arguing with refereeing decisions; you're never going to change their minds.

Accounts

There's no escaping from it: you need to know your numbers. At any point you should know how much money you've got in the pot, how much you owe, what you're committed to in orders, any salaries you might be paying, how much your assets (stock, website and equipment such as computers) are worth and, if anything, how much you're owed. You should know what you've taken that day (preferably that hour) and what you're going to make for the rest of the hour, day, week, month, year.

You should know it and you should understand it. Otherwise you'll have no idea how the business is performing and no solid financial base from which to make decisions.

The basics you should understand are how to read a balance sheet of your income and outgoings, called a profit and loss sheet. Here's an example:

Profit & Loss sheet example	£	£	£
Sales/turnover			60,894
Opening stock (1st of month)	3,000		
And purchases made	24,253		
		27,253	
Less closing stock (30/31st of month)		4,278	
Cost of goods sold		31,531	
Direct labour costs		7,364	
			38,895
Gross Profit			**29,363**
Overheads			
Rents and rates	3,294		
Heat, light and power	783		
Insurance	106		
Indirect wages and salaries	7,296		
Marketing costs	571		
Printing, stationery and consumables	1,951		
Computer costs	758		
Telephone	939		
Depreciation of assets	3,697		
Legal and professional fees	750		
Bank and finance charges	264		**20,409**
Net profit before tax			**8,954**

We'll cover the finances you need to know once you're up and running in Chapter 8.2.

To begin with you certainly don't need to know much else, though. Not everyone is great with figures and this is where accountants come in. If you pay for any outside help in setting up your online venture, an accountant with experience in the sector will almost certainly prove useful and offer the best return on investment.

If you think you'll need the services of an accountant though, find one early in the process. Too many people wait until the end of the tax year when the annual tax return looms, to sort out their accounts. By this time they are likely to have accumulated piles of paper. An accountant can sort this out for you but leaving it that long can make it an expensive and time-consuming process. Involve them early on and they'll get your financial data straight from the start and almost certainly find ways of making you some fairly significant savings. They can also give you some invaluable business advice in the early stages of your business when you might need it the most.

Paying yourself

Your business plan should include how and what you intend to pay yourself for at least the first year – and it's essential you include this in any borrowing that you take out.

It's true that banks and investors love to see you're making massive sacrifices to see your business get off the ground. If you can afford not to take a salary for the first few months or even the first year, they'll expect you to do this. It not only ensures all profits can be reinvested back into the business, but demonstrates just how badly you want to succeed and how determined you are.

That said, it's simply impossible for many people to do this and while an online business incurs relatively low overheads compared to other types of business, it isn't just for people wealthy enough to have six months' salary in the bag. If you can't survive without taking a salary out of the business, whatever you do, don't pretend you can. Trying not to pay yourself and hoping you'll somehow muddle through almost never works and is foolish to try.

Everybody has to pay a mortgage or rent; everybody has to eat; everybody has reasonable living expenses – and lenders do understand that. Not paying yourself a wage will just mean you end up borrowing elsewhere and, conversely, lenders can actually view that as bad management. Saying you can live on £500 a month when your mortgage is £1,000 a month isn't going to look too clever.

Lenders also dislike it when they lend an initial amount of money based on forecasts they've been told are realistic only for the borrower to promptly return needing more. Again that doesn't speak much for management or your forecasting skills.

It's far better to include your wage as a cost of the business. Indeed, it actually sets your business out on a solid model from the outset. Anyone who stepped into your shoes or acquired the business would expect to either earn a wage or pay a managing director a wage and your business model needs to be able to support that. For example, a business that claims to be generating a healthy profit of £50,000 but whose owners are effectively working for free, perhaps isn't as successful as it might first appear.

Having said that, don't expect to pay yourself a fortune. Investors won't appreciate you pulling up at the bank asking for a loan in a Ferrari dressed head to toe in Armani. If you're coming from a corporate background to escape the pressured rat race, be realistic. You're setting up your own online business and are expected to work hard first and reap the rewards later.

Startups Tips

So what's a realistic amount to pay yourself? There are very few statistics for average earnings for online businesses, but review your personal spending habits, assess how much you need to support your lifestyle, look at this figure and be conservative.

Startups checklist

- Consider your finance options carefully: What's best for you, straight loans or giving away a share of the pie?
- Make sure family and friends are clear about what they're getting involved in before you accept any cash from them.
- Be prepared when pitching: You need to know your figures inside out.
- Be realistic: It's better to ask for the cash in advance than ask for help when you're in trouble.

3

LEGALITIES

 # CHAPTER 3.1

Trademarks, domain names and copyright

Running a business comes with a host of legal obligations and it's essential that you protect yourself, your business and your customers from any potential legal threats. The internet is well established as a business model, but many related laws are still evolving so it's equally important to keep up to date with internet legalities as well as being aware of the basics.

The other point to bear in mind is that the internet gives you an instant global customer base – people from all over the world can log on to your site and buy goods or services. As such, you'll need to be aware of rules governing global e-commerce as well as regulations that relate to trading in the country you are based in.

While other areas such as cashflow, planning and PR (public relations) make your business, failing to stay inside the law – no matter how tedious it feels – can break it.

In this chapter we'll cover:

→ Trade names, trademarks and domain names
→ Securing your domain name
→ Privacy policies
→ Terms and conditions
→ Copyright
→ Legislation that affects you
→ Maintaining a database of customers
→ What can go wrong.

Trade names, trademarks and domain names

Trademarks are signs, symbols, logos, names and colours (things that can be described in writing) that differentiate your business from that of your competitors. It's one of the ways customers will recognise your company and its products, and businesses generally spend a lot of time and effort on names. The right name for the business or a product could help you stand out from the crowd; the wrong one could place you in a legal dispute.

Trademarks are powerful and valuable assets. Protecting your trademarks should be an important consideration whenever a new business or product is being launched. Trademarks help customers and other businesses identify your products and services and also the reputation and goodwill that has been built up. All too often others may wish to copy, and attempt to share your success. This may or may not have an immediate effect on turnover, but others using your name could prevent trademark registration and the exclusivity it offers. In addition, any adverse publicity or poor reputation your rival may acquire may affect your business if customers cannot differentiate between the two names.

To register your trademark, apply to the Intellectual Property Office. Do some research to ensure that no one else has applied for the same or a similar trademark and make sure you are satisfied with your choice, as you can't alter your trademark once your application has been submitted. List all the goods and services you want your trademark to cover, as again, you can't add any later.

Your biggest challenge with trademarks is likely to be ensuring you are not infringing someone else's. It's vital that you don't do this or that you take action if you think someone is using your trademark. A quick search on the internet will help point you in the right direction, but it might not be the definitive answer as to whether a trademark has been registered or not, so if in doubt, err on the side of caution. Follow up an internet search by carrying out an exhaustive trademark search. The more individual your trademark, the more likely it is to be successfully registered.

Startups Tips
You could also check with a trademark adviser to see if the name and logo you have chosen are not infringing any existing trademarks. If you have big plans for your website, it makes sense to register your trademark from the outset.

Having a trademark, however, does not mean you can automatically use this for your domain name. This is the term used to identify particular web pages and how people search for information on the internet. For example, in the website address http://nominet.org.uk/index.html the domain name is nominet.org.uk. Domain names are also used as part of an email address. Someone may have already registered the domain name you want for the same, similar or different goods and services. You can take legal action if you think someone is using a domain name to pass off their goods and services as yours or if someone has taken out your trade name as a domain name in order to try and sell it back to you. Nominet. uk is the registry for .uk internet domain names, and provides a dispute resolution service for .uk domain names (www.nic.uk).

 In my experience

We really didn't think about trademarks when we chose the name Wahanda. We were much more concerned about having a name that was original and that allowed us to express the full range of health and beauty areas that we cover.

Company: Wahanda.com

Owner–manager: Lopo Champalimaud

Securing your domain name

Assuming that no one has beaten you to it, anyone can register a domain name – UK ones are being registered at a rate of more than 200,000 a month. One you've chosen your domain name, you need to decide what domain name type or extension you want – this describes the ending of your domain name. There are various ones to choose from, the most common being: .co.uk, .com, .org, .net, .org.uk (generally used by non-profit organisations such as charities) or .plc.uk (used for UK public limited companies). Other options range from .info (for information providers), .me.uk (an individual domain name suffix), .ltd.uk (for UK limited companies), .biz (a shortened version of business), .tv (used by television broadcasters), .eu (open to residents and companies in the European Union) and the relatively new .mobi (for sites delivering services to mobile devices).

If you find that someone has beaten you to your domain name, don't despair, as there are ways you can buy a domain name from someone else – they are bought, sold and auctioned off like any other asset. Of course, your chances of securing a domain name for a website that is already doing business are very slim. If, however, the name is reserved but not obviously being used, then you could try and negotiate buying it. Many domain names have been speculatively snapped up by people hoping to sell them on at a higher price rather than use them for a business, so you may be able to buy a name that has already been 'taken', if you are prepared to pay for it.

Often, domain names that have been reserved will have contact details of the owner on the page, so you could try contacting them direct, or you could go to a site such as whois.org, which gives details of domain name ownership. You could also browse domain name auction sites, such as Sedo.co.uk or Pool.com to see if your desired domain name is up for sale or you can put in a request for the name you want and be informed when it comes up for sale.

> **Startups Tips**
> Domain names are normally registered through an agent known as an internet service provider (ISP). The price you pay (an annual fee) and service you receive will vary from agent to agent, but it's essential you use one that is registered.

Nominet.uk, the internet registry for .uk domain names, encourages companies and individuals to register a domain via an ISP. This is because the majority of ISPs are Nominet.uk members. Once you have registered with an ISP, they will then submit the application to Nominet.uk, ensuring a more thorough and secure process.

However, contractual terms, charges and service levels vary dramatically, so it is worth noting that shopping around is key to finding the best deal for you. Some ISPs offer domain registration, others include free web space and email addresses or more specialist options.

Startups Tips

Even if you are not going to use your domain name straight away, you should register it first. A list of accredited ISPs is available through the InterNIC website at www.internic.co.uk and you can carry out a search on the site to see if a domain name is available. Nominet.uk also provides a list of accredited ISPs.

Always read the small print and ask to see copies of the terms and conditions for domain name registration as well as your right to move across to another ISP if you are unhappy. If you don't register with an ISP there are around 6,000 companies who have domain registration facilities. It can often be worthwhile paying the extra to deal with an upfront reputable company that won't let you down.

There are some online packages and ISPs that will offer you a domain name for a small fee such as Microsoft's Office Live, which charges £10.99 every other year or £7.99 a year for more common domain name extensions such as .com, .org and .net. However, you may still wish to register the domain name independently. Once you have decided upon the company which is going to register your name, the process is generally swift and painless.

First, you will be asked to pay a fee to secure your domain. Once this is done, the company will then send you a template of your registered domain name to the network information centre (NIC). Each country has its own NIC, which is a centre where all the details of registered domains are held.

If your registration is accepted the company you have chosen will set up a domain name system (DNS) entry. Essentially, this means assigning your name to a name server that collates and keeps all registered names so that your domain can be found on the internet. The process takes between two and three days.

Once these stages are complete you are alive and kicking on the internet and are able to use your name.

What does it cost?

There are a variety of packages on offer. Some are cheaper than others and it often depends on what other services are included (for example, registration fees and support service fees). Fees can range from free to £200 for .co.uk names – but this depends on levels of service and support.

Prices will vary, depending on what your business needs, but there is an average price you will pay for single domain name registration.

To protect your brand, it's worth registering your domain name in both .com and co.uk versions, which are the top-level domain names for businesses. If you have high hopes for your online business, it might be worth registering several variations of the name, or versions in which it might be misspelled, to ensure you catch as many potential customers as possible.

Privacy policies

A privacy policy is information displayed on your website that lets your customers know what you do with their personal information. It's an important consideration – with the rise in identity theft, people are becoming extremely sensitive about how companies handle their personal data and are therefore cautious about exactly how much they reveal. If your customers submit details about themselves as part of a registration process or during a transaction (this could include personal and financial information or data related to their activity on the site), they will expect such data to be heavily protected. Failing to provide information on this will erode any trust you may have built up.

The policy describes what you will do with such information. For example, you may use it to help improve the customer experience on site, for your own marketing purposes or for records of transactions. A privacy policy is particularly important if you intend to run a website that collects personal data from its customers. Most websites normally include a link to their privacy policy on the bottom of the website homepage.

A privacy policy should ideally include the following:

- Description of a any information you might collect on your customers
- How you intend to use this information
- When you might use such details to contact customers
- Whether you will be disclosing this information to anyone else
- People's choices regarding any personal details they may have submitted, such as how to update or remove these
- Cookies and how your site uses them.

You can use this opportunity to inform customers that if they choose to opt in with their personal information, you may use this to send them marketing communications or to pass their details on to carefully selected third parties.

Terms and conditions

You need to include terms and conditions to give users information about your website content and what they can and can't do with it. These usually appear on a link at the bottom of the homepage – by using your website your customers accept your terms and conditions in full. The detail of these depends very much on what type of online business you are running but they should basically contain the following information:

→ An introduction to the site and who you are

→ Your limitations of liability (a disclaimer)

→ The fact that the website contains material which is owned or licensed to your business, and that reproducing it is not allowed unless it is in accordance with the copyright notice (see section below for more on this)

→ Any rules relating to use of chat rooms or forums, for example, you will remove any malicious postings or offensive wording

→ Rules relating to unauthorised use of the website

→ Contact details.

Startups Tips

You can download an example of different terms and conditions to use from www.businesslink.gov.uk.

Copyright

The growth of the internet has led to the infringement of copyright becoming more and more commonplace. Many people have fallen foul of copyright rules by inadvertently copying material without first asking for permission. As soon as a piece of work is created, copyright comes into force.

You have full rights of ownership over any content you create or have created for your website. An internet copyright notice sets out the copyright position of your website content, such as whether you will allow the material to be downloaded or distributed by visitors. An example might be: 'This website and its content is copyright of [business name] – © [business name] 2011. All rights reserved.'

Don't ever copy material from other sources to display on your website without first asking permission, although in some cases, this isn't necessary. This includes if the material is going to be used for teaching purposes, for news reporting and for reviewing, for example.

Legislation that affects you

Insurance

As you're yet to open the virtual doors to your business, it's unlikely you've much enthusiasm for thinking about all the things that could go wrong. However, while it's not the sexiest element of starting-up, ensuring your business has the necessary insurance cover will protect all the hard work you're putting in elsewhere.

Some insurance cover is required by law, others make total business sense even though they seem an expensive overhead to take on when first starting out. Instead of looking at what insurance will cost you now, you should consider the implications of a disaster on your business.

Employers' liability insurance (ELI)

If you employ one other member of staff you are required by law to have this cover or you could face a fine. This type of insurance helps you meet the cost of compensation for staff if they are injured while working. Policies generally start at around £10m worth of cover to include legal expenses. However, ELI doesn't mean you're untouchable. You must still honour all your health and safety obligations, carry out regular risk assessments and have all the appropriate paperwork to back this up. To find out more about your health and safety obligations visit the HSE website: www.hse.gov.uk.

Product liability insurance

Although not compulsory by law, if you are selling products online, you'd be very foolish not to take out this kind of cover, as it will protect you against claims made against your business by members of the public and you need to protect yourself should anything untoward happen. However, it's still your responsibility to ensure your goods meet all the necessary requirements.

Premises insurance

You might not have premises as such that your customers visit, but as your business grows, you may consider renting or buying premises to accommodate staff and technology developments. Your online business' chances of survival will be severely compromised if the actual premises are damaged. You can take out cover against damage as a result of any number of unforeseen occurrences such as floods, fires, or malicious damage. Landlords will sometimes cover certain aspects of buildings damage. The more measures you take to limit damage, such as CCTV and metal roller shutters, the easier it'll be to keep premiums down.

Contents insurance

As premises insurance only covers the physical building, you'll need to make sure the contents of your business are also adequately insured against damage or theft. This will cover stock, technology, furniture and anything else included in the policy.

Business interruption insurance

While covering you against the costs of repair and replacement, contents and premises insurance won't necessarily help with any income you lose while your business is closed as a result of unforeseen events. This is where business interruption insurance comes in.

When the Buncefield oil explosions occurred in December 2005 several companies with warehouses in the vicinity went out of business overnight. Online fashion retailer ASOS could easily have been one. It lost £3m worth of stock in its busiest week of the year, cancelled and refunded 19,000 orders and closed the site for six weeks. Fortunately, CEO Nick Robertson had the company insured to the hilt with a firm disaster recovery plan in place.

Business interruption insurance covered ASOS for the lost business and included provision for an extensive advertising campaign for relaunch.

When the site began trading again in late-January 2006, it took record sales on its first day.

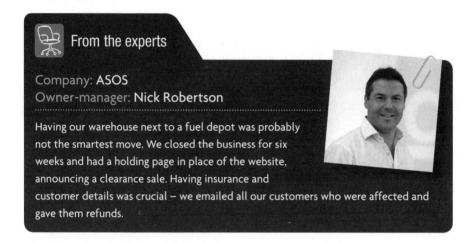

From the experts

Company: **ASOS**
Owner-manager: **Nick Robertson**

Having our warehouse next to a fuel depot was probably not the smartest move. We closed the business for six weeks and had a holding page in place of the website, announcing a clearance sale. Having insurance and customer details was crucial – we emailed all our customers who were affected and gave them refunds.

Online regulations

As an online trader you are subject to the same laws as other retailers, such as the Consumer Protection Act, the Sale of Goods Act 1979, and the Supply of Goods and Services Act 1982, as well as a few internet specific ones.

If you're planning to sell online you will need to be familiar with the Electronic Commerce (EC Directive) Regulations 2002. Nearly all commercial websites are covered by these regulations so there's no getting away from them, and no excuse for not knowing them.

To comply, your customers must have certain information including your business' name, physical address and email address. You must also give details of any professional body with which you are registered, and display your VAT registration number if you have one.

The Companies Act 2006 also requires all UK companies to state the company registration number, place of registration, and registered office address on all of their websites. You do not have to display this information on every single web page. It is commonly placed on the 'About us' section of the site.

As well as displaying the appropriate information on your e-commerce website you must also be aware of the Distance Selling Regulations. These regulations are designed to protect the consumer when they are not actually in the presence of the vendor during a sale. The regulations cover sales made via the internet, email, phone or mail order or digital television. However, they do not apply to business-to-business transactions.

Under the regulations, the seller is required to:

→ Give consumers clear information including details of the goods or services offered, delivery arrangements and payment, the supplier's details and the consumer's cancellation rights before they buy. This information must be provided in writing

→ Give the consumer a right to a cooling-off period to cancel the sale contract within seven working days

→ Give the consumer written confirmation of their order

→ Deliver the product within 30 days unless otherwise agreed.

There are however, some exceptions to rules surrounding cancellation of contracts for businesses offering accommodation, transport and catering or leisure services. This only applies where services have been agreed for a specific date or time period. Other exceptions include the sale of customised or perishable goods, sealed audio or video recordings, or opened software, as well as items or services bought via auctions.

You can find out more information on the regulations by visiting the website of the Office of Fair Trading at www.oft.gov.uk.

Maintaining a database of customers

One of a business' greatest assets is its list of customers, which is effectively a source of past sales and potential future revenue. A database can also help you identify key trends and important information such as your most and least profitable customers. With an internet business, your customer database is likely to (or hopefully will) contain thousands of email addresses.

Keeping this up to date can be time-consuming and challenging though. People's email addresses change on a regular basis and most people have more than one email address (for example a business and personal one) so it's essential to keep customer details up to date and ensure you don't duplicate. Email data decays rapidly – people can change from one email service provider to another with alarming frequency and with people changing jobs more often these days than in the past, work emails can quickly go out of date.

Getting up to date details of email addresses and other customer information that can help you with your marketing, such as age, marital status, and family situation can prove to be a challenge, though. Consumers are increasingly wary of providing any information about themselves while online, largely as a result of the rise in identity theft. There have been many instances, documented in the media, of criminals finding out people's personal details and using them to open bank accounts and get credit cards, loans, state benefits and documents such as passports and driving licences in these customers' names.

Spam is another reason people are reluctant to part with their email address. Most of us have experienced the frustration of entering our email address on one website and soon after receiving volumes of spam email. So what steps can you take to build and maintain a customer database, and encourage customers to part with their details?

→ Be clear at all times about how you will be using customer data. Your privacy policy should cover this in detail, and ensure you stick by what you say.

→ Safeguarding personal information you collect goes without saying. We'll cover this in Chapter 4.2, in the security section (see p.124), but try not to use obvious names for your database files such as 'customer details', 'email list' or 'subscribers'. Spammers are skilled in scouring the net for email addresses they can harvest and naming files in an obvious way is playing right into their hands.

→ Clean your database on a regular basis. As mentioned, email data decays far more rapidly than postal or telephone data. Every time you send an email newsletter or alert for example, make a list of bounced email addresses that you can clean your original list against. You might have an impressive database of 50,000 customers and their details, but it will be worth very little if only a small portion of these details are correct.

When things go wrong

In Chapter 4 (p.95), we will cover issues your business might face, such as security threats and the risk of hackers hijacking your customers' details

Cleaning your data

There's little doubt that email marketing campaigns are far more cost-effective to run than postal ones but if you don't ensure the email addresses you hold on your customer database are valid ones, you will be wasting time and money.

If your basic customer information is misspelt, out of date or inaccurate, you won't be able to gain your customers' trust. No one likes to receive an email where their name is misspelt – more often than not, it will be deleted. Clean data helps you to maintain good customer relationships by minimising the likelihood of annoying or offending your customers through data inaccuracies.

for identity theft purposes or harvesting their email addresses and sending unsolicited emails. US telecoms provider AT&T was the victim of a hacking attack in June 2010, when the email addresses of more than 114,000 Apple iPad users who had signed up to AT&T's wireless internet service were exposed. Monster.com too suffered a security breach in early 2009, during which time hackers obtained unauthorised access to its database and downloaded account logins, as well as the corresponding personal information. The website warned that the stolen data could be used to launch phishing attacks.

In such instances, it's imperative to react quickly to restore customer confidence. When running an online business, it can be tempting to try to sort everything out remotely. But don't just rely on email to sort things out, get on the phone if you have to and drag people out of bed if necessary – after all, this is your dream business and it could be your livelihood on the line.

When you make calls, ensure you record or take copious notes of discussions, including times that calls have been made, the content and the person you spoke to, plus their telephone extension.

Online retailer Amazon came under fire a few years ago when consumers said the retailer did not adequately protect customer details. Amazon responded immediately by promising that it would heighten its protection on customer data, refrain from selling its customer database to marketers and narrow the wording of its exceptions. The company also promised to provide specific examples of how data is used and what data it gathers from customers.

In my experience

Don't be intimidated by legal issues – you aren't the first person to start a business. Get a good solicitor and don't be afraid to ask for advice from those around you.

Company: Wahanda.com
Owner-manager: Lopo Champalimaud

Startups checklist

- Keep up to date with new legal developments, as the internet is a fast-moving environment.
- Look after your customer data: People will not trust companies where data breaches occur.
- Ensure your privacy policy is clearly written and easy to find on your website.
- Always contact your customers as soon as something happens that may affect them.
- Clean your data regularly: Consider outsourcing this if you don't have the resources in-house.

CHAPTER 3.2

Registering your business

Naturally your energies will be focused on getting your online business launched and trading – but before you can start this you'll need to register your business. What can seem an overly complicated and laborious process isn't actually that difficult once you've established the basics and gathered all the information you'll need to register.

You'll need to decide what legal structure your business will take, be it a sole trader, partnership or a limited company, complete the necessary paperwork and then submit your registration to Companies House, one of its licensed agents or HMRC. The legal implications and paperwork differ for each structure so make sure you pick the one that is best for your business and fulfil all the required steps to forming that type of company.

In this chapter we'll cover:

--> Sole traders and partnerships

--> Limited companies

--> Registering as a limited company, including how to name your business and the company officers you need.

The different legal business structures

There are essentially three legal or accounting structures you can choose from when starting your online business. You can go it alone by being a sole trader, team up to form a partnership or operate a limited company. Choosing the right structure is important, so you'll need to give it some serious thought. It is possible to switch between different structures after you've started your business. For example, you may start out as a sole trader, and then decide to register your business as a limited company or partnership. You will save yourself a lot of work if you establish the most appropriate business structure beforehand though. Below is an explanation of the different legal structures you can choose from when starting your online business and guidance on which structure is most suitable for both you and your web venture.

Sole traders and partnerships

Registering as a sole trader, essentially just you on your own, is relatively straightforward, record-keeping is simple and you get to keep all the profits after tax. As a sole trader you are the single owner of your business and have complete control over the way it is run. However, and this is quite a crucial factor, the law makes no distinction between the business and you as the owner. This means you'll be solely responsible from your personal wealth for any debts if the business runs into trouble. This differs to a limited company (which we'll come to) where debts, but also profits, are liable to the company not the individual.

If you choose to run your online business as a sole trader you must register as self-employed with HMRC within three months of your trading start date otherwise you could be fined and charged interest on any outstanding tax and National Insurance payments you owe.

If you're forming your business with one or more other people you need to register as a partnership. As with the sole trader model, each partner is responsible for any debts the business incurs. Each partner is also self-employed and receives a percentage of any returns from the business, which they are then taxed on. The partnership as well as the individuals within it must submit annual self-assessment returns to HMRC and keep stringent records on business income and expenses.

Starting an online business as a sole trader or partnership venture can prove the easier option initially, especially if you don't have ambitions for rapid growth. There is less paperwork involved and you will not need to register and send annual returns to Companies House. It is also much easier to withdraw funds from the business as essentially, all profits make up your own earnings. However, as well as the financial liability that lies at your feet, as a sole trader it is much more difficult to grow the business and you may find it harder when dealing with creditors and suppliers.

Limited liability companies

Registering as a limited (Ltd) company is probably the best legal structure to go with if you have any intention of growing your web venture beyond the smallest of operations. As well as offering you a degree of personal financial security should your business run into financial difficulties, it will also give you more credibility when seeking finance or credit. Registering your online business as a limited company also makes tax and succession planning a lot easier.

If you expect your online business to maintain a healthy amount of trade and return high levels of profit you will definitely want to go with the Ltd model. Profits will be subject to corporation tax, (up until March 2011, profits of up to £300,000 will be taxed at 21% and from April, this will drop to 20%, which is half the rate you could end up paying as a high-earning sole trader). Limited companies pay corporation tax on profits and company directors are taxed as employees in the same way as any other people you employ.

A limited company is very different from a sole trader model where there is no legal distinction between you and the business. A limited company is a separate legal entity to the people that run it. Profits and losses belong to the company, and the business can continue regardless of the death, resignation or bankruptcy of the shareholders or directors. Your personal financial risk will be restricted to how much you have invested in the company and any personal guarantees you gave when raising finance for the business. However, if the company fails and you have not carried out your duties as a company director, you could be liable for debts as well as being disqualified from acting as a director in another company.

You can get help with this from an accountant, of course, and if you have aspirations of your business employing staff and making healthy profits (who hasn't?) a limited company is almost certainly the structure for you.

Startups Tips

If you decide to register your business as a limited company you will need to allow more time to deal with the paperwork as it is a much more administration-heavy process than running a business as a sole trader. It will also require more stringent record keeping and auditing throughout the entire life of the business.

Registering as a limited company

To register your business as a limited company you must submit the appropriate paperwork to Companies House, the official UK government register of UK companies or one of its registered formation agents. What follows is a guide to the process, and documents and requirements involved in turning your business into a legal entity.

Although it is possible to register a limited company yourself, unless you have done it before you are probably going to need to engage the services of a solicitor, accountant, chartered secretary or a company formation agent. Formation agents use their own software that works directly with the Companies House systems. If you want to register your company electronically (most are registered this way) you will need to have the specific Companies House electronic interface – hence the need for a formation agent. However, you can still deliver the physical documents directly to Companies House without the need for a formation agent or specific electronic interface.

Startups Tips

Download all the forms you need to fill in at www. companieshouse. gov.uk. You can fill these in online, or send them to Companies House by post (see the website for address).

It can be far easier to register using an official formation agent and that's what most people do. There are lots of these agents listed on the Companies House website and all use slight variations of the same software. Look at several and pick one that sounds the most helpful or whose online system looks the easiest to use, providing the prices are sensible.

Finally, you can buy an 'off-the-shelf' company. You will receive a ready-made limited company that has designated company officers listed on the paperwork. You simply transfer your name and the names of any other company directors once you receive your documentation. The process can be completed on the same day and many accountancy firms will have several ready-made limited companies that they can sell to you. This is the quickest option, and with the exception of registering the company yourself, can often be the cheapest too.

Costs

Prices for formation agents can be up to £200 depending on the level and speed of service you require. A key advantage of using a formation agent is the advice they can give you on compiling the necessary documents and the right structure for your business. Companies House does not provide this service when registering, so if you are unfamiliar with the process it is advisable to get help to avoid errors. Going through the registration process yourself can be time-consuming, especially if you make a mistake, and Companies House staff will not advise you about specific matters such as the content of the documents you are required to submit.

Alternatively, you could also get assistance from an online registration company. The standard service usually costs £30–£100 including fees, but since some documentation needs to be posted, registration usually takes three to eight days, although there are a few same-day services now coming onto the market. This option is usually cheaper than using a formation agent, although you will not receive the same level of personal service.

Company officers

Once you have established whether or not you need help in establishing your company you will need to decide on who the company officers will be, and what your business will be called.

Limited companies are required by law to have named company officers. Company officers are the formally named directors and company secretary as stated in the Articles of Association, one of the documents you submit to Companies House that is explained in more detail below. It is a legal requirement for company officers to be in place at all times and for their names and current addresses to be written on the registration documents. If there is a change in company officers, Companies House must be informed straight away. All private limited companies must have at least one director and a company secretary.

Company directors

Company directors are the people that manage the company's affairs in accordance with its Articles of Association and the law. Generally, anyone can be appointed company director and the post does not require any formal qualifications. However, there are a few exceptions.

You are prohibited from being a company director if:

→ You are an undischarged bankrupt or disqualified by a court from holding a directorship

→ You are under 16 (this only applies in Scotland).

Company directors have a responsibility to make sure certain documents reach the registrar at Companies House. These are:

→ Accounts

→ Annual returns

→ Notice of change of directors or secretaries

→ Notice of change of registered office.

Startups Tips

It's worth noting that it costs as little as £15 to register directly with Companies House so what you're paying for is the service of an agent to help you through the process or an online agent's software.

Directors that fail to deliver these documents on time can be prosecuted and are subject to fines of up to £5,000 for each offence. On average, 1,000 directors are prosecuted each year for failing to deliver accounts and returns on time so it is not a responsibility that can be taken lightly or ignored.

Company secretary

This person's duty is not specified by law but usually contained within an employment contract. For private limited companies, secretaries are not required to have any special qualifications.

The main duties of a company secretary are to:

- Maintain the statutory registers
- Ensure statutory forms are filed promptly
- Provide members and auditors with notice of meetings
- Send the registrar at Companies House copies of resolutions and agreements
- Supply a copy of the accounts to every member of the company
- Keep or arrange minutes of meetings.

Naming your business

As well as establishing your company officers, you will also need to pick a company name to register the business with. The name of your business does not have to be the same as the name of your online venture, however. If you open three shops, all with different names, you can still run them as one limited company. You will need to establish your company name before you think about filling out your registration documents, as there are certain rules to consider.

The name you choose for your company must:

- Feature the word 'limited' or 'ltd' at the end. For Welsh companies the equivalent 'cyfyngedig' or 'cyf' can be used, but documentation must also state in English that it is a limited company
- Not be made up of certain sensitive words or expressions (listed by Companies House) without the consent of the Secretary of State or relevant government department

⤙> Not imply a connection with central or local government

⤙> Not be offensive

⤙> Not be the same or similar to one that appears in the Index of Names kept by Companies House.

You can search the index of business names already registered on the Companies House website free of charge. If your chosen name is too similar to another, an objection can be lodged within 12 months following the incorporation of your company and you could be forced to change it. See more about the process of choosing a company name and the legal implications that go with it, in Chapter 4.1: Identity.

Documents to submit

When registering a limited company there are three documents that must be provided to Companies House. These are discussed below.

Memorandum of Association

This document sets out the following:

⤙> The company's name

⤙> Where the company's registered office is located: England, Wales or Scotland

⤙> What the company will do: This can be as simple as: 'to conduct business as a general commercial company'.

Articles of Association

This is where you set out the rules for running your company. You must state how shares will be allocated and transferred, how the directors, the secretary and your meetings will be governed. And if you decide not to adopt the standard articles of the Companies Act in full (known as Table A) you have to submit your amended version when registering. Once your company is incorporated you can only make changes if the holders of 75% of the voting rights in your company agree, so it pays to get this right at the outset.

Application to register a company (Form IN01)

This replaced the old Form 10 and Form 12 from 1 October 2009. There are various sections to fill in relating to details of the company's registered office, the details of the consenting Secretary and Director(s), details of the subscribers and, in the case of a company limited by shares, details of the share capital. A statement of compliance will also need to be signed to ensure that all the information submitted on the form is correct.

The new form is considerably longer than the previous Forms 10 and 12 and the level of detail required means you may need to fill in information on additional sheets of paper. Make sure to take copies of Form IN01 before sending off the originals, as Companies House will charge you for issuing copies of submitted documents. Once all that's been submitted your online business is a fully-fledged limited company, but don't forget: the legal structure you choose when you start trading isn't set in stone. You can alter your structure, or even float on the stock market should your business become successful enough. For now though, you can concentrate once again on the launch!

Startups checklist

- Assess your business structure options carefully: It may be cheaper to stay as a sole trader but are the risks to your personal finances worth it?
- When registering as a limited company make sure you've gone over your documents meticulously before submitting them. If you make a mistake you'll have to submit them again.
- Search the list of submitted business names on the Companies House website before you get your heart set on one. It may not be available.

4

SETTING UP

CHAPTER 4.1

Identity

Building an identity for your company is one of the most enjoyable aspects of starting an online business and is probably an area you have devoted a great deal of time to. The identity, including the business name, website URL, branding, style and image of your online venture is what creates the experience for your customers and helps to make your business stand out from the competition.

Think of your website as a virtual shop window. It's the first thing customers will see and what they will base their impressions on. The identity of your website will be the first step in the realisation of your desire to start your own business so make sure it reflects what you set out to do in owning your own online business.

In this chapter we'll look at:

➙ *Choosing a name/website URL*

➙ *Establishing your identity*

➙ *Style and design*

➙ *Branding your site, this includes your logo should you choose to have one.*

Choosing a name/website URL

What's in a name? Business names are funny things and their importance polarises opinion. It's easy to understand the ambiguity. Think of any successful online retailer, brand or product that you buy from and in almost every instance, the name is the very last consideration and least important factor in your conscious buying decision.

That said, business names are how we all identify and refer to those online businesses and products and it's often what we remember most. And while some names bear little significance to anything, the smartest names undoubtedly form part of the branding and identity that pulls us in.

It's safe to assume that you won't improve a poor online business with a great name, and a great one shouldn't suffer too badly from an average moniker. Let's face it, what you sell or provide, for what price and how good your service is will determine whether people like your business or not.

But that doesn't mean names aren't important.

A good name will:

→ Draw attention and attract people to your site

→ Communicate a clear message about your business' identity

→ Lend itself well to PR and set you apart from the competition.

A poor name will hinder all of the above. So these are the basic principles you should work on when planning a name.

Website names

A website name is known as the URL (uniform resource locator) or the domain name (see p.75 on how to secure your domain name). This is what your potential customers will use to find your website. It needs to be something that is memorable and ideally not too long. It also needs to be easy to spell, to eliminate the chance of customers making typos. If your business is selling baby accessories, you'll want to include the word 'baby'. A straightforward domain name, for example, www.leathershoes.co.uk will not only instantly signal to customers what your business is about, but will also be useful for search engine optimisation and marketing purposes. When your traffic logs show people typing your site's name into the search engines to reach you, it's a good indication that your site is developing a strong brand.

Don't make the mistake, however, of naming your company simply because it's a well-searched word or term. It's not about appearing on the most searches, just the right ones and near enough to the top. Andrew Selby had to rebrand his iPod accessories company because the original name, I-magine (a clever enough name as a shop), returned nothing but John Lennon search results.

Admittedly, many of the best domain names have already been taken so you'll need to exercise some creativity and do some careful research. Ideally, your business should have one name and this will be used for the domain and to name your website, becoming your brand. This will be the main way that customers will know your business. When it comes to domain names, the advantages and disadvantages of using a short or a long one have been hotly debated. There are several arguments to support both sides. A long domain name is likely to rank higher on the search engines and you'll have more room to describe your service or product offering. A short domain name, however, is easier to remember, faster to type into a browser and chances are it will be spelt correctly.

You can use up to 67 characters (61 characters plus the six characters for the extension, such as .com or .co.uk) although few websites' names ever use that many, as you run the risk of people misspelling the address and being directed elsewhere, and long names tend to be less punchy and memorable. As mentioned previously, there are various one to choose from, the most common being: .co.uk, .com, .org, .net, .org.uk (generally used by non-profit organisations such as charities) or .plc.uk (used for UK public limited companies). Other options range from .info (for information providers), .me.uk (an individual domain name suffix), .ltd.uk (for UK limited companies), .biz (a shortened version of business), .tv (used by television broadcasters), .eu (open to residents and companies in the European Union) and the relatively new .mobi (for sites delivering services to mobile devices). Try to choose a domain name with .com as this is still the most popular extension.

As a new online business, it's likely that your ideal name has already been 'taken' or registered by another company, but there are certain tricks of the trade that can help you get around this. Many businesses have simply added in a hyphen to names that have already been taken. While this means that search engines can distinguish your keywords better, your potential customers may not realise your website name has a hyphen and will simply type in the words, so you run the risk of sending them somewhere else entirely. You'll have to weigh up just how important that name is and whether it's worth using with a hyphen.

Startups Tips

When thinking about names that'll work on the internet, think search. Nine tenths of visitors to all websites arrive at your website via a search engine. For search, read Google.

Startups Tips

Make a note of several domain names that you like and test them out among friends and family. Ask them questions such as: do they like the sound of it? What comes to mind? Is it catchy and memorable?

99

Choosing a website URL

- Register a domain name which has a popular keyword that is relevant to your sector
- Have several domain names in mind as your preferred choices may already be taken
- Keep it short and therefore memorable
- Ensure the URL is easy to spell.

> **Startups Tips**
>
> If you decide to incorporate your business you need to make sure you pick a name nobody else has. If you run your business as a sole trader this is not as much of an issue but you still need to be aware of the legal implications of choosing an offensive moniker, or one with certain banned words. Check Chapter 3.2: Registering your business for more on the legal aspects of choosing a name.

Establishing your identity

When you decided to start your online business, you probably had a vision of running a virtual company, selling goods or providing services that you are passionate about. You shouldn't lose site of that vision. It's quite possibly changed a little from the planning stage where you further identified USPs, pricing strategies and differentiators, but essentially it's still that vision, combined with these factors, that makes up your online business' identity.

 In my experience

The best way to establish your business identity online is to give your customers a reason to talk about you.

Company: Wahanda.com
Owner-manager: Lopo Champalimaud

It's certainly not just the products you sell, the prices you charge or the services you provide that will determine whether people visit your site and part with their cash. You'll need to create a site that attracts customers and encourages them to spend.

Don't neglect your USPs

Keep going back to those USPs: other than products it sells or services it provides, what is your online business? What will it look and feel like? If it's upmarket premium goods you're selling to a customer with a high disposable income then the identity, from logo to design, price to packaging should reflect that. In turn, if you sell eco goods or ethically sourced products you'll want that to be entwined in all that you do.

Many businesses talk about core values and many entrepreneurs like to draw up a list of values that reflect their online business identity as a reminder to themselves and staff. It can certainly pay to constantly revisit them to ask: is this what we're about? Are we sticking to our USPs?

Once you sacrifice those USPs – start selling different products or offering new services simply because you think you can make a nice return or compromise on quality to generate sales, for example – your business stops becoming what you started out to be. This can be particularly difficult during the early days of trading and site development, but your whole sales story has been built on a unique identity and losing sight of it is a major, but commonly made, mistake.

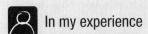

In my experience

The worst sites to me are those inhuman, large corporate sites, where there is never a mention of a person's name, no address, no telephone number, or sites that hide behind a nameless, faceless 'brand'.

Company: Country Products
Owner-manager: Mark Leather

Branding your site

Branding differs from identity as it focuses more on what people think of your business and what it stands for. Whether you like it or not, people will form opinions about your site from the moment it launches. They'll have views on what it looks like, the products or services it offers, the customer service and assign it, consciously or not, among the other brands they're exposed to and buy from.

The likes of Disney, Nike, Apple and Coca-Cola have distinctive brands that are instantly recognisable and which speak for the sector they are in. Think Disney and family and entertainment spring to mind. Apple, meanwhile is linked to technology, innovation and cutting-edge products, while Nike is not just about running shoes but about the sporting industry and athleticism. Brand names also need to be catchy and memorable. eBay founder Pierre Omidyar had originally named the business Echo Bay Technology, but when he tried to register it, he found it had already been taken by a Canadian mining company. So he chose the next closest name by shortening it to eBay.

How much you care about branding is likely to be dependent on how much you intend to grow your business. If your sole ambition is to make a nice living from it, you probably don't need to think too much about building a brand, simply maintaining your reputation should suffice. If your intentions are to expand and to one day establish a heavyweight presence online, then branding needs to be at the forefront of your thinking.

Either way, return sales will be crucial so you should be thinking about how people think about your business, and that means more than having a flash site. A great internet brand comes about from creating a great user experience. It's the way you treat customers, the level of interaction you look to have post-sale and how you communicate this in your advertising or marketing. This is particularly important for online businesses – as all transactions are carried out remotely, the whole notion of customer service can seem rather anonymous, with queries dealt with via email or through a call centre, rather than face-to-face, as in the case of a physical shop. Take Amazon as an example. The online retailer has built its reputation partly on the back of its customer service, delivering goods when promised and replying promptly to customer queries.

Deciding what your brand should stand for is about considering how you want people to view you. That should come, essentially, from who your customers are and what you're looking to sell. If you've researched your customers fully you should have a clear idea of their tastes, the ways they prefer to shop, the experiences they like and in turn don't like, and that should give you a clear idea of how you should look to position your brand to them and the outside world.

Your logo

One of the key aspects of brand-building is having a logo that is simple, distinctive and which is recognised beyond the boundaries of language, using either words or images. Coca-Cola for example uses a text-based logo whereas Apple's is marked by a symbol. Consider the likes of internet brands eBay, YouTube and Google. eBay is known the world over for its colourful logo – it's instantly recognisable. Google may be the most popular search engine in the world, but its multi-coloured logo can probably lay claim to equal levels of popularity. Its logo changes with the seasons, or to mark a famous person's birthday, so much so that people are attracted to the site just to see what logo is being used on that day. Video-sharing site YouTube's distinctive red, black and white logo was designed by its founder, Chad Hurley.

As you establish your brand, the logo and colour scheme for your site should be consistent and clearly visible on every page. If you look at various other websites, you'll notice that most logos are displayed on the top left of the pages. You should scope out the identity of your business before you commit time or funds to a logo, as it should communicate identity and your USPs to your customers at all times.

Your logo is one way people will remember you and it's certainly how many customers will form their first impression of you. Images and colours are very powerful methods of communicating messages and you want to think carefully about the logo that should emblazon your website and how this will be translated offline. Your brand shouldn't just exist in cyberspace – ensure that it is reflected offline, such as on your business cards, stationery, packaging and any promotional items.

That said, don't rush out and commission a brand identity group. It's often just a case of finding a logo that simply and clearly radiates your business identity. The fuller the brief you can write about what your business is, who your customers are and what your USPs are, the more a web designer will be able to produce something close to what you're looking for. It's a subjective decision of course though, so it's always an idea to give an example of logos you like and don't like. You could consider seeking the advice of a professional consultant who can carry out some market research around designs that work online and with focus groups. It won't be cheap, but you'll be getting professional advice.

Alternatively a logo created by a freelance designer or small design company might give you the independent edginess that makes you stand out. For most of you you'll have no option but to pursue this route. Another option is to ask local design colleges or students to submit entries, incentivising them with a prize or vouchers for the site once it's open. There are a number of websites for budding, freelance or small design companies where you can pitch such competitions or request enquiries, with www.logosauce.com probably being the best. Just post your brief (remember to be as detailed as possible), set a deadline then wait for 'bidders' to upload their best efforts and contact the ones you like.

Startups Tips

Having a number of designs to choose from certainly helps you decide what works well, so even if you decide to give the project to one person or company ask them to give you at least a couple of options and colour schemes. You're likely to favour one and then ask to see several variations of that until you're happy.

Logos should work well in a number of sizes; whether it applies to you or not, think postage stamp and billboard. Forward plan to ensure what works for you as a start-up will work for you as a burgeoning online business. Even if this isn't your goal, it'll almost certainly be how many of your customers will want to see you.

Don't make the mistake, however, of thinking everyone shares your idea of good taste and smart design. They won't. This isn't your house you're choosing a theme for; it's your online business. While it might be 'yours' its success will be dependent on others wanting to go there, so unless you're selling the type of product that lends itself to the weird and wonderful, remember that niches are niches for a reason. Instead, apply the property development mantra: design for the broadest range of people you're looking to sell to as possible.

Startups Tips

As a rule create a detailed brief, get a number of designs to choose from and go with what works best for your customer, not you.

Do your research, go online and look at how your competition style their identity and check out popular brands to see what they have got right. Also force yourself to study a successful website whose identity doesn't particularly appeal to you and consider what it is that makes it work for its customers.

Branding for you as a start-up online business owner shouldn't be a massive preoccupation but as it's closely aligned to what your identity and overall sales story is, it is a very worthwhile exercise trying to draw up a list of words you'd like others to describe you with. This will make a useful reference document to look back at when making buying decisions and help form marketing decisions and eventually, a fuller branding strategy.

Style and design

Think of your website as a virtual shop window – in order to attract customers, you'll need to work on the style and design. It's one of the most important aspects of any web business, as it's the first thing your customers see so it's easy to understand why so many entrepreneurs invest time, effort and money into the look and feel of their site.

In my experience

The style and image of a website is very important. Have a look around at different sites and see what you like, make a hit list of different types of different sites for your designer and take some screen grabs.

Company: Glasses Direct
Owner-manager: Jamie Murray Wells

Good design isn't just about making the site look good or attractive – it's about making it functional, reliable and easy to navigate round. There's little point in having an attractive, attention grabbing, iconic website if it's not user-friendly – your website has to be both appealing and functional. Sport clothes retailer Boo.com famously went bust in 2000, a victim of style over substance. Its website could not be seen by people who used Macintosh computers and the heavy use of graphics and 3-D images meant that only those people who had a high bandwidth internet connection could access the site.

Online customers also tend to be rather impatient and choosy – with the amount of sites available on the world wide web, there's little reason for them to persevere with your site if it fails to deliver to their expectations. So it's crucial you get the style and design right from the start. Of course, the benefit of an online business is that tweaks and changes can be made if necessary as your site develops, but you want to get the look and feel right from the start and ready for launch.

With the myriad of sites available online, it can seem that the more research you do into competitive and non-competitive sites, the more varying types of styles and design you uncover. Don't get put off by the vastness of style choice available – there are some basic rules of website style and design you can follow. These include ensuring that there is enough white space between text so your pages do not look too cluttered, keeping fonts consistent across pages, and ensuring a navigation bar is visible across all pages so your customers can get round the site with ease. It's also about using the same colours and logos across all parts of the site and making sure that graphics and texts are well-placed on the page.

Startups Tips

Good design isn't just about making the website look good or attractive. It's also about ensuring that it is functional, reliable and easy to navigate round. You want your customers to keep on coming back – if they have a good experience on your site, they are more likely to return.

Startups Tips

A cluttered website will turn customers off. You need to strike a balance between a website that is both aesthetically pleasing and functional – ensure that there is enough white space between the text so that pages can be easily read.

Startups checklist

- Identity must go hand-in-hand with every aspect of your planning.
- Don't agonise over your business' name but do give it careful consideration.
- Spend some time on your logo, but not necessarily lots of money.
- Keep your branding as consistent as possible.
- Always design with your customers in mind.

CHAPTER 4.2

Technical issues

The technology you choose will play a vital role in the success of your online business. With the amount of choices available today, it can seem quite daunting choosing the right software packages and deciding which equipment to invest in. With the speed at which technology changes today, another worry is that whatever you choose to invest in will date quite quickly. The bottom line is that you should invest in what your budget dictates – it's easy to be seduced by the latest deals, gadgets and computers with a sleek design, but you need to maintain a practical head and buy what you need for your business and what will most benefit your customers.

In this chapter, we'll look at:

→ What equipment you need
→ How to select a web host
→ Creating your website
→ Security issues
→ Content
→ Accessibility
→ Testing your website
→ Payment systems
→ Shipping options
→ Returns policy.

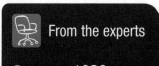
Equipment needed

Hardware

The price of IT equipment has reduced substantially in recent years, which is good news for anyone thinking of starting an online business. There's a huge selection available in the market, however, so it's important to be realistic about your needs as well as keeping a sensible budget in mind. Don't be tempted to buy more than you need, in terms of both hardware and software. Many businesses, for example, make the mistake of investing in more server capacity than they need from the start, when the reality is that you can save money by buying only what you need and adding more server capacity at a later stage, as your business grows.

From the experts

Company: **ASOS**
Owner-manager: **Nick Robertson**

We used to buy our IT kit and servers off eBay – it wasn't the prettiest option but it did the job.

Startups Tips

Set out your budget before you go in search of your IT needs. It's easy to become carried away with the array of equipment available and to buy more than you actually need.

Essentially, you'll need a computer, modem, printer, monitor, scanner and image-capturing devices. When it comes to purchasing a computer, you may be tempted to buy one of the most up-to-date models but a basic computer will probably suffice just as well, as long as it can support the latest software. You'll need equipment you can rely upon as you will be using it to perform a range of tasks, such as handling customer queries, checking emails, writing correspondence and checking and maintaining your site. Shop around to see if you can get a deal on hardware that also includes some free or reduced-price software. Aim to get at least three quotes on the equipment you intend to buy. You could also try to negotiate a deal on software packages when you purchase hardware. As a rule of thumb, expect to spend no less than £500 and anywhere up to a few thousand. Second-hand equipment is also an option but ensure you check all the devices thoroughly before committing.

Hard drive

Hard drive storage is an important consideration. The hard drive stores information such as text and audio files and most hard drives on the market can now store many gigabytes (GB) of information, at the very least 60GB, which should be more than adequate for the needs of your business. You can also buy portable hard drives on which to back-up information and this is one area you shouldn't skimp on. It's essential you back up as much information as possible, in the event of any data loss caused by power outages, theft or damage.

Startups Tips

Data loss can cripple your business so think long and hard about what storage capability you might need – not just now but in the future as your business grows.

Monitor

It's also worth spending some time choosing the right type and size of monitor. Bear in mind that most websites are optimised for monitors of between 17 and 21 inches in size, although obviously, you won't be able to have any control over what size monitors your customers have, and how much of the website they can see. Flat panel LCD monitors are all the rage now, they take up less room than more traditional ones and prices are very competitive.

Image devices

The other essential piece of equipment you will need is a device for capturing and transferring images, particularly if you are launching an online retail business. Pictures of your products are one of the main ways you are likely to attract customers to your site, so it's essential that any pictures you use look professional, attractive and represent the product in its best light. To do this, you'll need to use either a digital camera or a scanner. Digital cameras have dropped in price in recent years, and you can pick up a fairly decent one now for as little as £200. Check out the following criteria before you buy: can you download images from the camera to your computer using a USB device? Can you download images to a memory card? (This will enable you to transport the images and download them to different computers if necessary.) Scanners cost from around £50 – you place an image on the scanner and it reproduces it on screen for you.

Software

The good news for anyone starting an online business is that there is plenty of free software to download from the internet, particularly for security and firewall purposes (see p.126 later on in this chapter for more on software options in this area). Make the most of free tools provided by the likes of Google, many of which are useful for marketing purposes, such as Google Analytics, Site Maps and Product Search (we cover this in more detail in Chapter 5, p.175). The benefits of free tools are that they are readily available and can be more cost-effective, depending on your needs. More often than not though, there won't be a free or low cost tool that will serve all your requirements, so assess what value such tools will bring to your business.

 ## In my experience

In the early days when money was limited, we used free tools from Google, so make the most of these if you can.

Company: Glasses Direct
Owner-manager: Jamie Murray Wells

Web browsers

In terms of other software needs, web browsers will be your first port of call – this is the interface through which content on the web is displayed. There are four main options to choose from. By far the most popular is Microsoft's Internet Explorer, the latest of which is version 8, launched in 2009. Other choices include Firefox 3.6 from Mozilla and Safari, from Apple. Search engine giant Google has also launched a product in the browser space, with its offering Chrome. Deciding which browser to go for is mainly down to personal choice, so test the browsers out and see which one best fulfils your needs. It's also a good idea to test whether your site is optimised across all browsers, as you can never be sure which browsers your customers will be using.

 ## From the experts

Company: **LinkedIn**
Owner-manager: **Reid Hoffman**

The key thing for all businesses, and especially technology businesses or businesses that employ technology as a key kind of strategic advantage, is you always have to be investing in the future.

Browsers: What to bear in mind

- Always focus on the user experience
- Test, test and test again. Ensure that your website is optimised across all browsers without the need for user intervention
- Compare the relative percentage of browsers that hit your website to statistics on overall browser share
- Users have a wide choice of browsers so you need to make sure they get the best experience possible, regardless of the browser they choose to use
- Think about both the context of your offer and your customer when approaching browsers.

Startups Tips

There is an array of free software that can be downloaded from the internet. Much of it can be useful for marketing or web design purposes, but assess what value each tool will bring to your business before downloading.

Other useful software

You should also invest in tools such as web page editor and graphics software. Web page editor is a software application for creating web pages, formatting text and adding images and you don't need to know HTML or any other code to use it. Graphics software such as Adobe Dreamweaver will be useful if you intend to create your website yourself, as you can use the application to create and edit images. Count on paying about £450 for the software.

You can quickly and easily set up an online shop if you invest in shop-front software. It will automatically build a professional-looking store through a series of templates, even if you have no design skills. Many of the shop-front software options available enable you to start off by using just the basic features at first so it's ideal for someone who is new to the concept. Features include shop design and layout, shopping cart options (see p.120 for advice on this) and sales and marketing support. On the downside, these can be expensive to invest in so weigh up whether this software is something you truly need. As they use templates, they can also be quite restrictive.

One other type of software that is essential for any business is accounting software – it will help you to keep on top of your finances and enable you to manage your costs more efficiently (see Chapter 8, p.255 for more on this).

Connectivity

Bandwidth, the amount of data that can be transferred from one point to another over a given period of time, is also an important consideration for any online business. Broadband describes the bandwidth of your internet

In my experience

The quantity and sophistication of free software tools is remarkable and the marketplace is evolving quickly. We have used Google Analytics from the start and have found it a remarkably powerful tool for

> Company: Wahanda.com
> Owner-manager: Lopo Champalimaud

managing our business. We have also been users of OpenOffice, Ubuntu and Google Docs.

connection and there are some very attractive deals available, where you can have a cost-effective connection on a monthly basis. You'd need to have a very good reason to use a dial-up connection instead – it may be cheaper than broadband, but the amount of time you waste waiting for pages to load up will more than cancel out any savings you make on costs. Your bandwidth requirements will normally be handled by your web host provider (see the section below on web hosting for more information).

 ## In my experience

You don't want to be worrying about your hosting provider so find someone you trust. If you can, use some of the cloud providers (where storage and software is available via the internet) such as Amazon's EC2. If you

> Company: Wahanda.com
> Owner-manager: Lopo Champalimaud

need to have more control (like we did) find somewhere that has a good track record but is not too expensive and where you can get to easily – inevitably, you will need to get to the hosting centre at some obscure hour.

Web hosting

Web hosting involves housing, serving and maintaining files for a website – essentially you rent space online in order to make your website visible to your customers. It basically means you can run an online business without having to incur the expense or carry out the legwork of maintaining your own server, as web hosts provide you with access to servers. As well as housing your website, your web host will also be providing you with email accounts, bandwidth and technical support.

Choosing the right web hosting service can seem quite a daunting task, given the number of providers vying for your business. There are many deals that look too good to be true and the reality is they often are. There are a few factors you need to take into consideration when selecting a web host, such as exactly what capabilities you want your website to have. Price can vary from free to several thousand pounds so be clear from the outset what your needs are as it's all too easy to get talked into paying for a web hosting service that offers much more than you require at present.

Assess your needs

If all you need is a simple brochure site with basic information about your business, hosting your site will be relatively easy and won't cost you anything.

So how do you get it on the internet? As is often the case in the virtual world of the internet, you don't need to have the server in your office. In fact, it's very unlikely that you will. The cheapest and easiest option, and the one which most small businesses choose at the start, is to have a virtual host.

Types of host

Having a virtual host basically means getting a third party to host your site. The files for your website are stored on the hosting company's computer along with the files for other websites and their server deals with requests for your website and others. This is called shared environment hosting. Currently in the UK there are hundreds of companies that will host your site in a shared environment. If you already have a website and domain name you may have already come across offers of free web hosting.

Your ISP (the company through which you access the internet such as BT or Virgin Media) will often give you a small amount of space on which to host a website. Alternatively, the company that registered your domain name will often provide access to a free or low-cost hosting service. It may be a natural step to use one of these companies to host your website since you already have a business relationship with them. However, you need to be aware of the restrictions that they may place on you in terms of space, features and support.

You should bear in mind that the main activity of an ISP is connectivity – that is, getting and keeping businesses and individuals connected to the internet. The resources of these companies may not be prioritised on keeping your website up and running.

Startups Tips

There are hundreds of web hosting companies offering their services so shop around to find the best deal and don't be afraid to negotiate if some of the deals don't quite offer you all the services you want.

There are, however, companies that have been set up solely for the purpose of hosting websites. Some of these have invested a lot of money in technology and support services to ensure the sites that they host are secure and always accessible from the internet and that their customers are given all the necessary support.

If you just have a simple brochure site that needs little maintenance or technical support, using your current ISP or a free package is likely to be sufficient. For this type of website, your main concerns will be how quickly the page appears on the screen and whether there are any occasions when it doesn't appear.

Startups Tips

There are plenty of web hosting services available so assess your business needs now and in the future and get a quote from at least three different providers before making a decision.

One of the best ways to find out how good a service is, is through trial and error. You won't be paying a great deal if anything at all for the service, so experimenting won't be expensive. You can always move on if you're not satisfied. If, however, you are serious about running an online business and one with e-commerce capabilities, you're likely to need a web hosting service that stretches beyond what your current ISP can offer, as you'll require features such as additional webspace, email addresses, adequate bandwidth and most importantly, support, in the event of anything going wrong. A basic, shared web-hosting package will generally cost around £40–£50 a year, but expect to pay up to £100. A dedicated server can cost in the region of £40 a month.

Email addresses and webspace

Check out how many email accounts you are allowed to set up. In the early days of your business, you may require one, but as your business grows and you employ staff, you'll need email addresses for them as well. You might also want to set up some generic email addresses, such as 'sales@. . .', 'customerservice@. . .' and 'info@. . .' The amount of web space you can get will vary, but is generally from 5 megabytes (MB) to unlimited. You'll find that 5MB will cater for a site that has about 8–10 pages, so you'll probably need more than this if your site is particularly complex or is likely to have a lot of graphics. Ensure that your web host will allow you to increase the amount of space you need as your business grows.

Bandwidth

Working out how much bandwidth you need can be tricky, as you're never sure how many people are likely to visit your site in the early days and numbers can fluctuate as your business grows and you are fine tuning your marketing strategy. You might be incredibly lucky in the early days and have more traffic than you anticipated – if this is the case, check with your web host to find out what penalties you might have to pay if you exceed your bandwidth allowance, and whether you can upgrade this easily and quickly if necessary. Some web host providers offer unlimited bandwidth allowance, but check the small print carefully, as this may be conditional on the type of data you are transferring.

The bigger and more expensive your web hosting service, the more likely it is to have a better connection to the internet, enabling pages from your site to be downloaded faster by your customers' browsers. Consider how many of your customers are likely to be using a broadband connection as opposed to a 56k modem for example, as they won't really notice any difference in speed if they are using the latter. Nowadays, it's quite likely that most people have a broadband connection, as prices have reduced in recent years and broadband is now often bundled in packages with television and telephone deals.

 ## In my experience

In recent years, technology has got cheaper and cheaper. When we started out, good e-commerce products weren't as readily available as now, it was mostly more expensive merchandising software. But if it's more economical, consider building it yourself. I put a notice on the board at my university for a web developer and he worked side by side with me.

Company: Glasses Direct
Owner-manager: Jamie Murray Wells

Reliability and technical support

Reliability and technical support goes without saying. You need a web host who can guarantee that their servers are well maintained — just think of the amount of business you could lose or trust that can be eroded if your site was down for any period of time. It will obviously cost you more to invest in a reliable web hosting service, but it's a small price to pay for peace of mind and to ensure your website is online at all times.

Choosing a web host

You've worked out your web hosting needs and made a list of all the requirements you're after. So what is the best way to go about selecting one? Barry Mills, founder of digital marketing agency Netstep says that unless you are developing the site yourself and really know what you are doing, you shouldn't select one. Instead, leave the selection to whoever is

The effects of downtime

The effects of downtime can be extremely negative, as auction site eBay found out to its cost in the early days of its trading history. In June 1999, following a site redesign, eBay suffered a number of breakdowns in its service, with one lasting 22 hours. This had a severe impact on consumer interaction with the site and knocked more than $8 off the price of its shares. Further outages occurred and company revenues took a severe hit – according to reports at the time, the service interruptions cost eBay $3.9m of its second-quarter revenues, as it refunded listing fees and granted extensions on auctions.

At the time, the 22-hour outage was one of the worst internet crashes in history and a backlash quickly ensued as users wasted no time registering their complaints on an internet newsgroup dedicated to the site. Others raised questions about the robustness of the technology.

helping you to develop and support your site (see Creating your website below). That way, there's no doubt about whose responsibility it is when the site stops working. If your developer doesn't have their own hosting service, then set up a contract with the hosting company that they chose direct, so you aren't unnecessarily locked in to the developer. But make the same party responsible for maintenance, support and hosting.

You should oversee the selection though. Take up references, and in particular find out if any of the web host's existing clients have experienced downtime and how it was handled. The reality is that it's only really when something goes wrong that you find out how good your support is. Don't sign any long contracts unless you are dealing with one of the market leaders, and don't make a selection based on price. Remember that if your website host's business folds, your site will go down too, so do a thorough background check looking at how long the web host has been established, its client list and the nature of support offered.

It can be awkward thinking about changing suppliers before you've even got the relationship started but it's worth learning to recognise when it might be time to switch web host providers. Poor performance or a change of developers or technology are some of the signs that it might be time to change. The main thing to do is to plan ahead. Always retain control of your domain name. Make sure it's registered to you, and unless you have a very strong relationship with the developer it is safer not to let them manage it for you. Also, make sure you have current backups of your site files and any live database content.

Creating your website

As a virtual shop window, your website will make or break your business, so it's essential to get the design and functionality right from the start otherwise it can be a costly and frustrating exercise if you have to continually tweak the site. The first decision you'll need to make is whether you will be designing the website yourself or hiring a web designer to do the job for you.

Glasses Direct: Founder Jamie Murray Wells initially built the site together with a web developer

Tailor-made or off-the-shelf?

You don't need to have design or technology skills to work on your site. Improvements in technology mean that there are plenty of cost-effective web build tools at your disposal, most of which lend themselves to being used by complete novices. In fact, you could find yourself creating a professional looking website in a matter of hours. But should you opt for a tailor-made solution or invest in an off-the-shelf one?

There are many factors to take into account when deciding between a tailor-made e-commerce site and an off-the-shelf solution. Advocates of bespoke systems point to the advantages of a tailor-made website, while boxed e-commerce providers argue that the usability and speed of their products make them superior. Your decision will probably be influenced by finding a balance between cost, functionality and ease-of-use of both options.

Off-the-shelf

An off-the-shelf e-commerce package is easy to install and often easy to use. It is almost certainly likely to be cheaper and quicker than having a bespoke e-commerce site designed for you. However, updates can be expensive and sometimes unavailable. Another downside is that off-the-shelf packages only have so many templates and functions, so you could find that your options are somewhat restricted. The other disadvantage is that your site could be similar to that of your competitors and you will have no control over how and when functionality is updated, and so it will be difficult to differentiate your offering.

Tailor-made

A bespoke system will allow you to present your products in the most appropriate and effective way for your business. This is especially important if you have complex products, or product ranges with multiple components. A bespoke system can often be more easily integrated with existing IT systems and web services as it is developed from the ground up to meet your specific needs. This kind of system can help set you apart from competitors and you will be able to add additional features quickly and easily.

You will have to consider what you need from an online shop very carefully before you commit to either package. Another option, if you cannot afford the time or cost of your own online shop, is to run your online shop within a wider e-commerce community such as eBay or an online shopping mall (see p.227 for more information on this).

Commissioning a site

If you are serious about building an online business that includes features such as a shopping cart and integrated payment systems, then you are probably better off commissioning a web designer. Costs can be substantial, but you will be able to have the site built to your exact specifications. The good ones are expensive, but they will be worth it. On top of the costs of site build, you may also have to pay an annual maintenance fee, but again, this means you can get problems fixed if necessary, and by someone you are familiar with and who knows the site well.

Startups Tips
Commissioning a web designer does not come cheap, but it does mean you will have control over the look, feel and functionality of the site. You'll also be able to exercise more flexibility when it comes to testing the site and make any changes that are necessary.

Have a look around the web to get a feel for the kind of sites available and bookmark a few that you like the look of and that you feel could be effective for your site. Check they have the kind of features you're after – such as an e-commerce facility, good navigation and clear signposting, for instance. Then, find out who's behind them: usually they will be credited on the site. If not, you could get in contact with the business itself and ask them who's behind their build.

This approach is a good option and quite safe, because you have already seen the web designer's work and like it. You could also ask around business associates and colleagues to see if there is anyone they can recommend. Alternatively, you could browse through directories of web designers and there are plenty of resources on the web where you can start looking.

 In my experience

Use a small local firm, build up a relationship with your designer – someone who doesn't talk too much jargon, someone you can meet and speak with face to face.

Company: Country Products
Owner–manager: Mark Leather

Web design: Where to look

- The UK Web Design Association: www.ukwda.org
- Web Design Directory: www.web-design-directory-uk.co.uk
- FreeIndex: www.freeindex.co.uk
- The Chartered Society of Designers: www.csd.org.uk.

Good web design, however, isn't just dependent on getting a professional web designer on board. It's as much about functionality and reliability but it's also important to establish a rapport with your web developer. It's likely that the run-up to the site launch will incur long nights, stressful times and continual testing so it's important to have someone on the technical side who is supportive and committed to helping you launch your business in the best way possible. You will also need to keep your customers' needs foremost at all times. Revisit your market research from your business plan and make sure that before you start thinking about your website you are really clear about what you are selling, who you are targeting, and what your unique value propositions are. Then you should brainstorm what you think customers want.

Features for your website

Shopping carts

A shopping cart is a page on the site where visitors can store one or more items before they actually commit to buying them. It lets consumers purchase more than one item from your website in one transaction. Shopping carts can be relatively inexpensive or even free depending on what kind of e-commerce software package you go with.

An online shopping cart gathers up items in the same way that an actual shopping basket or trolley would. The difference is an online cart will calculate the total value and added delivery costs.

Shopping carts can clearly improve the user-experience of an e-commerce site and they add an element of functionality, meaning you would be foolish not to consider one for your site.

Carts can be added to your site relatively easily, even if you don't have a boxed e-commerce package. Many carts can be incorporated into your site by adding some simple code to the links on your site that passes the product information straight into the basket.

Online catalogues

If your site has a large quantity of different products then you'll probably need to display them in an online catalogue form.

Online catalogues work in much the same way as a department store does. Shoppers can browse hundreds or thousands of products according to categories. This makes it easier for shoppers to find exactly what they're looking for, minimising the chances of them missing a product on your site.

There are four main types of online catalogue which vary in price and functionality.

→ **ASP: Application Service Provider:** With this type of catalogue you are given a user account and password that give you access to the site through your web browser. With this option you don't need a separate hosting site and you can make changes and updates from any computer connected to the internet.

→ **Software:** With this option you load the software onto your own machine, and then load it onto your shop from there.

→ **Open source:** This is a kind of cooperative service where you use software which has been developed and given away free by developers. However, there may be some hosting costs associated with this type of system.

→ **Free products:** There are free catalogues out there but with these you often only get the software itself for no charge, and are liable to pay fees on the transactions you make when using the software. Be careful with these catalogues as they may restrict your site development in the long run.

 In my experience

Don't penny pinch – go for value. Just because it's the cheapest certainly doesn't mean it's the best – but at the same time don't get talked into things you don't need.

Company: Country Products
Owner-manager: Mark Leather

Style matters

In terms of style, such as images, typeface and logo, the key is to keep things simple. Don't make it too fancy, don't use gratuitous animation or graphics, and don't let designers show off. Think about search engines, or make sure your designer does (see p.201 for more information on search engines). Keep all your key information and navigation above the fold (this

Shopping carts allow customers to purchase several items in a single transaction.

means ensuring it is visible on the page without the need to scroll down or sideways). Generally navigation menus should be top and left – that's where users expect to find them. Use visual navigation aids within the central window of your homepage to guide users into your site.

Treat your website as a continuous project. Barry Mills from Netstep believes that the mindset of building a site and then thinking it's finished

ASOS: For a fashion website the style is important

until it looks tired and ready for a redesign after a few years is completely wrong. You should be continually analysing your website traffic using analytics, developing ideas for improving the site, and testing, testing, testing. It's also important to listen to customer feedback.

 ## In my experience

Creating a distinct visual style is important but the voice you use on the site is even more important. It was one of the most important things I learned from Lastminute. com.

Company: Wahanda.com
Owner-manager: Lopo Champalimaud

123

Security issues

In March 2010, payment service provider Sage Pay surveyed 2000 e-commerce businesses with the aim of benchmarking the factors that contribute to success online. Of those surveyed, 62% were either retailers or wholesalers and the remaining 38% fell into the following sectors: information and communications, leisure and entertainment and technology. E-commerce performance data was used to work out the average rates of purchase initiation and completion for respondents, and then compared across four categories: marketing (getting people to your site), influencing a purchase, making it easy for people to pay and security and fraud.

The survey found that many of the tactics used to attract visitors to websites, such as advertising or use of social media, may have limited impact on visitors' behaviour once they arrive. In general, the survey found, those e-tailers using a variety of marketing techniques are attracting people to their site but are not able to entice the shopper to buy – the average e-commerce success rate (completed sales on a website compared to the number of visitors to a site) is low at 7%. The survey concludes that by reviewing checkout processes and online reassurance factors, such as money back guarantees and approaches to card data security, e-tailers can ensure that their marketing spend is not wasted.

Indeed, online security issues continue to make the headlines and it's vital that you are aware of the various security threats that can harm your business. These relate to the site itself and to how you deal with information such as customer details and payments. Your site could be susceptible to fraud and hacking and your customer details could be compromised. Online fraud is a growing business – it's often said that those who carry out fraudulent activities are always one step ahead of the technology being used to combat levels of fraud, so it's important to keep up to date with the latest solutions available.

According to Sage Pay's report, security policies have a considerable impact on sales: 65% of retailers interviewed for the survey have a security policy clearly displayed on their website. When this figure was compared to the retailers' conversion rates, businesses with a security policy were 16% more likely to make a sale, proving that e-shoppers are concerned with card fraud and security and are looking for extra reassurance.

Your website isn't necessarily a one-way street. It can also open the window to the heart of your company – the network, including the storage facilities that hold its data files, its most priceless asset. Lax security that enables hackers to break in can lead to embarrassment, and waste your time and money. And in extreme cases it could mean the collapse of your business.

What can go wrong?

A security breach can paralyse an entire network in a matter of minutes and/or result in privacy controls becoming ineffective, as several high profile brands have discovered to their cost. In 2008, for example, a lapse in security at social networking site Facebook resulted in strangers being able to access the personal photos of site subscribers. The incident was all the more embarrassing for the company as it came only days after Facebook had beefed up its privacy options. Meanwhile, online clothing retailer Cotton Traders, suffered a security breach during which its customers' credit and debit card details were stolen. It is estimated that up to 40,000 individual sets of card details were stolen when its website was hacked into.

The financial cost of putting matters right can be very high. In addition, the impact on customer confidence can result in a severely damaged business reputation, taking months or years to reverse. You might not know immediately that this has happened though, but the repercussions from security breaches could last some time.

As well as spreading abusive graffiti, hackers can alter catalogue details and prices, or steal all the customer details, including their home addresses and sensitive information such as medical treatments. Apart from the embarrassment to your brand, this would be in direct contravention of the data protection regulations, and could lead to prosecution and fines.

Hackers often seek connection bandwidth, because this can be used to damage other businesses in so-called 'distributed denial of service attacks'. These involve numerous computers bombarding an internet server with data, overloading it and causing it to stall or crash, resulting in your website being unavailable for a certain period of time, all of which could mean lost orders and frustrated customers.

In the worst case, hackers can get hold of customers' credit card details (as in the case of Cotton Traders and numerous other brands that have been the victim of hackers) in which case the bank that handles transactions could withdraw and the site owner could be liable for the debts. A fraudulent credit card charge leaves the holder only liable for £50 or so while an improper business-to-business transaction could bankrupt a company.

Credit card criminals are increasingly turning their attention to smaller e-commerce sites, using stolen credit cards to buy goods online, so it's imperative to have the right level of security in place. If your business accepts online payments, you need to ensure your site operates a secure online payment system and if you are taking note of customers' details, you need to keep their details safe. As a rule of thumb, no cardholder data should be stored unless absolutely necessary.

Virus protection

One big worry for traders and customers alike on the internet is the threat of viruses. Headline-grabbing monster viruses such as Melissa and the Love Bug brought mighty corporations grinding to a halt, generating spurious emails in such numbers that the networks collapsed. Other varieties can corrupt data files or stop computers working altogether.

Ensure you install anti-virus software; virus experts such as Symantec and MessageLabs analyse viruses the moment that they appear and can quite often have a fix ready within a matter of minutes, that can be downloaded over the internet in time to provide protection. Your internet service provider should also have anti-virus software for your use. Ensure you keep up to date with viruses as versions are updated on a regular basis.

If your business is affected, it could mean several hours of downtime that could result in loss of trust and trade. There's no guarantee you'll escape a virus attack, but there are measures you can put in place to help lessen the risks. Viruses can be spread in a number of ways such as via email, instant messenger programs or infected files. Be especially wary of emails with attachments from people you don't know. Often, a virus infects people's email address books and the email appears to be sent by someone you know. If in doubt, don't click on the attachment – delete the email.

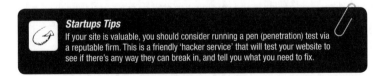

Startups Tips
If your site is valuable, you should consider running a pen (penetration) test via a reputable firm. This is a friendly 'hacker service' that will test your website to see if there's any way they can break in, and tell you what you need to fix.

Firewalls

Installing firewall software will also help to protect your systems and your customer data. This can come either as a hardware device fitted as part of the system or as software, or a combination of both.

It's an application that filters the information coming through the internet connection into your network or computer system, so that if the filters flag a packet of data, it is not allowed through. A firewall is effectively a policing system which stands between a computer and the internet. It blocks unauthorised programs and viruses trying to hack into the computer.

Firewalls are also increasingly found as a default standard in products such as Microsoft's Office XP and e-commerce programs and any decent hosting service should include firewall protection for your site – hosted web services often market themselves on their claims to offer tough security. As with anti-virus software, ensure any firewall protection you have is up to date.

Stand alone units suitable for small businesses are provided by companies such as Sonicwall, ComputerLinks (formerly known as Unipalm) and Watchguard Technologies. These typically cost a few hundred pounds and are relatively easy to install.

Public key encryption

Many users will only give out personal details if the website they are using provides encryption technology; this is represented by a padlock sign on the internet browser. You may have come across the term SSL encryption and wondered what it stands for. SSL stands for Secure Sockets Layer and is a type of technology that protects your website, making it easier to build trust between yourself and your customers. Essentially, an SSL certificate enables the encryption of sensitive information (such as a customer's credit card details) during online transactions. It establishes a private communication channel enabling encryption of the data during transmission. Encryption scrambles the data, essentially creating a private message. You'll need to use SSL if your online business accepts credit card payments, you have a login or sign in facility on your site and you are dealing with sensitive data such as credit card details or addresses. VeriSign (www.verisign.com) is one of the leading providers of SSL certificates and secures more than one million servers.

E-commerce sites will also be protected by the encryption used by payment clearance providers such as PayPal, which process credit card payments. This ensures that customer details remain secure and also mitigates liability if the worst happens.

Making sure your site is secure is vital if you want to instil confidence in your customers. If they are in any doubt that their personal information is not secure, it's unlikely they will enter details such as credit card information on your site.

Content

The way in which people react to online shops differs from how they approach shops on the high street – those who browse the web tend to be more impatient and don't waste time looking at sites that download slowly. The way in which users approach web content also differs from how they would look at printed matter. Typically, people tend to scan content on the web rather than reading it word for word and there are certain guidelines you can follow when presenting your content. Here are a few suggestions:

⇢ Make sure any text you use is broken up into easily digestible chunks, with enough white space so that the page and text do not feel too cluttered.

⇢ Break up text with headings and images.

⇢ Bullet points are also useful for listing characteristics of products or for drawing attention to a piece of content.

Startups Tips

Content isn't just about the words you use on the page, it's just as much about how the words are presented. Test a variety of fonts, backgrounds and colours and ask your friends and family for their opinions.

What you are aiming for is content that is easy to read and that is easy on the eye, so avoid creating pages where your potential customers will need to scroll either downwards or sideways in order to read them, as this will distract them and potentially put them off your site.

Consider carefully what colours you will use on your site and research other websites to see what colours might work best. You'll notice that there aren't many websites with yellow text on a white background for example. This is because together, these colours are not easy to read and can put a strain on the eyes. The same goes for choice of font – choose one that is clear, simple and easy to read.

When it comes to supplying the copy for your website, the easiest and cheapest way is to write it yourself and as it's original, you will own the copyright. It's a good idea, however, to get a friend or two to proofread the content before you go live. Content that is misspelt and which does not read well is not going to appeal to your customers. Depending on the type of website you are operating, and the amount of content you might need, you could consider using a freelance writer to supply the copy for you. For more on writing for the web, and how to optimise your content for search engines, see Chapter 5.2: Working with search engines.

Accessibility

Making your website accessible involves tweaking your site to make it as easy as possible for everyone to get the information they want.

According to Netstep's Barry Mills, the law relating to website accessibility is rather unclear. Generally, if your customers can use the site, you should be okay. But you may have disabled or partially sighted customers, so think about their needs. Accessibility isn't just about catering to the visually-impaired either; some users may have movement and coordination problems, which means they have to navigate sites using only the keyboard.

Designing websites for those with disabilities shouldn't be seen as a restriction of your creative development plans – if anything it should ensure your web development team comes up with more creative ways to address accessibility.

As well as evidence of compliance, accessibility is often very sound business practice and generally sites that are good for accessibility are also good for search engines, so it's in your interest to make your website as accessible as possible. In addition, making your website more accessible means it can be viewed by those users with older browsers who won't have technologies such as Flash installed. Making a website accessible, however, isn't an overnight job; it takes time as you'll need to test the site and review accessibility when the site has an update.

The W3C guidelines are widely regarded as best practice for accessibility and you can find out more by logging on to: www.w3.org.

Testing your website

Take every opportunity you can to test your concept. It's likely you'll still be tweaking it a year from launch, but by then you'll have overheads, time constraints and running responsibilities to deal with, so take every chance you get while researching and starting-up to test, test and then test again. It's true that websites can be changed relatively easily, but it's expensive to do this so it's important to get the main part of the design fixed and then add features if necessary at a later stage.

Get your friends, family and business contacts to visit your site (if you have a basic version up and running) or explain the concept to them and ask them to give feedback. Website design has an important effect on how people interact with your site, which then has a bearing on sales and levels of 'stickiness' and we'll be covering more of this later on (see p.204). If you don't have a basic version of a site that people can link to (all you really need is your homepage), design a mock up that you can send out and invite comments and criticisms. Consider conducting an email survey – after all, you are launching an online business. If you intend on selling products online, give them away in exchange for honest feedback. It's important to try to sell as well. You'll quickly find out if your prices are too high, or on the flipside, if you're shifting units like hotcakes, then perhaps you're not charging enough.

All of the above can ensure that your content and design can be the best it can be at the launch stage but all of this will count for nothing if technical aspects of your site, referred to as your site's functionality, are not working. You'll need to ensure any glitches are corrected before launch and there are certain steps you can take to ensure that this doesn't happen. You'll also want to make sure that your site is optimised for search engines the moment it goes live. This is because many websites that are hosted on internal servers can present problems when they go live online. If you have hired a professional website design company, it should have a complete quality checklist against which it will check the website it has designed prior to delivery.

Whether you have used a company or not, it's well worth your time to carry out some checks yourself. Ensure your site can be accessed through a variety of browsers. As mentioned earlier, the main ones to be aware of are Internet Explorer (up to version 8), Safari, Firefox and Google Chrome. Every single link should be checked to ensure that an error message does not appear, which will come up as a '404 page cannot be found error'. Not only will this result in your website looking unprofessional and potentially alienating customers, but it will severely hamper your chances of getting an effective search engine ranking. There are plenty of free tools you can use to test broken links, such as Xenu's Link Sleuth and W3C Link Checker.

Proofread your site again and again – and get your family and friends or even a freelance proofreader to do this too – not just the text but phone numbers and contact details too. Ensuring that your website contains exclusive content will help boost its search engine ranking. Exclusive content can relate to the way in which you describe the products you are selling, for example. You can check how unique your content is by using a free tool such as Copyscape (www.copyscape.com).

Feedback

For any concept testing you do, make sure you record the results, it's all good for tweaking your model and also compelling evidence to use in your business plan and when pitching for finance; even for PR.

The founders of Innocent Drinks constantly refer to the day they tested a selection of initial smoothie recipes out on visitors to a jazz festival asking people to place their empty cups in either a 'yes' or 'no' bin under the banner 'Should we quit our jobs to make these smoothies full-time?'

The more feedback you can get, the closer you'll be to selling products people actually want once you're open and hopefully you'll be building customer and brand awareness along the way.

Payment systems

With online shopping set to grow further in the next few years, more and more people are shopping online and they'll expect the majority of websites to have online payment systems in place. If you want to be one of the businesses to benefit from the increasing popularity of online shopping, online payment systems are an absolute must.

 In my experience

Give yourself time on these... Although it should be the easiest thing to do, depending on your line of business, payment systems are always more complicated than you anticipate.

Company: Wahanda.com
Owner–manager: Lopo Champalimaud

According to Sage Pay's *E-Business Benchmark Report*, giving people choice in how they want to pay can increase conversion rates, but it's not a guaranteeing factor.

As Sage Pay outlines, most online businesses accept debit and credit cards as primary payment types. Respondents to its survey say that on average over half (54%) of payments are made with credit cards and 34% on debit card. The remaining 12% of payments are via additional payment types such as AMEX, PayPal and Google Checkout. Analysis revealed that there was a marginal difference overall between those top performing sites and those with lower conversion rates. Only 7% more of the top performing sites in the survey offer one or more of the additional payment types listed above.

In the 1990s, when the internet was emerging as a retail platform, online payments were dogged by instances of fraud and systems that were less than secure – but today, the technology and security options have come a long way. To accept online payments, you'll need to work with a payment service provider (PSP – see below for more information on this).

There are a number of ways to accept payments online and it's a good idea to consider these as you build your website, choose your e-commerce platform and shopping cart. Thinking about all of these elements at the same time will help you to make the right business decision. For example, you'll need to make sure that your shopping cart is compatible with your chosen PSP and that you have the option to provide a range of payment types and services. According to Sage Pay (the UK's largest independent PSP), the following are the most common ways of collecting payments.

-> **Regular payments:** This is instant and is the fastest way to get to your customers' money.

-> **Deferred payments:** This is a method whereby you can capture payment and authorisation for a specific amount without immediately taking the funds. For example, this payment method works well for those who have longer lead times to dispatch goods, or those who are building bespoke goods. It's also important to note that there is a finite timeframe for settling a deferred payment; this is usually within three to six days.

-> **Repeat payments:** These work in exactly the same way as regular payments, but stored card details (either by the vendor or the payment gateway) can be used to trigger a second, third and fourth payment.

-> **Refunds:** A payment has been taken, but needs to be allocated back to the customer. This is usually used in the case of returns or faulty goods.

-> **Token payments:** This is a method whereby your customers' card details are captured by the PSP and stored as a token or card number 'alias'. The PSP securely stores the card details and passes back the Token to the merchant. It can then be used to process transactions as and when required. Tokens can also be used to create a single click checkout.

 ## In my experience

We were recommended our payment system, Sage Pay, by our web designers. I would consider it one of our best business moves ever. The biggest benefit is the costs and charges, which are far more realistic and

Company: Country Products
Owner-manager: Mark Leather

reasonable than our former supplier, the settlement times are far speedier, but I always look to far more than the old pounds and pence – the system is simpler; the reporting is far better, easier and clearer which benefits our customers.

Advice from Sage Pay. . .

Payment systems: what is settlement?

All payments are split into authorisation and settlement. Getting authorisation means that the card is valid, hopefully not reported stolen, has funds available and is a genuine card number. However, funds are not actually removed from the customer's account until the payment service provider (PSP) has sent the payment data to the relevant acquiring bank (your merchant bank) – this is what is known as settlement. This usually happens at a specific time each day. It is important to note that with the regular payment option, although authorisation is immediate, the money will not leave the customer's account until the transaction has been 'settled'.

www.sagepay.com

Types of payment service providers

Independent payment gateways

These have no affiliation with any bank and will work with a whole range of acquirers (a high street bank or other financial institution that offers credit and debit card accepting/processing services). The benefits of choosing an independent payment gateway are:

- ⇢ If you want to change banks, you don't have to change your payment service provider, so there is less disruption and the PSP will just fit in with your new requirements.

- ⇢ Pricing is very competitive.

- ⇢ Funds are usually released quickly.

- ⇢ You can integrate other payment types (eg PayPal) into the same system, making reconciliation much easier.

- ⇢ Most can help you to get an internet merchant bank account – which you need to accept payments online – and could save you money.

Bank associated gateways

These are associated with a specific bank and therefore must be used in conjunction with a merchant account/number from that specific bank. Here, your business bank account, merchant number and gateway are all under one roof so it can be easier to manage, but if you change banks you may be forced to change your gateway too.

133

eWallet services

eWallet systems, such as PayPal (see below for more information), allow a merchant to accept payment from a customer who has an account with the particular eWallet provider. A number of eWallet solutions are integrated with independent PSPs, so that you can take advantage of a variety of payment methods. The benefits of choosing an eWallet service are the following:

⇢ They don't use actual card details, instead they use funds placed into the eWallet account by the customer. These funds can be added to or 'topped up' by the customer at any point through the eWallet interface, meaning card details are neither collected nor divulged at any point.

⇢ Research shows that many shoppers regard eWallets as an extra pot of money that they willingly use to spend on online shopping. For example, if they've sold something on eBay themselves and the money is in a PayPal account, they are more likely to spend that online. For this reason many merchants choose to accept eWallets as well as credit/debit card payments.

Startups Tips
eWallet services, including the likes of PayPal, Google Checkout and moneybookers.com (merchant services), are suited to those businesses that don't anticipate a large number of online transactions and which don't have internet merchant accounts. You also have to rely on your customers having an eWallet account.

Setting up a payment system

Once you have registered your domain name and chosen how you are going to create your website, try to consider your shopping cart and payment options at the same time. That way you can make sure you get exactly what you want.

When choosing the right online payment system for your business, you should first think about the product you are offering to your customers and the manner of payment you would like to allow your customers to use. For example, purchasing a shopping cart that does not facilitate deferred payments when your business is based around deferred payments wouldn't make sense. Equally, signing up to a payment service provider that does not allow American Express, when you have a particular necessity or interest in accepting this card type, will cause problems and cost you money.

Advice from Sage Pay. . .

What you need to accept online payments:

- *A shopping cart:* These can be tailor-made by web developers or simply purchased 'off-the-shelf' – they allow customers to select items and proceed to purchase as well as allowing the vendor to monitor stock and inventory and track orders.
- *An internet merchant account:* Getting one of these is crucial if you want to accept a variety of cards and payment types. You won't be able to trade online without one. Merchant accounts are available from a range of acquirers (banks). The internet merchant account gives you, the merchant, the facility to get authorisations on customers' cards and have funds transferred into your business bank account. Some payment service providers can also help you to set up your merchant account. As they buy in bulk, they will usually have negotiated good transaction rates with the bank. A merchant account is a banking facility and obtaining one is generally not a quick process. It can take between four to six weeks to set up, so plan well in advance and make sure you have a business plan at the ready.
- *Payment service provider (PSP):* The PSP will facilitate the process of capturing credit card details and will securely transmit those details to your chosen acquirer for authorisation. The PSP will often also be able to offer fraud screening facilities as part of the payment gateway package.
- *A business bank account:* This is where the funds taken online will be deposited, pending agreement with the chosen acquirer (your merchant bank account). www.sagepay.com

Costs of payment systems

Think also about the price. The cost of processing a transaction soon adds up so look at what options are available to you and make sure you account for these when pricing your goods. These are a list of potential charges you may have to pay.

Merchant bank

The bank/acquirer will charge you each time you process a payment. The fee varies, so check whether it is a percentage of the total transaction or a flat fee. Different acquiring banks will have different rates and if a payment service provider can negotiate a better deal for you, then it's worth investigating.

Payment service providers (PSPs)

There will be a small fee for the authorisation process; however, there are considerable pricing and service differences between providers, so shop around for the deal that best suits your business. Some will quote you an all inclusive monthly fixed rate for a set number of transactions, while others may quote for the transaction only, but add charges like set-up fees or fraud screening. The good thing is that there are choices, but make sure you choose what is right for your business.

Fraud

Most PSPs will be able to provide you with fraud protection; however, there are different levels of protection, so again look at what is available and don't pay for more than you need. Some PSPs will include basic fraud screening as part of their offering and this can work out to be more cost-effective.

PCI compliance

The Payment Card Industry Data Security Standard (PCI DSS) is a set of requirements designed to ensure that all companies that process, store or transmit credit card information maintain a secure environment. It's not yet a legal requirement in the UK and the cost of compliance depends on the number of transactions that you process and whether you decide to capture your customers' credit card details or let your PSP do this. If your PSP is collecting the data and they are PCI compliant, it shouldn't be too expensive. Your PSP and qualified security assessor (QSA) like Trustwave (www.trustwave.com) will be able to advise you further. Again, some PSPs may be able to negotiate rates so it's worth checking with your PSP too.

If you find the issue of compliance a challenge, then you are not alone. Over a third of e-tailers in Sage Pay's *E-Business Benchmark Report* that claim to collect, store or transfer card data say they have not reached the required data security standards, showing that regulating and compliance is still causing confusion.

Advice from Sage Pay. . .

Why compliance is important

Compliance is important to prevent hackers and security breaches and lessen the risk of fraud. Any potential weaknesses in a network can be used by hackers to gain unauthorised access, and in the worst case, capture sensitive card information. Any breaches of this nature would not only compromise your technology systems, but also have a severe effect on your reputation in the eyes of your customers. In the online world, it's not a situation customers forget very easily, and with the high level of competition on the net, they'll simply go elsewhere.

There is also a moral perspective to think about. Companies that capture and store sensitive card and cardholder information must be aware that in the event that this information is accessed by an unauthorised source, their actions could cause untold damage to their customers.

There are four levels of PCI Compliance; information on these levels is as follows:

1. Any merchant: Regardless of acceptance channel – processing over six million Visa transactions per year. Also includes any merchant that Visa, at its sole discretion, determines should meet the Level 1 (those who process more than six million transactions anually) merchant requirements in order to minimise risk to the Visa system.
2. Any merchant: Regardless of acceptance channel – processing one million to six million Visa transactions per year.
3. Any merchant processing 20,000 to one million Visa e-commerce transactions per year.
4. Any merchant processing fewer than 20,000 Visa e-commerce transactions per year, and all other merchants, regardless of acceptance channel, processing up to one million Visa transactions per year.

PCI compliance can be an expensive ongoing cost, so you should seek out the alternatives. For example, choosing a PSP that is Level 1 compliant and getting them to host your payment pages will mean that you only have to be compliant to the most basic level. This approach will often save you money and a lot of hassle.
www.sagepay.com

Online shopping malls

An online shopping mall collates a number of smaller e-retailers together on one site. The mall will host your shop as well as process the payments for you. Although they are relatively quick and easy to set up, there are some drawbacks.

They are generally the most expensive way of selling online, and may ask for both a joining fee and a monthly or annual fee. You are also less likely to have any control over the way your shop looks, as it will go through the mall's own templates.

All about PayPal

This is one of the most popular payment processing companies as it's owned by eBay but your customers aren't obliged to have an account with eBay to use this payment method. As with most PSPs, this system enables you to receive or make payments anywhere in the world. There are various ways to add a PayPal facility to your website. You could add a button, a shopping cart (one of the most widely-used options), use a PayPal-approved partner solution (which you can do if you have used an e-commerce partner to help build your site), or choose the customer integration route, which requires some technical knowledge. PSPs like Sage Pay include PayPal integration too.

Please note requirements change regularly so you should always check with your PSP/QSA.

Micropayments

These are means of transferring very small units of currency in situations where collecting such small amounts of money with the usual payment systems is impractical, or very expensive, in terms of the amount of money being collected. They've never really been that popular with consumers, but if you want to find out more about how to use micropayments, log onto www.mppglobal.com, a payment technology provider, for more information.

> **Startups Tips**
> There are a host of payment options available, so do shop around for the best deal for you. Find a payment company that offers your customers an efficient service, and that provides you with support and an easy to use system.

Protecting against fraud

Online fraud can destroy a business. Recent research shows cardholder not present (e-commerce) payments represent the sector of fastest growing fraud in the UK, accounting for 15% of all fraud. According to Sage Pay's *E-Business Benchmark Report*, fraud prevention is an important consideration among those businesses surveyed, although they say it is not the most frustrating aspect of the payment process. Those surveyed said that they experienced varying levels of fraud and those not using basic fraud tools like 3D Secure (see below for more on this), are likely to experience five more chargebacks a year from their merchant bank. A chargeback is the return of funds to a consumer, forcibly initiated by the consumer's issuing bank. This means that the consumer does not lose out financially if their card is stolen or cloned – it is the merchant who ultimately has to foot the bill.

Startups Tips

Online fraud should be a constant and ongoing consideration – vigilance is essential at all times.

Fraudsters are ever-more inventive and although systems are developed and employed to tackle online fraud, fraudsters will always work to find a loophole. They'll also find new areas to attack and new inventive methods of fraud.

Online fraud can take place through stolen cards and identity theft, but can also be as a direct result of poor security on the part of the vendor: you. A website without proper security measures could allow a fraudster to obtain details from a genuine customer. Even poor security within an office environment could up-scale a minor office break-in to a full data breach, resulting in card numbers used by genuine customers being compromised and used by fraudsters for their own ends.

Sage Pay gives the following example of how online fraud can affect a business: a vendor who has no level of vigilance or awareness towards online fraud and accepts a payment from a card which is later reported as stolen, will not only lose the value of the goods he has shipped, but will also be held responsible for refunding the monies to the real credit card owner. He'll also have to pay an additional fee to the bank which retrieves the funds, forcefully, from their business account. Go to www.sagepay.com for more information from the experts.

By signing up to initiatives such as 3D Secure (which good PSPs will offer for free), you can ensure that your online payments will be protected against chargebacks – this will reduce your own risk and subsequently the risk of jeopardising your business.

Common fraud screening tools

- **AVS (Address Verification System):** This system checks the numerics in the billing address of the card against the address at which the card is registered.
- **CV2, CVC, CVV (Card Verification Code):** This is the three/four-digit authentication code on the back of credit or debit cards.
- **3D Secure:** Similar to an online version of Chip and PIN, where instead of a PIN number a user generated password is required. It aims to reduce the possibility of fraudulent card use by authenticating the cardholder at the actual time of the transaction and subsequently reducing your exposure to disputed transactions and chargebacks of this type.
- **Third party checks:** Some PSPs work with a third party that runs secure background checks on card data supplied from many sources. For example:
  1. Contact details match, eg telephone number matches the postal area
  2. Delivery to a high-risk postal area
  3. Multiple addresses have been used by the same person or card.

Fraud screening tools may vary in complexity and effectiveness and it is worth noting that any results you get are only ever as good as the information you provided in the first place. If a transaction containing no details about a customer is run through a fraud screening system then the transaction may be marked as 'safe' or 'low risk' even if this is not an accurate representation of that customer. The more detail you gather about a customer or a purchase and provide to your PSP or fraud screening company, the higher the effectiveness of the fraud screening results.

Cardholder information is validated against huge databases, including card address, number of cards used at the address, card issue numbers and card security value.

Training your staff

Online fraud and fraud screening should be at the forefront of your payment policy and vigilance by yourself and other members of staff goes without saying.

Fraudsters may even strike by calling members of your staff to gather information about real life customers, a process known as 'social engineering'. Social engineers attempt to garner information gradually, one phone call at a time. By slowly making notes and building up a database of titbits of information provided by the company over the phone, they can eventually contact the company and provide detailed information relating to a particular individual/company with the aim of passing all security checks and having unrestricted access. This demonstrates the importance of staff awareness and training and also management awareness around how fraud can be an internal problem.

Infrastructure is also very important; it is wise to always ensure that you are getting the best out of the security you have at your disposal. If you have a security feature on one of your networks, ensure that it's being used.

Shipping options

So you've got as far as persuading customers to actually buy from your site. Unless you're selling certain digital products that can be downloaded online, you now have the important task of getting the sold product into the hands of the consumer.

The key with shipping options is to make it fair and sensible for your market. Rates will depend on where you are located as well as where you are sending the goods. Experiment with different policies, such as absorbing shipping costs into prices and offering free shipping, or free shipping on certain order sizes to encourage larger baskets.

 In my experience

We really don't ship very much as nearly everything we sell is electronic which of course may well be the best advice... deliver it electronically if you can.

Company: wahanda.com
Owner-manager: Lopo Champalimaud

If your business is relatively small, you may want to send items individually using a standard service such as that provided by Royal Mail. The most important thing about shipping costs is to make sure that they are transparent throughout the buying process. Few things kill more sales than a hefty carriage charge that only appears unannounced at the very end of the checkout process.

The speed and service you offer in the delivery of products can make or break your business. According to Sage Pay's report, the most influential factor in encouraging a purchase online is next day delivery. If a customer isn't happy with how long it took to have the item they bought reach their hands, or it didn't arrive in good condition, it's very unlikely they'll order from you again.

You have to perfect your delivery strategy and work out a system that is both cost-effective for your business, and of a satisfactory standard for your customers.

There are several options to look at when planning your strategy for delivery. The first is to deliver items yourself, or hire someone to do it. This is probably only a cost-effective option if you sell locally, or sell a limited number of big ticket items.

 In my experience

My advice on shipping options is to use the best you can. There are others in the market who will be cheaper, but with every pound you save, you could lose a customer.

Company: Naked Wines
Owner-manager: Rowan Gormley

Outsourcing

The most viable options are probably going to be using a postal service such as Royal Mail, or courier/distribution services. If you choose to outsource your delivery you must ensure you choose a partner who can meet the standards your customers expect, and fits in well with the way you operate your own business. With the e-commerce industry increasing at such a dramatic rate, there are many different delivery outsourcing companies to choose from, so make sure you shop around for the right partner for your company.

Tracking

Keeping your customers informed about when to expect their purchases is one way of elevating the level of customer service you offer. Nearly all couriers offer online tracking of parcels. This works by allocating an ID number to the order which can then be used by the consumer to track the location of their order online.

The use of order tracking will probably only be really valued by consumers if the item they have ordered is urgent or expensive. For most small or low priced purchases an email from you telling the customer their item has been dispatched, and a delivery estimate, will suffice.

Returns policy

In the UK you are obliged to offer a no quibble seven-day refund on any hard goods, and clearly state that on your website. If you don't, the customer will have an automatic right to return the goods and be refunded any time up to three months after purchase, under the Distance Selling Regulations (see p.81 for more information).

Startups checklist

- Determine a budget for your technology needs before you source the equipment.
- Make the most of free software available to download from the internet.
- Research different web hosting options: Get at least three quotes.
- Check out the best practice guidelines for website accessibility.
- Online fraud could cripple your business so ensure you take the necessary precautions.
- Shop around to find the best payment options available for both you and your customers.
- Offer a variety of shipping options if possible and gauge customer demand.

 CHAPTER 4.3

Managing the business and accounts

Launching an online business is what you set out to do and without doubt that's where your energies are best served. However, as a small business owner, you'll no doubt find yourself involved in many different aspects of your business and there's a substantial amount of administrative duties to be aware of. Many online businesses are started from home, but as your business grows, you may need to consider investing in premises. If you are selling goods over the internet, you'll also need to think about issues such as posting and packaging, as well as your after-service model, including managing returns. It is often the new financial aspects of running a business which people find the hardest to get used to. You'll always need to put time aside for the financial aspect of running a business.

In this chapter we'll cover:

→ Property needs
→ Storerooms
→ Packaging and sending
→ Managing returns
→ Accounting systems
→ Profit and loss
→ VAT.

Property needs

Many an online entrepreneur has set up shop in their spare room, bedroom, kitchen or garage. It's likely that your business will also be launched this way and you may find that you can run the business from home indefinitely. You might, however, require more space, particularly if you are in online retail, as you'll need space to store goods. You'll also have to consider premises if you are looking to hire employees.

In my experience

We started Wahanda around my dining room table until we became too big and my wife put her foot down (I don't blame her). We then rented desks for the first six months from a larger company while we were getting going.

Company: Wahanda.com
Owner-manager: Lopo Champalimaud

If you can, this is a great option as you really don't want to be dealing with a lease and office furnishings when you are getting started.

Startups Tips

You can tweak your website, change suppliers and introduce new product lines. Property, however, is likely to be where you have least flexibility and at the most cost, so you'll want to get it right first time.

Finding commercial premises, however, incurs considerable expense, so it's not a decision to be made lightly. Revisit your business plan and consider your cashflow and future forecasts. You'll need to consider exactly what you'll need from your premises. How much floor space will you need, for instance? And how much space and what special requirements will you need for stock and storage?

You can always create the necessary number of rooms and install special requirements but first and foremost you'll need to ensure you've got enough space overall – and, just as important, you're not paying for more than you need.

Lease or buy

You've two options when searching for premises: to lease or to buy. For many of you there won't actually be a choice because you won't be able to afford to buy. Even if you can, especially in the current climate of declining property prices, it could be smarter to keep your money in your pocket and not saddle your business with a sizeable mortgage.

One major consideration should be the current state of the property market. While commercial property tends to withstand fluctuation better than the residential market, retail and office lets are at their lowest levels for 10 years, while many landlords have seen the value of their portfolios decrease over 2009 and the early part of 2010. Basically, it's a far better time to be renting than owning.

Buying

Even given the current state of the property market buying does have its advantages. You'll have an asset to play with and the freedom to not have to go seeking your landlord's approval every time you make a change. Ask yourself the following questions before you decide to buy a property. If you can't answer yes to all of them, buying isn't for you.

→ Is the space in the best location you think you can ever afford?

→ Do you plan to keep to the same size indefinitely? Does it meet your needs now and in the future?

→ Do you have both a sufficient deposit and the budget for a mortgage, or enough cash to purchase the property outright?

If you're in a comfortable enough position to buy premises, then there are several advantages associated with buying a property. The first and most obvious is that you'll own it, have the freedom to do with it as you please, and not have to answer to a landlord. Another major advantage with owning your own premises is you'll have a major asset, either to secure loans against or think of as an investment.

Startups Tips

Do as much research on the building and area as physically possible because if something's not right with it once you've got the keys, it won't be easy to just pack up and move on.

As with any property purchase, domestic or commercial, you'll need to carry out the appropriate checks before you agree to buy. Bring in a reputable surveyor, get the place checked with the environmental health officer and find out what your business rates will be.

Leasing

Leasing is far more common than buying, for the simple reason that it gives you more flexibility in both a physical and a financial sense. If you expand more quickly than anticipated and need more space, you can move at relatively short notice, provided you negotiated the right kind of contract when you took out the lease. Also, there are a limited number of properties on the market to buy and you'll find your options are far more open when looking for leased property.

A lease can be negotiated for any length of time that you and the landlord agree on but typically will last anywhere between three and 25 years. The landlord will be looking for a reliable tenant that will run a successful business and consequently be able to pay the rent on time. You may be asked to present a business plan and have your own financial history checked up on. If you don't have any trading history then it's not unheard of for the landlord to ask for anything up to a year's rent in advance, so bear this in mind when budgeting.

However, you have just as much right to do your own checks on the landlord. If possible talk to the current or previous tenants. Find out why they're moving on. If their business failed, was it because of something wrong with the property, or even as a result of a difficult landlord? These are the kind of things you'll want to know before signing a lease.

That said the one advantage to the current economic climate is that the power could be swinging back to you as a tenant. It's not uncommon for a landlord, especially if they're struggling to fill a space, to give you an incentive to move in. It's all about supply and demand and don't be afraid to fight your corner just because you're a start-up business. See if you can negotiate a period of free rent to help your business establish itself and use the argument that it's in both your interests for that to happen.

Here are a few tips and things to consider before signing a lease:

- What kind of rent rates are similar businesses in the area being charged, and is yours a fair rate in comparison? The simplest way to find out is to ask: you'll find most businesses will be just as interested to know if they're overpaying the current asking rate so will be happy to play ball.
- Is the length of lease suitable? If it's too short your online business will lack security but if it's too long and you don't have a break clause, you may find yourself stuck.
- Is the building sound and in a state of good repair? It's advisable to bring in expert help to check there are no serious faults.
- Will the landlord offer a rent-free period if there are repairs to be carried out?
- Do you need planning permission before you can build or alter the space according to your designs?
- Who is responsible for insurance? What's included in the rent, and what cover will the landlord expect you to take out yourself in addition?
- This is by no means an extensive list of everything you should check before signing a contract. It's always advisable to have a solicitor or property expert check over the small print for you.

Storerooms

Web shoppers are impatient and expect instant gratification – if you display items that you don't have in stock, it's likely you'll lose that customer pretty quickly and they will move on to another site. So maintaining inventory – and having space to stock it – is an important consideration. As a start-up, it's not easy to gauge what potential demand may be, but instead of ordering the bare minimum, order a bit more so you have enough left over. Having too much inventory is better than running out, but don't order in huge quantities unless you are absolutely sure the product is likely to fly off your virtual shelves, otherwise you may find you are left with stock that is impossible to shift and which you are paying rent on.

Keeping track of how much inventory you have and what is pending can help you decide whether you need to rent storage space or whether, as many entrepreneurs do to start with, you can stock the goods at your home initially. You could choose to do your stock control manually or use software. The manual option is likely to be the cheapest but you won't be able to access and retrieve records as quickly as if you were doing this through electronic methods. Most accountancy software packages include inventory management, so if you have invested in a package, it's worth seeing if it includes a function for stock control (see p.281 for more on accountancy package options). A computerised inventory control system is also worth investing in if you have many different types of stock. Before you invest in software, get two or three quotes from providers and assess your business needs now and in the future.

Startups Tips

Efficient stock control allows you to have the right amount of stock in the right place at the right time.

If you are looking to rent storage space, bear in mind many of the guidelines that apply to leasing property also apply to renting storage space – check out whether the rates are suitable and see if you can negotiate terms.

Guide to inventory control

- Netsuite (www.netsuite.co.uk) offers inventory management software that is integrated with customer relationship management, enabling customers to view updated inventory information on your online store.
- OrderWise (www.orderwise.co.uk) provides stock control software that integrates with many accountancy software packages.
- InventoryOps (www.inventoryops.com) is a website with information on inventory management.

Packaging and sending

You've got your online shop up and running and built the transactional part of your website. The next area you need to turn your attention to is order fulfilment – the packaging and sending of items purchased. It can seem like one of the least exciting parts of running an online business, but the fulfilment of orders is often the most important aspect for your customers.

 From the experts

Company: **ASOS**
Owner-manager: **Nick Robertson**

Logistics is never far from my mind, it's such an important part of running an internet business. You have to keep an open mind as to what needs to be done in this area.

Deciding how you fulfil orders will depend very much on the type of items you are selling and where you are sending them to, but there are basic rules to stick to regardless of what type of online business you run.

⇢ Use strong packaging to ship items: There's nothing worse than sending something, only for it to be delivered damaged. This is one of the quickest ways of losing customers.

⇢ Take advantage of the shipment and place a small token, thank you letter for ordering and your business card inside the package, it will remind people of your site when they open it up.

⇢ Product packaging can add value to your product and boost brand awareness, so consider what design you can use on your packaging to increase its impact.

 In my experience

We've outsourced our warehousing because we've grown very rapidly.

Company: Naked Wines
Owner-manager: Rowan Gormley

Managing returns

It's important to set restrictions on when people can return goods and expect a refund or exchange. Many businesses, for example, say that goods need to be returned within 21 or 30 days and that they should be unopened or undamaged. Your returns policy should be stated clearly in your website's terms and conditions.

Accounting systems

If you decide you're going to manage the books yourself you'll want to get yourself some accountancy software. Whoever's job it is, yours or an accountant's, the person balancing the books, chasing invoices, managing suppliers and paying staff doesn't need to be worrying about the latest technology and it's probably the last thing on their mind. It's perfectly possible to work with an Excel spreadsheet but buying an accountancy software package can slash the amount of time and effort you put into managing your finances. Expect to pay from £500 for a system that supports two to three users.

From reminders for chasing payment to generating invoices, a good package is like a virtual accounts department. It can tell you how much you are owed and by whom; how long it takes you to pay your bills; what you have in stock and what you have in the bank at any moment in time. More importantly, it could also give you those vital breakdowns of how much you are making on each service, day or month. Of course, there's nothing stopping you or your accountant working from a basic Excel spreadsheet, but bear in mind that a good accountancy software package can drastically reduce your accounting bill every year.

There are a multitude of different systems on the market. Choosing the right system at the right time is critical. What is the right system? There is no easy answer to that question. System selection will depend on a number of criteria. Professional services firm RSM Bentley Jennison recommends that you ask yourself the following questions:

- → Budget: How much do you have to spend right now?

- → Compatibility: Will the system you choose 'talk' to the online software you have created for your business? The last thing you need is to re-key the electronic information already collected into the accounting system.

- → User friendliness: Who will use the software and how accounts literate is the user?

⇢ What information do you need from the system and in what format?

Leaving aside the manual bookkeeping systems, there are two broad types of software:

⇢ Software that is hosted on a stand alone PC

⇢ Web-based systems (often referred to as 'software as a service' or SaaS).

According to RSM Bentley Jennison, the latter are becoming more popular as they are anytime, anyplace so you don't have to be at the office to either process data or obtain reports. There are a number of different 'families' of accounting software systems; each offering different packages from basic to sophisticated. It is worth choosing the one you think will best fit your needs in the medium term, at least, because upgrading within a family is far easier than changing from one to another. Here are a few examples:

⇢ Sage: www.sage.co.uk

⇢ Access UK: www.theaccessgroup.com

⇢ Netsuite (web-based system): www.netsuite.co.uk.

Advice from Sage...

What types of accounting systems are available?

There are many different types of software that can help you manage your accounts. Very basically, they break down into desktop, server and online systems, to help you decide what's best for you, here's a brief description.

Desktop software
This is software that you load onto your computer from a disk or download from a website. You access the software locally on that computer and all your data is stored in the same place. Sage Instant Accounts and Sage 50 Accounts are examples of desktop software.

How desktop software differs:

Data held locally: The user holds their own data on their own machines, servers or hard drives. This helps with accessibility, up time, backing up data. Some customers prefer desktop software because of security as they are not sharing their data with a third party. However, some customers like online software as they share it with a third party that is responsible for their data.

Ownership and licensing: You tend to pay a one-off fee for desktop software then you own the software outright, whereas with online software you would tend to pay an ongoing monthly subscription fee.

Integration with other desktop products: More developers build for desktop than online but that trend is shifting quickly. This means you can integrate your accounts software with Outlook, e-banking/payments, payroll etc.

Server-based software
With server-based software, you still use your computer to access the data, but everything is stored on a central server. It makes it easier for several people to share information and access the same data at the same time.

Online or hosted software
You access online or hosted software through the internet. Your data may actually be stored miles away, but you can work on it from anywhere with an internet connection. www.sage.co.uk

Cashflow

Many of you would have heard of the saying 'cash is king'. Of course, in the long run, you have to be profitable to have a successful business but the mistake many businesses make is that they do not know whether they will run out of cash. Their systems are not robust enough, or the information from them not timely enough, to project forward to see where the cash holes are.

From a cashflow perspective, there are two fundamental questions to consider:

Startups Tips

Web-based accounting systems are becoming increasingly popular as they enable you to work on the accounts without being tied to the office.

→ Do you know when you should expect cash to come in from customers?

→ Do you know when you have to pay your suppliers?

It's still surprising how many businesses still don't know the answer to these questions. Once you have discovered the answers then, with the aid of a simple spreadsheet, you can forward forecast income less expenditure and discover where the holes are.

Profit and loss

Understanding whether you make a profit or a loss is one of the most critical key performance indicators of any business. If you're not making a profit, there's little point in being in business. Understanding what your income drivers are, and the associated costs, will enable you to have a firm grounding to understand the profit and loss account. Many accounting systems will produce a profit and loss report but, without the understanding behind the numbers, they are just that: numbers on a page. See p.67 for an example of a profit and loss sheet.

There are many online resources that can be found to explain how to interpret a profit and loss account. You may be able to find courses at your local Business Enterprise agency (such as the Chambers of Commerce). The best way to find out how your profit and loss account works is to ask your accountant! After all, they are there to help.

VAT

Supplies of goods and services via the internet have become commonplace; however, for a new business the VAT rules can be complicated. Businesses trading via the internet should also be aware of HM Revenue & Customs' (HMRC) ability to track the sale of goods from a particular address. One professional services firm, for example, says that several of its clients have received visits from the VAT man armed with lists of items sold on eBay. An appreciation of the rules is therefore essential if an unexpected bottom line cost to the business is to be avoided.

Goods sold via the internet tend to be treated like any 'normal' supply of goods and should not present a problem where the rules are understood. A supply of services made via the internet can, however, be more complicated.

As RSM Bentley Jennison outlines, four basic conditions need to be met for a supply of goods to be subject to VAT in the UK, namely:

- ⇢ The supply must be a taxable supply (at the standard or reduced-rate) made by a 'taxable person' (a natural or legal person registered or required to be registered for VAT in the UK)

- ⇢ The supply must be made for consideration (normally money but does include barter arrangements)

- ⇢ The supply must be made in the furtherance of a 'business'

- ⇢ The supply must be made in the UK.

Whilst the first three conditions are normally self-evident the fourth can be more problematic; however, the basic premise is that the place of supply of goods is determined by where they are located when they are dispatched to the customer.

Sales made via the internet by UK suppliers (where the goods are located in the UK when they are dispatched) to a UK customer are subject to VAT under the normal rules (zero-rated supplies made in the UK by taxable persons do not attract VAT).

Supplies of goods made by a UK business (where the goods are located in the UK when they are dispatched to the customer) to business customers in the EU or abroad are zero-rated, subject to the normal rules and should not present a problem to a business trading via the internet.

Where a UK business supplies and delivers goods to a non-VAT registered person in another EU member state (typically private individuals), the supplies will attract UK VAT, subject to the normal rules, unless the volume of sales is in excess of the 'distance selling threshold' for that member state. In this case, a liability to register in the particular member state may arise with a resulting requirement to charge VAT at the local rate. A liability to register in several EU member states could therefore arise where trading spans the EU.

The place of supply of installed or assembled goods is in the country where the goods are installed or assembled and a liability to register and account for VAT at the local rate may arise in the EU, although a simplified procedure may be available to allow the VAT registered customer to account for VAT instead.

Startups checklist

- Make sure you analyse your property needs thoroughly: Is buying or leasing better for your business?
- Carefully plan your packaging and sending processes: The fulfilment of orders is one of the most important aspects of your relationship with your customers.
- Be thorough in your record-keeping: The better organised your figures are, the better organised your shop will be.
- Don't try to manage all yourself if you don't have the time or skills: Hire an accountant if you need one.
- Check out the different types of accounting software available: It could reduce the amount of time and effort put into record-keeping.
- Be cautious in your forecasting: It's better to underestimate trade than overestimate. Be aware of your cashflow and profit and loss figures at all times.
- Make sure you are aware of all the regulations surrounding VAT and goods sold over the internet.

CHAPTER 4.4
Finding suppliers

Good suppliers and good offers won't just turn up in your inbox. You'll need to do the research, negotiate and put considerable effort into finding the right suppliers and the right products at the right prices. If you're planning on launching an online retail business, the type you choose will largely decide how and where you source your products and goods, and the type of suppliers you need to speak to. Mostly though, you'll buy through wholesalers, direct from manufacturers or suppliers, or from abroad.

In this chapter, we'll look at:

→ Wholesalers
→ Going direct
→ Trade fairs
→ Sourcing goods from abroad
→ Maintaining relationships
→ Building good credit.

Wholesalers

Wholesalers specialise in certain types of goods and tend to cluster together in industrial areas of cities. In London, for example, most are located to the west near Wembley and Park Royal, making them more accessible for the rest of the country. The centrality of the Midlands also makes it a logistical hub for distributors and wholesalers.

Wholesalers are fairly traditional in how they advertise themselves and you're just as likely to track them down in the Yellow Pages as online. Slowly but surely, however, they are beginning to use the web to reveal their whereabouts and even advertise their goods.

Before you set off on a visit, phone ahead to check about the products they've got on offer and in stock and for their best prices. Get the person's name that you speak to so you can find them when you get there. It'll make you seem more experienced and they'll be more inclined to help you find what you're looking for – and maybe even give you a discount.

Negotiation is the norm when it comes to buying in bulk and the wholesale warehouse floor is where the deals are made. The prospect of battling it out with a cockney 'Del Boy' might terrify some of you but it needn't be anywhere near so scary. Simply open negotiations by asking something such as, 'If I take three batches of this instead of two, are you going to give me x% discount?'

Remember, it's in a wholesaler's favour for you to make a healthy profit to ensure your business prospers and you keep coming back for more stock, so there's always room for negotiation on advertised prices. Obviously, the more you buy the more flexible wholesalers are likely to be. A £200 sale

Startups Tips

Some wholesalers will require you to have a trade or membership card, but don't be put off by this. It's usually something you can fill in at the counter with proof of business status such as a bank statement.

Startups Tips

www. thewholesaler. co.uk is the most established site for UK wholesalers.

From the experts

Company: ASOS
Owner-manager: Nick Robertson

At the beginning, no one wanted to deal with us and we walked around Great Portland Street in London with a plastic bag. Now people knock on our door.

isn't a big deal to them so be realistic. That said, discounts of up to 20% are commonplace when a deal's there to be struck.

It's also possible to get credit from many wholesalers. The process differs little from applying for any other form of credit and just involves filling out the relevant forms and undergoing a basic credit check. It's definitely an option many online retail businesses take advantage of but you should probably stick to using bank debt to begin with as it's a lot easier to keep control of your finances if they're all in one place. You'll also want to make sure you're happy with a wholesaler's service before you start taking credit from it.

Startups Tips

Most warehouses are open Monday to Friday and for part of Sunday. As inconvenient as it might be, they also tend to close from Christmas Eve through to 2 January, so check times before you set off.

Direct from manufacturers or suppliers

As opposed to physically visiting a wholesaler and bringing your newly acquired goods back to your home or premises, you can also buy directly from manufacturers or suppliers who'll deliver to you.

Your decision to buy directly from a manufacturer could be because you specifically want to stock a certain brand or product. If they don't sell through wholesale most large companies will have a department set up to deal with direct sales and distribution and you should look to contact them directly.

Most suppliers welcome any trade and while you might struggle to get credit with them as a start-up, they'll be happy to supply you. Others though, and most often in the case of branded products such as clothing, will want to see evidence that your business profile fits their brand. You'll be expected to go to their premises to pitch to become an official reseller and prove you understand the way they'd like their goods to be sold. Certain brands are deliberately picky and, silly as it might seem, you'll have to work hard to earn the right to sell their goods. If they don't already sell through an online channel, this could improve your chances of getting them on board. If they do already have a web sales channel, find out which other resellers they use and see if you can improve on this service or at the very least, match it.

In turn, you'll find it'll work the other way round as well and you'll be approached by salespeople asking you to stock their products. As the shoe is on the other foot you should be able to negotiate free or heavily discounted products for your first order to see how well they'll sell, so use such opportunities to practise and refine your negotiation skills.

157

When buying direct from suppliers or manufacturers you may also be able to negotiate or even be offered a 'sale or return' deal. This means you'll be refunded for any items you don't sell within an agreed period of time. However, most 'sale or return' will see you earn a commission of 10%–20% per unit sold, instead of the larger mark-up you'd expect from buying wholesale. It is a sensible way of testing the market for goods though before risking a large outlay.

In my experience

We asked our partners, friends at other start-ups and of course investors. When you are small and starting up you want a supplier who will take you seriously and share your dream and a personal recommendation sometimes helps.

Company: Wahanda.com
Owner–manager: Lopo Champalimaud

Trade fairs

The other way you'll find direct suppliers and manufacturers is through trade fairs. Here companies showcase their products and the latest ranges and it can also be a good hunting ground for networking purposes. It's always worth attending the main trade fairs in your industry, even if it's only to keep an eye on emerging trends and new suppliers who might be able to cut you a better deal in order to secure your services. Trade fairs also present the opportunity to find smaller suppliers that otherwise weren't on your radar and to pick up something unique. Exhibitions.co.uk is a listings site for the main UK trade fairs but you should also make an effort to find out about industry specific events by reading trade magazines covering your business sector and asking your suppliers which ones they attend and recommend.

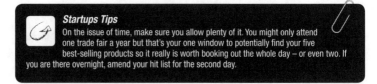

Startups Tips

On the issue of time, make sure you allow plenty of it. You might only attend one trade fair a year but that's your one window to potentially find your five best-selling products so it really is worth booking out the whole day – or even two. If you are there overnight, amend your hit list for the second day.

Buying from abroad/importers

Why is it attractive to buy from abroad?

There are quite simply huge savings to be had from buying produce from abroad. In fact, it's not just savings, you'll find items that you can't buy anywhere else and which will have a mark-up far in excess of anything you'll buy and sell from a UK manufacturer or wholesaler.

China and India are the booming economies of the world; however, their export trades are very much geared to supplying big business and they rarely ship items in quantities less than 40ft containers. Smaller amounts are easier to source from countries such as Thailand and Indonesia, specifically Bali, where there's a good variety of products that are very saleable in the UK market. Increasingly, online businesses in the UK are importing everything from jewellery to clothing and interior design products, at rock bottom prices that make it mouth-wateringly tempting.

However, while international trade is becoming far more commonplace among small business owners, it remains laden with risk for a start-up like you. There are also significant costs to consider that will counter-balance what initially seem like massive mark-ups. In addition to purchase price, factor in the cost of finding suppliers, packing and transportation, insurance and customs duty.

You'll also need to account for a degree of leeway in this, as when you're managing large imports even a slight fluctuation in transport charges or exchange rates can eat massively into your profits.

Startups Tips

Relying completely on goods imported from abroad is a riskier strategy than buying from home simply because there are more factors beyond your direct control.

Finding a supplier abroad

You've got two options for finding overseas suppliers, either seek them yourself and buy directly or go indirectly through an importer. Buying directly offers you the greatest mark-up but you'll have to find them, arrange the deal, transportation and maintain all lines of communication on your own. Using an importer is far less risky and taxing but, predictably, the profit you can make is nowhere near as high, while the chance of you importing something truly unique is also reduced.

If you're thinking of importing directly, the first thing you need to do is find a supplier. You can fly out to the countries you know specialise in your goods on a fact finding trip and go seeking suppliers yourself, much as you might plan an exploratory trip to West London warehouse depots. If you do this, try to plan as much as you can in advance so you can make the most of your time. Research regions that specialise in export supply, look for clusters of suppliers, try to contact UK business networks in that country and ask all your contacts for advice. Has anyone else you know been through the same experience and what recommendations and advice can they give you? While expensive it could also be worth taking a translator with you.

A safer and easier way to begin is either by using a supplier recommended via word of mouth from someone who has already successfully imported with them or by consulting trade bodies in your sector that might have a list of recommended international suppliers. Likewise, each country's embassy should have a commercial department. See the Foreign and Commonwealth Office website (www.fco.gov.uk) for more details.

Startups Tips
To ensure you're buying from a legitimate supplier look for a proven track record of supplying goods to the UK, ask for the name of UK customers so you can check this, and ask to speak to the main sales agent you'll be dealing with to ensure there will be no insurmountable language barriers.

Striking a deal and protecting yourself

The key here is to be absolutely clear about what you're buying and for how much. Get it all in a legally binding, bilingual contract and leave nothing unaccounted for. If you can, try to be there or have a representative present when goods are packed or transported. Chances are you'll be fine but there are plenty of horror stories of business owners who sign off and pay for goods only to see something that bears little resemblance arrive in the UK a month later. If you're in any way suspicious, first question why you're doing the deal. Second, order a small amount as a test.

Don't scrimp on insurance. Get some good advice from an insurance broker on product liability insurance for the goods you're importing, marine insurance (which covers you for all transportation) and look to cover goods for the contract price plus an extra 10% to account for the extra costs you'll incur if something goes wrong.

Transporting goods

Aside from cultural obstacles and the dangers of being ripped off, the main problem is the unreliability of affordable transportation. Shipping is the cheapest option but involves taking out a container (20ft is usually the smallest, with 40ft the standard size) that runs the risk of being delayed at both ends of departure and arrival. You simply can't afford delayed delivery times, particularly if you are selling online – people expect almost instant gratification from the internet as a sales channel. The same applies to posting items, sending them by airfreight or loose cargo can be massively expensive as you'll pay by weight.

Startups Tips

By far the best way is to carry items back with you as luggage, but of course, this will only apply for goods such as jewellery, where you are able to carry substantial quantities with ease.

Paying customs duty and legal responsibilities

There are various legal obligations you'll need to comply with, depending on what it is you're looking to import.

There are limitations, quotas and special controls governing the import of certain products such as foods, medicinal products, plants, animals, metals and textiles. In some cases you'll require an import licence, in others you'll need to provide proof of country of origin, while many items are subject to inspection.

You'll also have to pay any duty and VAT that applies to the goods you're importing under UK and EU law before they are released to you. Your freight transporter can sometimes pay this re-invoice you for it; otherwise you'll need to seek advice from HM Revenue & Customs (HMRC) or an accountant on what you need to pay. Make sure you do this in advance so you're clear about the real cost of the goods you're buying.

Is it really worth it?

In brief, while it's massively tempting, for most of you buying from abroad is better put on hold until you've established your business and can survive if an order is massively delayed or, worse still, doesn't arrive at all.

If you do go ahead, be as thorough as you can possibly be. Without doubt you shouldn't buy without flying out and visiting the supplier to see the goods. Indeed, you'll usually only find the best deals by doing this and it can be far more reassuring to see the products in person.

Maintaining a relationship with suppliers

Once you've established a network of suppliers you're happy with and can rely on, it's important you maintain a good working relationship with them. It's not just about paying your bills on time.

→ Try to deal with the same sales representative or agent whenever you order. Building a relationship with one person is more likely to inspire trust and the odd favour when you need it.

→ Keep a check on prices and review your bills against what other suppliers are offering. Even if you don't want to change suppliers you may be able to negotiate more competitive prices. Don't be afraid to do this; suppliers will understand your need to get a good price and be grateful for giving them the chance to match it rather than lose your trade to a competitor.

→ Remember not to judge a supplier solely on price. Ensure levels of customer service, flexibility and, crucially, quality of product, don't slip.

Advice from Sage ...

Managing suppliers

Make sure you have clear terms and conditions stated upfront that both parties have agreed and understood. Clear invoice and remittance documents can also ensure there's no confusion over payments.

Using software that enables you to log all your communications history with a customer or supplier means that you can see exactly when you made a phone call or sent a letter to them. And having a good stock control system can also help. If you know you're running low on items, you can let your suppliers know in plenty of time to reorder them.

Finally, using BACS (see below) can speed up the time it takes for you to make payments to your suppliers, something which will always help the relationship!
www.sage.co.uk

Building good credit

In an ideal world we'd all be paid the minute we invoice and be given as long as we want to pay, and some companies, often the big ones with lots of weight to throw around, take that attitude. It won't even be an option for you as a start-up as suppliers will look to be paid promptly, but view this as a positive opportunity to build trust and earn the right to greater flexibility going forward.

Advice from Sage Pay. . .

Using BACS

BACS (Bankers Automated Clearing Service) is an automated payment method. It is used for batch payment and runs by using a link within your accounts software connected to your bank account.

The benefits of BACS are that it:

- Automates regular payments
- Reduces the time and cost of administering bulk payments
- Helps manage cashflow and improve financial control
- Reduces risk of loss, late payment and theft for customers.

It's an easy and inexpensive way to start improving procurement efficiency.

www.sagepay.com

If you do buy on credit, ensure that keeping payments up to date is prioritised. Falling behind with repayments is the best way to ruin an otherwise good business relationship and if a supplier suddenly withholds delivery or demands payment of what you owe in full, the future of your business could be in real jeopardy.

Startups checklist

- Have a clear idea of what you are looking for, especially price and quality.
- Try to buy in bulk, or ask for discounts.
- Build up a mutually beneficial relationship with your supplier.
- Make sure you consider both the benefits and risks associated with importing goods from abroad.
- When researching importing, don't forget to add up the costs of transport and customs duty.
- If you buy on credit, make sure you keep up to date with your payments or you risk jeopardising relationships with your suppliers.

 CHAPTER 4.5
Hiring staff

Many an online business is operated by one person, with the occasional ad hoc help drafted in to support busier times of the year, for example. But at some point in your website's growth, you may need to consider whether you need to hire staff to help on a more permanent basis. If you are focusing on a retail model, it's likely you'll need to hire people to help with customer sales, order processing, stock returns and after-sales support. If you are running a service-based online business, you may find you need to employ staff to handle customer queries as your business grows. Recruitment is a tricky area, and one that ends up being extremely costly if you make the wrong decisions.

In this chapter we'll look at:

-> Identifying your staffing needs
-> Writing job descriptions and adverts
-> Interviewing
-> Training up your new recruits
-> Ways of attracting the best talent
-> Pitfalls to watch out for
-> The necessary paperwork.

What are your requirements?

Your business plan should have included an idea of how many members of staff you'll need to run your online business smoothly, but will also have taken into account what you can afford. Ask yourself the following questions:

- ⇢ What level of technical expertise do your staff need?
- ⇢ Does it make sense to employ them part-time to start with?
- ⇢ Will you need more staff at certain times of the year?
- ⇢ What will be your busiest or most staff intensive hours?
- ⇢ How much can you increase sales by adding an extra member of staff?

Once you've established exactly how many members of staff your online venture needs you will have to make a decision on what you can afford to pay them. You'll need to strike a fine balance between being practical and not stretching your budget too far, but also being realistic about what you need to pay to attract the right kind of talent. Growth in the online sector means that salaries are competitive and demand for skilled employees — particularly web developers — can be high.

From the experts

Company: ASOS
Owner-manager: Nick Robertson

I wasn't tech-savvy when we launched the business but I was fortunate enough to employ people who were. This was back in the days when technology failed a lot. We spent a lot of money on our website and it would take a while for sales to catch up.

Distinguishing job roles

Website manager

For many people, the whole point of starting an online business is running it on a day to day basis. It might be a desire to exploit technology or work with family. Whatever the reason, they want to be in control, involved, the epicentre of all activity. For others though, often those online business owners looking to expand quickly or with outside interests who don't intend to be involved with the site full-time, there's a need for someone else to fill the website manager's role.

It can be a tricky role to fill – after all the hard work you put into starting the business, this person will have a major say in its success. The key starting point for any successful recruitment is a clear job description. However, aside from experience and skills, you'll need to find someone who you get on with, can trust and someone who shares your vision for the business.

You'll need your site manager to be motivated to drive sales and the obvious way to do that is through commission and bonuses. Better than a straight percentage are staggered bonuses or commission incentives above certain target thresholds incentivising them to keep striving for the next level.

Technical staff

Your technical staff will play a big role in your site's performance and the experience of your customers. Technical roles can cover everything from web developers, to coders to site maintenance staff. They could be responsible for both the front and back end of the site, the way the pages are displayed, the navigation of the site and the checkout function.

In my experience

Building a team from the start is tricky, especially when creating a web business. From the beginning, we had limited resources. If you employ a web developer, it's the difference between succeeding and failing, otherwise you could be making it up as you go along and it's critical you get it right.

Company: Glasses Direct
Owner-manager: Jamie Murray Wells

Flexible workers

Many online businesses rely on temporary staff, especially for peaks and troughs in trade such as weekends and holiday seasons. It's also a sensible way to start recruiting if you're not entirely sure you need anyone full-time.

An ideal situation is to try and establish a flexible team of reliable casual staff who you can call upon when needed and whom you could possibly employ full-time if the opportunity arises. Students can make great casual staff as well, both during term times and those returning home for the holidays.

Startups Tips

Look at what types of incentives and perks you can offer staff ranging from discounts, commission, drinks down the pub, flexi-time, fun days out or sponsoring sports and charity activities. Keep it varied and try and set new targets for individuals and teams to be aiming towards.

Recruiting staff

The key to successful recruiting is to put the homework in up front. Start by drawing up a detailed job description of the duties and responsibilities of the role and the attributes, skills and experience needed from candidates.

From the experts

Company: ASOS
Owner-manager: Nick Robertson

Looking back I would have recruited better staff earlier on. I might have struggled to get them but they would have been more experienced in areas I wasn't skilled in.

Writing job descriptions

Therein lies the crux. Your job description (and advertisement) should lay out the criteria by which you will carry out your recruitment process. If you have specific requirements that you can legally justify, then providing you detail them in advance and expose every candidate to the same criteria you cannot be accused of discriminating against one candidate.

Once you've established firm criteria and requirements for the role prioritise them into primary and secondary requirements. This will give you a firm matrix to compare applications and interviews so that if any legal objection was ever raised you'd have clear written evidence that the process was fair and above board.

Advertising for staff

Once you've made a detailed job description, creating an ad should be easy. List all the job requirements, criteria for applicants, information about your online business and also state the salary or wage you'll pay. Just as important as what you detail about the job role, is the information on how you want people to reply. Be specific. Ideally you want everyone to reply in the same way so you're making a fair and direct comparison of applications. The best way to do this is to use application forms but you might not have the time to draw one up or deem them not personal enough. If you want CVs then ask for a personal letter as well.

Startups Tips

Courtesy, people skills and technical experience are all likely to be important so perhaps ask applicants to explain why they have those attributes in their letters.

Where you advertise will depend on the role and type of online business you're running and it makes sense to advertise online, through online message boards such as Gumtree for example. For more senior positions such as site manager or web developer it might be that you target people already working in these positions through the technology press, recruitment websites or agencies that can prove they have candidates with the necessary experience on their books. Targeted advertising can make more sense than more general options, but be careful about what you're spending. It could be that networking contacts and job centres could be just as effective. Most likely, a combination will produce a decent response.

From the experts

Company: **LinkedIn**
Owner-manager: **Reid Hoffman**

Forming ties with a group of people around you where they help you grow as a professional, solve problems, get opportunities, and you help them, is the foundation of a strong, modern career.

Shortlisting candidates for interview

You'll already have done the hard work and this is where your matrix should pay dividends. Simply pass all your applications past your primary and secondary criteria ticking each attribute that they meet. If you've three candidates that meet all the primary boxes they're clearly the best suited for the job. If you have none then start consulting the secondary options and so on.

Be careful that you use these criteria and these criteria only. After all, you devised them. It is likely confusion will occur when an applicant meets most of the criteria but either lets themselves down in some way such as poor spelling or incorrect information supplied, or you have a gut feeling the person could give you more in an interview than on paper. It's unrealistic to pretend gut feeling doesn't exist – it's very important because after all you're going to have to work closely with this person so it can't be a purely mathematical choice.

Look to make a manageable shortlist but remember it's very risky to reject someone for an interview if they've met the same criteria as everyone else unless you've got a very good reason you'd be prepared to stand in front of a tribunal to defend.

Interviewing

Successful interviewing requires certain skills. If you've never employed people before you may find some training helpful. For more information on training contact the Chartered Institute of Personnel and Development at www.cipd.co.uk. There are various courses available to teach you effective interviewing techniques, but if you can't spare the time or finances for these, the basics are covered here.

Preparing to interview candidates

Interviews must be planned extremely carefully. You only have a short window of time to elicit all the information you need from a potential recruit. Not only do you have to ascertain their relevant levels of experience, you also need to gauge accurate impressions about whether they fit in with the kind of atmosphere and work environment you're trying to achieve.

Set aside some dedicated time to do the interviews – make sure there are no unnecessary interruptions such as ringing phones or other staff or even family members vying for your attention.

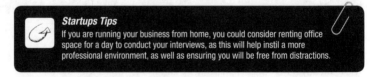

Startups Tips
If you are running your business from home, you could consider renting office space for a day to conduct your interviews, as this will help instil a more professional environment, as well as ensuring you will be free from distractions.

Remember, the interview stage is just as much about selling yourself and your business to them as the other way around. The best candidates are always going to be in high demand so you'll need to impress them too if you want to attract them to work for you.

Conducting the interview

Prepare your questions in advance by returning to your initial job specification. Include general questions regarding their personality, as well as questions that probe more deeply into how well suited they are to the job, but, again, make sure you ask all candidates the same questions that are likely to be decisive in your decision. Ask open questions that encourage fuller responses.

Include any written or practical test you think might be relevant but it's usually fair to tell candidates about this beforehand. Give interviewees the opportunity to ask you questions, but don't feel you need to answer anything you aren't comfortable answering and never immediately reveal how an interviewee has got on.

If you think it's appropriate get the serious candidates in for a second interview and if you have someone else in the business at this stage, consider involving them for a second opinion.

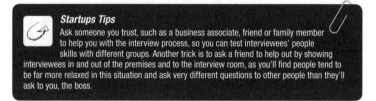

Startups Tips

Ask someone you trust, such as a business associate, friend or family member to help you with the interview process, so you can test interviewees' people skills with different groups. Another trick is to ask a friend to help out by showing interviewees in and out of the premises and to the interview room, as you'll find people tend to be far more relaxed in this situation and ask very different questions to other people than they'll ask to you, the boss.

Throughout the process keep clear notes that relate directly back to the primary and secondary requirements you first set out.

The selection process

Once you've completed the interview process, if you've done as outlined, you should have one clear candidate and it's likely because you've been so clear in your thinking throughout that your gut feeling will be closely aligned to what's on paper. If there's not one clear choice then it's time to study your feedback and make a decision. Once you've done that and you're happy you've got the right person then contact them by phone, set a start date and confirm this in writing.

The paperwork

Becoming an employer for the first time can seem a little daunting. There's a whole raft of administrative duties you'll now be responsible for, and neglecting them is not an option.

Your first port of call should be to contact HMRC's New Employer Helpline on 0845 60 70 143 and request a starter pack. It contains everything you need to set yourself up to recruit staff.

Nearly everyone that will work for your online business will count as an employee, which means you need to be aware of your obligations for tax and National Insurance contributions. You must keep detailed records of every single member of staff right from the very beginning. All of the following types of staff count as employees in the eyes of the taxman:

-> Directors

-> Full- and part-time workers

-> Temporary or casual workers.

Even if a worker claims to be self-employed and will pay their own tax and National Insurance, as an employer it is your responsibility to confirm that. HMRC will offer you guidance on how to do this in the starter pack.

Make sure you also know your legal responsibilities regarding:

-> Statutory sick and maternity pay

-> Working time and pay regulations

-> National Minimum Wage

-> Redundancy pay

-> Employing foreign nationals

-> Part-time workers' regulations.

Startups Tips
You can find out more about legal responsibilities on Startups.co.uk and the following websites:
■ www.direct.gov.uk
■ www.bis.gov.uk
■ www.businesslink.gov.uk

Induction and training

Think ahead to your new recruit's first day. There's nothing worse than starting a new job and it being clear nobody's really ready for you. You're a start-up so it won't do your new person any harm to learn quickly that they'll have to take situations as they come, but it's important to set out clear expectations from day one.

On their first day, sit them down, detail what you expect from them, how you'll assess their performance, how they will be rewarded, who they will report to and all the other information you'll need to cover such as holidays and pay.

Ensure that you train people for any jobs they need to do or tasks that are likely to invoke health and safety legislation and make frequent and regular assessments to identify training needs.

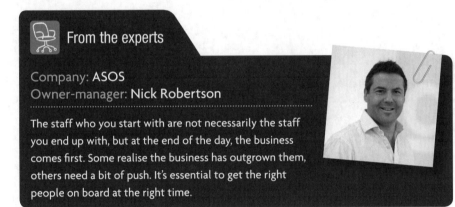

From the experts

Company: **ASOS**
Owner-manager: **Nick Robertson**

The staff who you start with are not necessarily the staff you end up with, but at the end of the day, the business comes first. Some realise the business has outgrown them, others need a bit of push. It's essential to get the right people on board at the right time.

Startups checklist

- Try to keep a flexible approach to staffing numbers when you first start: You may need to keep some staff on stand-by while you get a feel for the average number of customers to expect.
- Work out exactly what you require in each role before you start recruiting for the job and come up with a clear job description.
- As well as agencies and job adverts, use online networks such as Gumtree to recruit staff.
- Be careful not to fall into any interview traps regarding questions about personal or family life: It could land you in hot water and contravene employment law.
- Make sure you fulfil all the legal responsibilities required of you as a new employer.

ESTABLISHING YOUR PRESENCE

↪ CHAPTER 5.1

The launch and early marketing

Making your site live is the day you've waited for and worked so hard to get to. From raw idea to writing a business plan, designing a site, testing it, sourcing suppliers and buying in stock, you're finally ready to start trading and, hopefully, make some money. Before you can do that, however, you need to establish your presence and get customers to your site.

In this chapter, we'll look at:

→ Preparing the site for launch
→ PR, such as writing press releases
→ Advertising, both online and offline
→ Organising the launch
→ Attracting customers
→ Marketing techniques
→ Measuring success
→ Post-launch publicity
→ Forming relationships with the media.

Preparing the site for launch

While you've been designing your site, sorting out the copy and images, choosing payment systems and sourcing stock, you've no doubt been testing it at each of these various stages. Before your site officially goes live, however, you'll need to carry out a final risk assessment and test your website once more to ensure it is ready for launch. Once it's live, it will be visible to both your customers and your competitors, so it's important you get as much right as possible at the very beginning. It's true that in the online environment, mistakes can be rectified fairly quickly, but glitches can also occur fairly rapidly and escalate if unnoticed, which could damage your reputation as a business and result in fewer customers and sales.

Ensure that all the right content is in the right place and that the links work when you click through on them. Test and test again to catch and iron out any technical glitches, such as images not loading properly. It's also important to ensure that your website works across different browsers, as it's impossible to predict which ones your customers are using. If your site doesn't load properly in a browser, the customer is likely to see a page that loads slowly, with images missing – something that is likely to be unattractive and uninviting, so you risk alienating that customer if you don't test the site across different browsers.

Final checks aren't just about the site. Depending on the type of online business you've established, you'll need to safeguard some other areas pre-launch. Ask yourself the following questions: do you have the right amount of stock in place, and can you get hold of more goods easily if necessary? Are your delivery systems in place and reliable? Are your contact details correct and do you have processes in place so that you or someone is available at the times stated, in the event of any customer queries? Does your email address work and are you able to send and receive communications? You'll also need to ensure that you have web traffic monitoring systems in place so you can assess how many customers are visiting your site and where they are coming from (see p.215 for more information on this).

In my experience

We're always looking at ways to make the site more interactive – if you are looking to add new functionality to a site, it's vital to test, test and test again.

Company: Glasses Direct

Owner–manager: Jamie Murray Wells

PR and advertising

If you're reading this heading thinking, 'but I haven't got much (if any) money left for advertising', you're actually very sensible. Throwing money at advertising a new online venture isn't always the most sensible approach, especially until you've ironed out the creases that'll inevitably crop up in the first few months of trading.

When you're first starting out there's a lot of PR and self-promotion you can do for relatively little budget. If you're adamant you need to start paying for ads from day one, you'll need a clear strategy to ensure you're getting maximum return on your investment and are able to measure the effect your spend has had.

PR

PR is coverage of your business in magazines, newspapers, websites or TV, radio and in blogs, tweets, podcasts and webinars. For publications with any credibility, it is promotion you can't buy and so is hugely influential. Compared to advertising where you're simply paying to appear on a page billboard or web banner for example, it's assumed your business is being written about because someone thinks it's worthy of coverage. Providing the reason for that is positive and that the reader respects the publication, that's a very powerful endorsement.

Press releases

Journalists receive thousands of press releases from new companies looking for PR coverage. Many of them result in profile pieces, news stories and features offering months of free publicity to businesses that have literally just opened their doors. Admittedly, though, many press releases go straight in the bin.

The difference between those covered and binned rarely has much to do with the actual business. Sure, if you're opening the world's first money tree shop you'd probably make a front page splash no matter how screwed up the press release, but most of the time, for ordinary businesses, it's about pointing out the one thing which makes you not so ordinary – and if you've followed the planning section you'll have plenty of USPs to plug and promote.

Pitching to journalists shouldn't be too different to pitching to the bank. You're looking to inspire them and tell them what they need to know to do business with you. They need to hear what's so great about your story and there's a story in every business somewhere, it's just a case of digging it out.

179

The key is finding the angle. It's not news that you're simply launching an online business selling designer clothes as that idea has been done many times over. It is news if you have secured some exclusive deals with well-known designers and the designs are available only in your online store. It is news if you have designed the clothes yourself and fashionistas such as Victoria Beckham and Paris Hilton say they like the site and your designs.

If you're blankly thinking, 'but I don't have anything interesting like that', then the answer is to engineer an angle. It is news if you're going to preview a new designer's collection or if some designs have become coveted by the stars and are selling out online. Think niches as well; if you're using eco packaging, this might be interesting to an eco title; if you're offering ethically sourced clothing target the appropriate magazines; if your online business has a celebrity following, point that out to the local papers. Every business has a PR story, it's just a case of sculpting it and pointing it out to the right people.

You should always start by doing this yourself. Try and get as many of these little unique stories saved in your head as possible because you'll find them invaluable when talking to a whole range of people, not just journalists, about why your business is so great. For actually getting coverage, you've two choices: go direct yourself or use a PR company.

Using a PR company

If you've got the budget, PR companies can be massively useful. The two key elements you'll be paying for are their wealth of contacts and their management of the whole process. Any PR company worth its salt will keep up to date on who occupies all the key editorial positions in all media organisations, will have strong working relationships with them and can get a story to the right person. They should also look to apply

Startups Tips

Consider writing some press releases yourself and ask your friends and family to critique them and offer you feedback. This will give you some idea of whether your content is newsworthy.

In my experience

We have had a PR agency from nearly the start but it was a rocky beginning and we wasted a lot of money finding a partner who understood us and what we wanted to do. Ultimately we did find the right partner for us and I would say it has been one of the better investments we have made.

Company: Wahanda.com
Owner-manager: Lopo Champalimaud

Tips for writing a press release

- Make sure the wording is correct, the message is clear and direct and the correct information is provided so that a journalist will be able to use it even if they do not contact a member of your company or PR team.
- Your release should convey a sense of importance but not seem over-hyped. You want to provide information about your firm in a newsy format, not a marketing letter. Besides, if your announcement is worth sending a release out, it can probably stand on its own without marketing hype.
- All press releases should answer the journalist's five basic questions of: Who, What, Where, Why and How. This will require you to put yourself in the shoes of a journalist and chances are, answering those questions will give you a clearer idea of what you want to write.
- A punchy headline should be included that matches the release's first sentence, or lead, as those in the trade call them. The headline should be factual. It shouldn't try to make a joke or be smart.
- The first sentence should be direct, relate what is going on, convey a level of importance of the news and start off with the name of your shop.
- Include a quote from you about why you've decided to launch your online business. Quotes personalise stories and give journalists an idea of who to speak to. Most journalists will seek their own quotes by following up releases with interviews, but including a quote gives journalists the option to use it.
- Contact details for journalists who want to find out more can either go at the top of the release or the bottom and you can also include any additional, relevant information in 'Notes to Editors'!

their expertise to manage a full publicity campaign, staggering stories in different publications to achieve maximum exposure over a period of time. With all the other elements of running an online business to take care of, it's highly unlikely you'll have time to do this yourself and will end up snatching at publicity from any title that bites. PR companies should also be able to write a good press release – but for sanity's sake, you should ask to check everything before it goes out.

If you can't afford a PR company from day one, which is the case for many a start-up, have a go at doing it yourself. Target the titles you think should be most interested in your story, call them up to ask who the best person to send press releases to is, then put one together and send it off. Jamie Murray Wells of Glasses Direct wrote to lots of journalists he thought might be interested in the business, asking them to write about him. The media started to pick up his story and an article in *The Daily Telegraph* gave the company a much-needed boost.

From the experts

Company: moneysupermarket.com
Owner-manager: Simon Nixon

PR can drive traffic to your site cost-effectively and help you with your brand. Find a good PR agency in your particular sector. We now have around 20 people in-house who manage our PR and liaise with our agency.

One thing to remember is journalists get inundated with hundreds of releases and sometimes even the best ones get overlooked, so don't get upset if you don't get a response. If you haven't heard anything within a couple of days, call the person you sent it to and ask them if they thought it was relevant. If it wasn't, ask them why so you can tailor it closer to their needs next time.

In my experience

The article in *The Daily Telegraph* gave the business a massive boost. If you have a genuine hook or interesting story, persevere with getting some strong media coverage. It's one of the best ways to get a business going.

Company: Glasses Direct
Owner-manager: Jamie Murray Wells

Advertising

Online advertising

It goes without saying that you'll be using online advertising to promote your website and in terms of measuring return on investment you won't get a more accurate medium for advertising, as digital marketing is one of the most accountable forms of marketing. There are a range of techniques you can use, from banner advertising (a box containing graphics which a consumer can click on to link to a site), to search engine marketing, to pay-per-click advertising such as Google AdWords (the small advertisements you see down the right side of Google). More than 90% of web traffic comes from search, and for search Google is the main provider. While you

In my experience

It has taken us a few years of work to get our heads around online marketing, site optimisation and building above-the-line awareness of the business. In the days when money was limited, we made the most of free online advertising tools.

Company: Glasses Direct
Owner–manager: Jamie Murray Wells

should look to optimise your website to appear in the central, natural Google search, one of the easiest ways to advertise your website online is using Google AdWords.

If you choose to invest in banner advertising, there are a number of different styles and sizes to choose from – expect to pay more for more prominent positions and length of time the advert is running. The most common size is 468x60 pixels and you can vary the content too, from using one static image to using several animated images to rich media banner ads, which use audio and video tools.

Offline advertising

Many web businesses concentrate their marketing efforts solely online, which can be a missed opportunity – your customers could be just as likely to find you flicking through a local newspaper or directory as they would by performing a Google search. Sage Pay's *E-Business Benchmark Report*, for example, showed that using a variety of promotional tactics definitely has an influence in getting customers to your site. While 80% of these are online, many of the top performers surveyed use viral campaigns and a combination of on and offline advertising to drive sales. There are a host of opportunities for offline advertising and some will be more cost-effective than you might at first think.

Offline advertising such as print ads can give your customers something tangible to hold on to and to pick up, prompting brand recall. Print has been around for a lot longer than the web, and therefore customers are more likely to trust that medium. Many online businesses find that using some form of offline advertising helps to make their business less anonymous. The other advantage of using press ads to drive traffic to your site is if you are looking to tap into a local customer base rather than a global one.

Startups Tips

If a publication calls you and say they'll feature you for a cost, don't do it. Paid for articles have zero credibility and regardless of what the person on the end of the phone tells you, aren't read. Politely refuse.

From the experts

Company: ASOS
Owner-manager: Nick Robertson

Press advertising has worked well for us as it reaches our core target market. We started off advertising in celebrity magazines such as *Heat* and then moved on to more fashion-based titles such as *Grazia*.

Print ads

The most common forms of print advertising that small businesses use are:

- Local/regional/national newspapers or magazines
- Trade journals
- Trade directories
- Telephone directories eg *Yellow Pages*
- Miscellaneous items such as calendars, local tourist information.

Newspapers and magazines should provide an audited readership profile, which can be matched to your customer profile to identify if they'll attract the right kind of customers to your site. They should be able to provide you with information on their circulation, which is the number of copies that go out. Avoid advertising in publications without this kind of audited data.

> **Startups Tips**
> While it's important to do your research on the circulation of the publications you advertise with, bear in mind that free newspapers and magazines may have a readership lower than the official circulation. In contrast, those with a cover price usually have a readership larger than circulation.

In terms of size, generally, the bigger the better if budget permits, although putting editorial onto the page either at the bottom or the left-hand side can actually help. You should also bear in mind that as print ads are repeated the impact lessens. It can, therefore, be better to spend the budget on a few high impact ads than a lot of small ones. But test the waters slowly. Don't blow your whole marketing budget on a massive ad campaign in the local newspaper only to find print ads aren't the right medium for you.

Publishers will quote you different rates for different positions and sizes. Prime spots such as near the front or in the news sections, right hand pages, or tops of pages cost about 20% more but, as a rule, are worth the extra investment because they're viewed by the most readers. If you're going to splash out on an advert to let people know you're open for business you could use the opportunity to run a special offer.

Sample prices

- A quarter page advertisement in a local paper can cost upwards of £250 depending on its circulation.
- A full page advertisement in a national paper such as the *Daily Mail* can cost in the region of £30,000.

Always negotiate. The first price is never the best price. Find out when the last possible deadline is before the publication goes to press then phone back. While you might not get your preferred slot, most sales people will give you heavy discounts on unsold slots just to get them filled.

Radio/TV advertising

As the web has ploughed ahead, the development of digital radio and TV has meant prices to advertise have tumbled, while the choice of audiences has widened. TV will possibly be outside your price range as a start-up, but if you'd like to explore this option then contact a small local production company experienced at producing broadcast advertisements on limited budgets.

You'll need to take a similar approach for radio, which can be effective at a local level. For radio particularly, it's worth speaking to the sales teams of stations to ask the optimum length and style of ads and any recommendations for production firms to work with.

Yellow Pages/directories

The days where if you were running a business then you simply had to be in the *Yellow Pages* are long gone. That said it can still be very effective if your firm provides a relatively unusual service people naturally need to search for. Directories work best for companies where people aren't automatically aware of their existence or don't use them frequently, so it may work well if you are planning to launch a niche online business, or one that is focusing on providing services to a particular area or location.

If you think you'd pick up business from the *Yellow Pages*, negotiate a trial period to see what success you have. If they don't agree to this, negotiate until they do as they'll almost always prefer to give you this than put the phone down without 'a sale'.

Listings and guides

Getting yourself listed in a local directory doesn't have to cost anything. Most directories such as *Thomson* or the *Yellow Pages* will allow you to have a basic entry with the name of the business, the web address and phone number for free. If you want a bigger advert with more prominence you will have to pay; however, you can expect to get a free trial for the paid-for premium services even if it means you pay for one month and get another free.

There are other smaller and more regularly updated local guides and directories which are often put through letterboxes or left in public buildings such as doctors' surgeries, information centres or local authority properties. These printed guides or directories will have details on how to get your business listed within them. There are also online versions which have details of how to list for free or how to pay for greater prominence. Examples include, thebestof.co.uk, Welovelocal.com and Toplocallistings. co.uk.

Organising the launch

Many online businesses can get it spectacularly wrong during their first few weeks so be wary about shouting your arrival from the rooftops too fervently. While you certainly want people to know your site is up and running, trading and more than happy to take customers' money, it might make sense to leave it a couple of weeks before you 'officially launch'.

Launch doesn't have to equal 'day one'. Far better to do a soft launch as they're called, to spot all the little problems and have time to put them right than risk problems you could have sorted out with a little more time.

Get your site up and running and start trading, get feedback from your friends and family and customers about how they find the site and what they'd like to see. If you have employed staff, use the first few weeks to make sure they are trained properly and are providing the right level of customer service.

Try to offer a few incentives during these first few weeks to get customers in and garner their feedback. Offer introductory discounts (be careful not to make this look too much like a desperate sale), free gifts if they spend a certain amount or even run a competition where you can collect customers' contact details in return for some gift vouchers.

Startups Tips

Keep the first few weeks nice and relaxed (even if you're feeling the opposite inside) and keep your eyes and ears open for any way you can improve the service you're offering.

The launch party

Just because you've 'soft launched' it doesn't mean you shouldn't later have an official launch party. It's your first chance to let as many people as possible know about your new venture. See if you can negotiate hiring a venue for free in return for an advert on your website.

If you've hired a PR company, they should ensure local journalists are present, lured by the prospect of a great story and a glass of bubbly (wine if budgets are really tight) and hopefully a local celebrity or council member. If you're doing it yourself, make a list of targets, send out some invitations (email is sufficient and appropriate for a web venture) and follow up with confirmation calls and a reminder email on the day.

If it's not feasible to hold a launch party, consider whether there are any local business events taking place near your planned launch – you could use the event as an opportunity to publicise your site and for networking purposes.

 In my experience

I am still waiting for our launch party! When we launched, Salim and I focused less on flashy launches and more on just getting the word out to the industry and the press. We spent a lot of time at industry conferences, and with bloggers and journalists and listened to what they had to say.

Company: Wahanda.com
Owner-manager: Lopo Champalimaud

Just as importantly, work hard to get your target customers to your site. Look at complementary associations or clubs where you can advertise

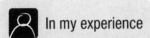
your launch, while even a poster in the windows of local shops that complement your offering or where your target customer is likely to pass by can work well, as can giving out leaflets on the street.

In my experience

We decided to print some leaflets promoting the businesses and I roped in some friends to help me hand them out to potential customers. We gave them out on a train so people would have our fliers to read for the whole journey.

Company: Glasses Direct
Owner-manager: Jamie Murray Wells

You'll need an incentive for shoppers so advertise a discount for a specified period of time for those who log onto your site within the first week of launch, for example. Print up some leaflets with a voucher code that people have to enter online, so you can track how effective these have been for future marketing purposes.

If you do have a launch party, on the night, make the evening as entertaining as possible. This is your one chance to make a first impression, so go all out. You should be on a complete charm offensive whether it comes to you naturally or not, and try to speak to every person, even if it's to simply introduce yourself and to thank them for coming.

Attracting customers

In order to attract customers, you need to look at several elements, such as any promotions you want to run, who your target audience is and how your creativity can help to convert sales. Hopefully, you will already have pinpointed your target audience through earlier research and created your website with them in mind – your task will now be to ensure they find your website and capture their interest.

To do this effectively, you'll need to define your target customer in more detail. Consider demographic characteristics such as age, income and location. You could carry out a survey of customers to find out more about their interests and what they might be prepared to pay for your product. You can then tailor your marketing accordingly.

After the launch

Identify sources of traffic

It's important to have your marketing and promotion plans ready straight after the launch of the site – unlike a bricks and mortar environment, you can't physically drag your customers in off the street or account for how many pass through your door, so you'll need to have a strategy to both market to them and keep them coming back for more. Creating a professional looking website is only half the story when launching an online business – how good it looks or what functionality you have built in won't really count for very much at the end of the day unless you can attract customers to your website and build some solid sales. To do this effectively, you'll need to learn how to promote your site in order to build up traffic, increase your customer base and ultimately, your sales.

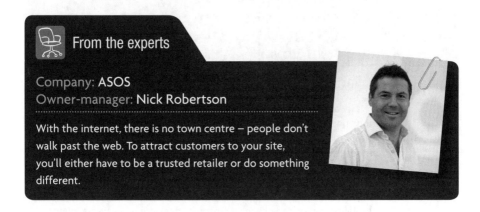

From the experts

Company: **ASOS**
Owner-manager: **Nick Robertson**

With the internet, there is no town centre – people don't walk past the web. To attract customers to your site, you'll either have to be a trusted retailer or do something different.

There are various ways for your customers to find you. This could be from simply typing in your domain name and arriving straight at your site, often prompted by advertising and marketing materials or by recommendations from friends and family. Or customers could use search engines, typing in words that are related to your company name or product. This is likely to be the most popular way for people to find your site and you will be reaching out to a broader audience base (see Chapter 5.2, p.201, for more on search engines).

It's all about you

Showcase what you sell, but make the website about you and your business as well. Have a page that talks about why you started up, what you hope to achieve and how passionate and determined you are to provide a great service. Try to keep the site updated daily, perhaps carry relevant news and definitely write a blog where you talk about running a business in your sector and activity in your specialist area. It'll bring visitors to the site and place you as an expert in your field.

From the experts

Company: moneysupermarket.com
Owner-manager: Simon Nixon

Lead with insight – you can get a lot of this from your customers and you can prioritise changes to your site accordingly. We carry out an ongoing review of our site with many people in our IT department responsible for making changes.

This means investing time and money into marketing activities – if you don't undertake any form of marketing, it's unlikely that you will build substantial amounts of traffic. Marketing isn't just advertising. It's the means by which your online business identifies, attracts, and keeps its customers; and that's such a powerful proposition it touches on almost every other element of your business. If carried out effectively it will not only ensure that your online business is seen and heard but will give it the flexibility to adapt to changing customer demands in an ever-evolving business environment.

Link building

There are some ways of attracting customers to your site which shouldn't cost a penny, one of which is exchanging links with a website whose business is complementary to yours. Link building refers to the process of getting as many relevant websites linking into your site as possible. The world wide web was designed to make it easy to flit from site to site and more than 90% of website traffic comes from other websites.

The more relevant links you manage to build up, the higher your chances are of getting your site ranked amongst search engines. Many of the main search engines now decide how far up the visibility scale your site should be, by the number of other sites linking into your site. This isn't the only distinguishing feature; metatag data (a tag that is used to store information about a web page, but is not displayed in a browser) and good content are still just as important. But quite naturally, some search engines feel that if loads of sites are linking into yours, then yours must be a good site, and therefore worthy of being high up in the listings.

Do some research into sites that you can exchange links with and ensure that you check your links on a regular basis – broken links are guaranteed to turn customers away.

The link building process

Begin with your local links. Local businesses are often happy to reciprocate links if they are not in direct competition with you. Email them requesting reciprocal links and try to build up a local network.

Think about your suppliers and customers. Which ones would be happy to put a link in to your site? If you've done a good job for a customer, try to get a mention somewhere on their site. The same goes for your suppliers. Do they have a list of clients on their site? If so, get on it. If not, suggest they set one up.

Now look at industry links. Are there any professional bodies that you are a member of? If so, they should hold a member directory online. Make sure you're on it. Look at all the unofficial resources for your business sector and try to get links on those. Typing some relevant keywords into the main search engines will help you find suitable linking partners.

Whilst some websites make their money from advertising and only exist to be a bigger and better directory, most sites that you contact will not be prepared to add a link to your site for nothing. At the very least, it takes up their time to add you, so why should they? You have to be prepared to give something back. This doesn't mean paying for links, but you should be ready to offer a link in return in an appropriate place on your site.

A successful link building campaign will make a real difference to your website traffic, which in turn should make a real difference to your level of enquiries through the website, which ultimately should lead to more revenue.

Creating a buzz

Despite your best efforts, your site might not be getting anywhere near the customer numbers you want, so it could be worth creating a buzz around your product or business to get people talking. You'll need to emphasise the benefits of your product, service and website and really push any areas you think make you stand out from the competition. Revisit your USPs and consider if there are some areas you are not pushing as much as you could.

In my experience

You need to create some kind of buzz with your website, there's only so much you can do with paid search and affiliate marketing. We've given out gobstoppers shaped like eyeballs with our glasses.

Company: Glasses Direct
Owner-manager: Jamie Murray Wells

Customer endorsements can help to get people talking about your site. Consider gathering testimonials from satisfied customers and creating space or a page on your website to showcase these.

Marketing plans

Marketing will help you understand who your customers are, what they aspire to and how you can position your business as the destination they're looking for. It will influence your buying decisions, how you price items, what packaging you use, the level of customer service you provide and the area you look to next if you choose to expand, perhaps by diversifying your product range or going global. Successful marketing is about accumulating knowledge and is an art as well as a science. You should be collecting knowledge from every day's trade and every transaction and purchase made should influence the next one, as well as govern how you try to promote yourself.

Whichever marketing techniques you use, it's important that you keep what your customers need uppermost in your mind and direct your efforts towards this. While your online business started off as your baby, for it to grow and achieve its full potential you'll have to allow your customers to dictate which direction it takes. You won't be able to do that, or bring in more like them, if you're not fully knowledgeable about who they are and what they want.

In my experience

Try to set yourself apart from high street expectations, select a customer wish list to try at home. You need to come up with customers' problems and try to solve them.

Company: Glasses Direct

Owner–manager: Jamie Murray Wells

But you shouldn't find the process daunting; keeping up with the changing demands of customers and finding new ways to get them to your site is to be embraced. If you've a great online shop offering what they want and know how to flaunt it, then marketing can be one of the most enjoyable elements of running an online business.

There are no hard and fast rules for creating a marketing strategy. It's up to you to set your own goals. However, as a general rule, you need to ask what you want your online business to achieve in a year, two years or even five years' time compared to where it would be without a marketing strategy.

Here are some tips to remember when devising your marketing plan:

- Start by setting clear objectives: Where do you want your online business to go?
- Set clear financial targets for these objectives
- Define your target market and identify your potential customers
- Decide on the brand and the values you want to communicate
- Plan your promotion strategy
- Set a budget
- Devise a schedule
- Decide how the strategy will be measured, for example, increased sales, direct responses, coverage in local press etc
- Implement the programme according to the schedule
- Monitor and evaluate results as an aid for future marketing decisions

In my experience

We care what customers say, what they
experience and how they think about us and I
think that translates into everything we do.

Company: Wahanda.com
Owner—manager: Lopo Champalimaud

Promotional ideas

One way of attracting new customers is to run special offers or promotions.
Online businesses, much like traditional shops, have end of season sales, but
there are other ways to incentivise people to log onto your site.

Loss leaders

These are items you sell at cost price to tempt customers onto your site so
they'll buy other items that are priced to give you the same overall profit.

Buy one get one free (BOGOF)

BOGOFs are now staple retail fodder. However, beware that you could
cheapen a product by offering it on such a deal or even set the wrong
tone for your brand – and make sure you can afford to give away a whole
unit for free. Chances are you won't find it as easy as the supermarkets do.

Limited special offers or introductory offers

Daily or weekly offers keep the homepage of your website looking fresh
and feel like you're offering an incentive or weekly special more than
trying to sell off stock that's out of season or end of line.

 In my experience

We didn't do any limited or special
introductory offers in particular to generate
traffic in the early days – we just focused on
getting the best range of offer we could find.

Company: Wahanda.com
Owner—manager: Lopo Champalimaud

Loyalty cards

While the Boots and Nectar cards are more about collecting customers buying habits, simple loyalty points can work as a way of attracting return customers. If your pricing allows you to, offer discounts or freebies after certain thresholds of expenditure or for a certain number of visits. You can then inform your customers about how many points they may have accrued through monthly email newsletters. Use this marketing tool sparingly though. Customers don't want to be inundated with junk mail (see below for more information on this). Collect visitor information wherever possible.

Competitions

A great way to collect customer data is through online competitions. Run competitions, ask people to sign up to receive special offers and use that data to provide a weekly or monthly newsletter telling them what's new on your site and prompting them to visit.

Or you could offer an attractive prize and get customers to enter by filling in their details online. You can then send an email thanking them all for entering and offering a call to action incentive – £5 off or 10% discount for example, to get them back.

More launches

Don't miss the chance to get your top customers and the press back for a drink (and shop, of course). If you start stocking a new range or brand of goods, contact your existing customer base to make them aware of the products and consider offering them an incentive to trial your new stock.

Partnerships

Seek out mutually beneficial partnerships with complementary online businesses or organisations. For instance, if you run a business selling pet accessories online, consider contacting kennels and dog-walking providers to promote each other's services. Look to local clubs, groups and companies used by your target customer and ask if you can put a poster up or distribute promotional material in exchange for providing them with a small discount. You'll find most will welcome this as a way of attracting members or employees.

Keep an eye on your diary and what's going on around you. If there's a bandwagon you can jump on, leap on it. If your town or local community is campaigning for an issue dear to your customers' hearts, you could flag this up on your website. If you can help local schools, help them. React to festivities and celebrations.

Post-launch publicity

We've covered the basics of advertising (see p.183), but it's important to consider the value of continuing to advertise. While initial advertising campaigns are good for attracting customers in the early days whilst you optimise your website for search engines, ongoing advertising can be great for flagging up promotions or new lines. However, this early on in an online business' life, you may not yet be breaking even, let alone have enough profits set aside to spend on advertising. That's where PR can prove the most effective route for promotion.

You may have had coverage in local papers or magazines when you launched but how do you keep the PR momentum going once you've been up and running a few months? Hopefully you've got more than one story to tell, so you can keep churning out the press releases. Remember, for everything that happens to your business and every new line your online business stocks, try to think of a newsworthy angle for it.

Another interesting way of getting your online business some free coverage in a local paper is to offer up your services to them. If you have a retail model, offer them a competition to win a £100 voucher to spend with you; even if you did it once a week chances are it'd still work out cheaper than buying an ad and £100 at sale value shouldn't be £100 at cost value.

Startups Tips
See if you can help out a paper or magazine by writing a column or advisory piece as a local business owner or as an expert in your specialist area. Mock up an example and send it in. Don't make it too hard sell and, as many welcome free contributions, they might run it as a regular feature giving your business a nice plug in exchange. Remember to include your website address on any piece you write.

Forming media relationships

There are plenty of ways to get free coverage but you have to make sure you're not a nuisance to the journalists who will potentially be writing about you. Here are some tips for getting the media on your side:

-> Buy them lunch to find out how you can provide content they want. If you've met and spoken to them face-to-face they're far more likely to give you the time of day later on.

-> Don't contact them too often. If you become a nuisance they may just start avoiding you.

-> Don't contact them with irrelevant stories. It's important you tailor any press releases, stories or promotions to fit in with their publications and what their readers want to see.

-> Find out when their deadline day is. If you contact a journalist when they're about to go to press they're unlikely to have time for you. Find out when their publication goes out and contact them straight afterwards as this will be the time they're most likely to listen to you.

-> Write a good press release. Journalists receive endless quantities of them so you'll need to make yours stand out if you are to get any chance of it being read, let alone covered. Have a look at the Marketing and PR channel of Startups. co.uk for more details on how to write a winning press release.

-> Ask magazines and newspaper supplements for forward features lists so you can see if the journalists will be writing about an area that's particularly relevant to your business.

 From the experts

Company: **moneysupermarket.com**
Owner-manager: **Simon Nixon**

It's critical to have media coverage – you want to be seen as an authority in your area and you want the business to be talked about.

There are plenty of other online review and listings sites dedicated to the retail and services industry. It's a good idea to check out the ones specific to your area and make sure you're listed on all of those too.

Measuring success

You'll need to have effective monitoring processes in place, to measure how effective your marketing is and which areas to address. Check what the competition is doing and review this on a regular basis. This might mean you will need to tweak your prices or offers and although this can prove time-consuming, as a new venture, it's important for you to remain competitive and to be able to offer something over and above the competition.

Keeping track of trends is equally important, particularly if you are running a retail site. And don't make the assumption that just because you are operating an online business, you don't need to consider an offline marketing campaign. A multi-channel marketing campaign, one that is run across different media such as print, radio, and online can ensure maximum exposure and response, although it does require a substantial outlay. Test different mediums to see which ones return the best response (see p.183 for more information on this).

If you've got several marketing or PR strategies happening at once it can be difficult to measure which ones are actually bringing in the customers. You're not going to advertise in a newspaper and then ask each customer that purchases online if they've done so because they saw an advert in the local rag. If you're not sure which marketing technique is giving you the best return on investment then why not try them one by one, then calculate any increase in customers or turnover for that period.

Of course the success of certain promotions, such as vouchers or discounts using codes are easy enough to measure because you can count up how many customers make use of the offers. However, it's important to remember that you need to bring in more custom as a result of the promotion than you spend on your marketing. It's no good offering discounts and doubling the number of visitors to the site if you end up making a loss on your products.

For each piece of marketing you do, set clear key performance indicators (KPIs) that will help you assess if it's proved worthwhile.

Startups Tips

Online marketing is very accountable and there are plenty of tools available to measure your online marketing activity, so it can be all too easy to get lost in a wave of figures and numbers. Decide from the outset what you are measuring and why.

Startups checklist

- Make sure you continually test your website to iron out any potential glitches before you officially launch.
- Have a clear and defined marketing strategy before you start spending your budget.
- Try sending out press releases or even having a launch party to promote the launch of your business.
- Also think about other forms of advertising such as print ads.
- Think carefully about what kind of promotions you offer and apply them to your slower days or times.
- Use PR sparingly but effectively: Don't become a nuisance to journalists.
- Look for strategic partnerships with local or complementary businesses.
- Monitor your sales regularly to keep track of how successful your marketing is proving to be.

↪ **CHAPTER 5.2**
Working with search engines

You've done all the hard work in terms of getting your site live. However, if your site cannot be easily found by search engines, you could be alienating many of your customers and missing out on potential traffic.

This is where working with search engines comes into play. If you're looking for something on the internet, it's likely that the first place you'll visit is a search engine such as Google. Search engines are one of the main ways people access content on the web and search marketing – a range of techniques used to increase the visibility of a website and brand on search engine results pages – is big business in the UK. An estimated £,1180.1m was spent on search optimisation in the first half of 2010, according to research from the Interactive Advertising Bureau. Search traffic can make or break your business, particularly as the online world becomes more and more competitive.

In this chapter we'll look at the following:

→ How search engines work
→ Submitting your site to search engines
→ Paid versus natural search
→ Search engine optimisation
→ Monitoring traffic/web analytics
→ Affiliate marketing.

How search engines work

Your online presence can prosper from the strategic use of search engines. But to take advantage of this you will have to understand how they work. As a search engine is automatic, it uses unique software to read and index websites and links on web pages, placing them in order of relevancy and frequency. The tool they use is called a spider. This enables search engines to crawl through the world wide web (www) looking at metatags and information and eventually storing them in a vast database.

Within the metatags the spider looks at words that appear frequently throughout the page called keywords (see below for more information on this), the page title, a brief description of the page, and the author as well as emphasised text and other aspects. Metatags can be viewed on any website by clicking onto the 'view' icon on the menu bar in Windows and then scrolling down the list to 'View Source' or via the 'page' icon on Internet Explorer 7.

Each search engine's relevancy methods are different to the next. For example, while some look at the title of your document, some are case sensitive and will give varying results, and others score words higher in their relevancy rating if unique spellings or characteristics are included. So make sure you pay attention to what tags you eventually use.

But beware, it is ill advised to try and repeat a particular word as often as possible in the opening paragraph to obtain a high ranking as it is something most established search engines frown upon.

Submitting your site

There's a vast array of search tools available today and your site needs to be found by most of them if you are to establish your presence online. Once your website has launched and is live (which means it can be viewed on the internet) there's a good chance it will be picked up by search engines within the first few months. However, it is always worth submitting your website directly to the search engines so that they are aware of your website. The most important element to bear in mind is that site submission is something you need to be committed to for the long term – it can take several weeks or even months to get your site ranked by search engines and securing a top ranking can take longer still. It's not something that can be done overnight but building your content and improving your links will help to boost your page rankings.

There are literally hundreds of search engines out there and submitting your website to every one of them is a time-consuming process. There are

In my experience

Search marketing is such a complex and opaque area that virtually every aspect is a challenge; however, creating a profitable search strategy is well worth the time and effort to get right.

Company: Wahanda.com
Owner-manager: Lopo Champalimaud

really only a handful of search engines that are worth investing time in, as many others have a low usage rate and therefore are not likely to drive much traffic to your website. On the plus side, you won't have to pay a penny to get into the major search engines.

The biggest challenge you face when using search engines is the breadth of competition. Most people will only look at the very first few pages of search engine results and if they can't find the answers they want, they are likely to use different keywords (the words that people type when performing a search, see p.209 for more on this area) and perform an alternative search. This means that if your business does not rank in the first few pages, potential customers will not be able to find you.

Startups Tips
The major search engines are the following: Google, Yahoo!, and Bing.

Google: How to submit your website

To submit your site, visit the homepage of a search engine and look for the 'submit link' or 'add URL' link where you can simply enter or submit your domain name for free. Google, for example, has a very comprehensive guide detailing how to submit your website, which can be accessed at www.google.co.uk/intl/en/submit_content.html

Getting your site noticed

Be professional: Your website reflects your company, so keep the content clear, concise and accurate, and enforce your branding and messaging. A high-quality website implies a high-quality company.

Content is king: Visitors want information and something worthwhile to read. Give them a reason to come back to the website again; constantly updated content and independent industry information gives users a reason to bookmark your website.

Be consistent: Keep the layout, design, and navigation the same across the website. Different fonts and styles should be kept to a minimum, but remain consistent throughout.

Be readable: Yellow text on a black background is not easy to read, and neither are long pages of centred, capitalised text.

Don't re-invent the wheel: Visitors don't want to learn a new navigation style, or have to understand a complicated interface. Imagine you are a first-time visitor; usability is more important than showing off the latest flashy effects.

Speedy access: Not everybody will wait for large image files or animations to load; most visitors will leave a site within a minute if the page hasn't loaded properly.

Email your visitors: Have an opt-in mailing list and contact the people on it regularly. This gives you permission to email them with special offers, which builds your potential customer database, reinforces your brand, and updates them with the latest news.

Be visible: A website is useless unless people can find it! Get your site listed in directories and on search engines, either through search engine optimisation techniques or consider using a search engine marketing company.

Compatibility: Check how the website looks on different computers, screen resolutions, and browsers. Is your website accessible by everyone?

Track your visitors: Use your server logs or tracking software to identify your visitors' habits, how they find your website and what browser and screen resolutions they use. Then fine-tune your website to match your visitor profile.

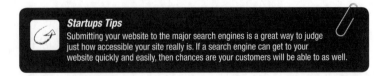

Startups Tips
Submitting your website to the major search engines is a great way to judge just how accessible your site really is. If a search engine can get to your website quickly and easily, then chances are your customers will be able to as well.

Some search engines such as Yahoo! offer paid directory submissions which can boost your visibility in its index. On the plus side, this means you can get your site submitted and registered quickly, but on the downside, your reputation could suffer among your customer base, as they may choose to trust the natural rankings rather than those that are paid for.

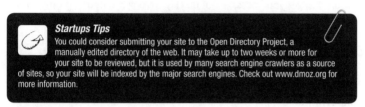

Startups Tips

You could consider submitting your site to the Open Directory Project, a manually edited directory of the web. It may take up to two weeks or more for your site to be reviewed, but it is used by many search engine crawlers as a source of sites, so your site will be indexed by the major search engines. Check out www.dmoz.org for more information.

Paid versus natural search

There are two ways for a website to become listed within search engines – paid (also known as pay-per-click) or natural (also known as organic) search. Most businesses use a combination of the two and there are several pros and cons for each, which are outlined below.

Natural (organic) search

Natural search is free and works by algorithms determining the pages that are most relevant to queries entered on search engines. The biggest risk with natural search is that over the long term, your brand or business is at the mercy of search engine index changes, which can simply alter ranking systems. Natural search offers little in the way of guaranteed results compared to paid search, although developments in analytics software are striving to meet this challenge. The other downside is the time it takes – it can be up to six months before you notice if any benefits have been reaped and whether your site has achieved a high enough ranking.

Paid or pay-per-click (PPC) search

Pay-per-click advertising focuses on specific keywords and enables you to list your site at the top of search engine results by advertising on keywords that best describe your product or service. These results appear above the natural listings or to the right of the page. The higher you bid, the higher your ad will be placed in the listings and you only pay if someone clicks on your ad and links to your site. This means you can control costs better and determine exactly how much of your budget you are prepared to spend in this area. Tools for tracking PPC campaigns are very effective so you can easily measure response rates.

As a rule of thumb paid search should be used as a tactical tool offering a responsive pricing or product-led call to action, with natural search listings more suited for a long-term strategy. Consider what your objectives are: are you using search marketing for a quick win to hit the market in a short space of time or is it more of a long-term branding exercise? PPC can ensure you get your message out quickly, making it suited to promotions and price-led creative, whereas natural search requires a longer time for changes to appear on the search results.

 In my experience

Wahanda has done virtually no paid search. Our focus was on building rich and relevant content that our consumers would find useful and the search elements would take care of themselves. I sometimes think that we worry

Company: Wahanda.com
Owner-manager: Lopo Champalimaud

too much about the search engine and not enough about the customer. That being said you can't totally avoid it so make sure that your site is well structured for natural search from day one.

Search experts also say that natural search offers access to a wider pool, citing figures such as 80% of search queries result in a click on a natural listing, as opposed to 20% on a paid one. Furthermore, with PPC, bidding on keywords can be an expensive business so if your company is in a competitive area such as travel and finance, you might struggle to see a return.

How PPC works

- Choose a PPC provider according to your business model, such as a search engine or price comparison website
- Do some research into keywords that best suit your product or service
- Bid an amount per click on each keyword that you believe will put you ahead of the competition (this is the cost-per-click – CPC)
- You pay your PPC provider the bid price for keywords you have specified when someone who has searched for a keyword clicks through the ad and is directed to your website. This is known as the click-through rate (CTR).

Search engine optimisation

These days, most people access the web via search engines rather than typing in a specific website address and there are certain processes you can undertake to ensure your website appears in as high a position as possible in the natural search results. Increasing and improving the volume of traffic to your site via natural or organic search is known as search engine optimisation, or SEO. This basically involves building and maintaining your website through the use of design and keywords. Keywords are the terms that people type into a search engine when they are starting a search (see p.209 for more on keywords). The aim for any SEO campaign is to enhance your search engine listing and placement without having to spend any money towards it. Sites that are well optimised can expect to gain a higher page ranking, which means you can expect to gain more traffic to your website, build interest and, ultimately, sales.

SEO is more of an art than a science as different search engines have their own rules when it comes to indexing sites; however, there are some general points you can take on board. In order to get the most from SEO, you'll need to bear in mind that you are not only designing and refining your site for the benefit of your customers, you are doing this for search engine spiders too. There are a few things you can do to optimise your site for search engines, such as submitting your site to the relevant directories, but bear in mind that it takes time to get results and you'll need to continually invest time and effort in SEO as your website develops, in order to maintain your ranking among the search engines.

Regularly updated content will improve your SEO ranking and give other websites a good reason to want to link to yours, not to mention ensuring that your website is maintained on a regular basis.

From the experts

Company: **moneysupermarket.com**
Owner-manager: **Simon Nixon**

We've perfected our search engine marketing over the last seven years – it doesn't come overnight. With search engine marketing, every penny of profit you get is critical, we have a team that is dedicated to getting us as high up as possible in the natural search rankings. In terms of our traffic on Google, around 60% is paid and 40% natural.

How to make your site design search-engine friendly

- Ensure your site navigation is as clear as possible, so consider adding tools such as a site map, particularly if your website has a number of pages
- Is your text easy to read? It might seem obvious to say that black is the most readable font colour, but you'll also need to ensure that the font is easy to read and that the font size is clear (most websites use a 12-point size)
- Images are great ways of attracting users, particularly if you are operating a retail site, but ensure that every image you use is relevant. If you have too many on the site, you risk users experiencing slower download times, which might encourage them to visit other sites instead
- Consider the kind of technologies you are using (such as Flash) and whether or not they add anything to the site.

Using an agency

If you have the right skills, you can probably manage your search engine marketing needs in-house, but if not you might have to pay for someone to write the content or use the services of a search engine optimisation agency.

There are a lot of providers available but any agency you choose will need to work with you very closely to understand your needs and help you to manage your site in the best way possible. Effective SEO requires a good understanding of your site, your sector and what you are trying to achieve, as well as your target audience.

As with choosing any supplier, when it comes to selecting a SEO agency, shop around, get recommendations from friends and peers and draw up an agency shortlist, as SEO can be an expensive undertaking. Ask for references or testimonials from previous customers. Remember that SEO agencies should want to know as much as possible about your site in order to create an effective working relationship. You'll need to be comfortable with any provider you choose as working with an SEO agency is a long-term commitment – search engine rankings change all the time so you'll need to be in touch with your agency on a regular basis and discuss ways of improving or changing tactics if necessary.

From the experts

Company: moneysupermarket.com
Owner-manager: **Simon Nixon**

We've always done our search engine marketing in-house, and have hired consultants to help us from time to time. If you outsource to an agency, you end up being just another client, so it can be difficult to keep intelligence in-house.

Keywords and what they do

If you've looked for something on the web, you've no doubt typed in a few words on Google describing what it is – these are known as keywords or search terms. If you've typed in one word, you've probably found that you get a whole host of answers, many of which are probably not relevant to your search. The more keywords you initially type into the search engine, the more refined your search is likely to be.

Keywords are crucial to the success of your website, as it's a free way of generating traffic to your website and is one of the main ways potential customers can find you. Imagine this scenario: you have built a site that is rich in content, with plenty of information and submitted it to a number of search engines. Week on week, though, you wonder where all your customers are, as traffic figures are disappointing. The answer is most likely that these customers cannot find your website as the keywords they are typing in are not on your website.

You'll need to aim for keywords that are often searched for and which therefore attract traffic to your site, but that are not so competitive that a top ranking becomes next to impossible. Research your competitors thoroughly and avoid choosing keywords that might end up directing traffic to their site, rather than yours. Ensure you use real sentences rather than just keywords in your content and don't use too many keywords in an attempt to improve your search rankings – search engines are likely to penalise you for doing this.

In my experience

Choosing the right keywords really depends on your business but there are two key areas. First, spend time looking at the search traffic for your business and focus on the most popular terms. If you are a business like ours

Company: Wahanda.com

Owner-manager: Lopo Champalimaud

long-tail terms (keywords that focus on less competitive niche markets) are also pretty important so think about the types of long-tail words that you think are important and make sure you are covering them.

To determine which keywords will work best for your site, put yourself in your customers' shoes and ask yourself the following: if they were looking for the products or services that your business provides, what words are they likely to type in? Review your website pages and note down all the words and phrases that might fit the bill. There's likely to be much more competition for the top ranking search engine results for single keywords, so think about phrases that appear on your website and which people are likely to type in. Consider words that are similar to each other too. For example, design and designer are similar terms but one or the other may rank higher when it comes to search and you may want to use both keywords if appropriate.

Startups Tips
Don't be put off if traffic to your site appears to be slow once you've identified your keywords and optimised them – it can take weeks and even months to process keywords. But ensure you keep a detailed record of traffic information so you can assess how effective your keywords are.

Opt for concise keywords, rather than those that are long and which may be difficult to spell. Keywords can appear in a number of ways, in your domain name and the content on your website for example. You could focus on optimising words on your homepage and in the headings or images – the more places your keywords appear in, the more exposed your site will be. There are tools available to alert you to the most frequently searched keywords and many of them are free to use. Check out Google's Keyword Tool, which can be accessed at https://adwords. google.com/select/KeywordToolExternal. This service enables you to type in keywords to see how popular (or not) they are.

How many keywords should you include on your web pages? If you are using natural search, the ideal number of keywords really depends on what sector you are operating in – the more competitive the industry, the more selective you should be with the number of keywords used, although use too few and you risk search engines not picking up on these keywords. Above all, keep monitoring your keywords and how they perform so you can determine if your web content needs changing.

Universal search

Search isn't just about web pages anymore. Over the last two years, the likes of Google, Ask, Microsoft and Yahoo! have all developed their services to offer listings based not only on web pages with text, but also on different types of media such as blogs, videos, images and maps.

For example, if you're looking for a pair of Nike running shoes and you type in 'Nike', rather than just getting a link to a list of websites, a search engine results page is now more likely to provide images of the shoes, blogs, reviews and videos on YouTube. This technique is known as universal or blended search and can offer your business improved levels of indexing. If you were launching a new product or service, one of the first things you'd want an online searcher to see would be a link to some positive reviews of the product, for example.

Depending on the nature of your products or the content of your site you could make use of universal search to improve your place in the rankings. For example, if your site is based around music or entertainment, you may have several videos that you could look to optimise too.

Monitoring traffic

Monitoring traffic to your website is much more than looking at the number of hits you get. You can track all the following elements:

- Information on the total number of visitors
- The different ways they navigate around your site
- What pages they view and for how long
- How any particular marketing initiatives have performed.

There are various terms used to describe the science of recording and interpreting website statistics: web metrics, web analytics, web stats and site stats, to name a few. 'E-metrics' refers to analysis of electronic businesses. The 'metrics' of web metrics refers to measurement – the science of measuring websites, specifically, measuring website 'events', and extracting trends. In this case, those 'events' are human clicks. By measuring these events you can answer questions such as:

⇥ Are there more or fewer people coming to your site this week than there were last week?

⇥ Is your site doing better or worse this week?

What should your stats tell you?

Your stats will inform you about numerous aspects of your traffic, such as the number of (returning) visitors to your site, and how visitors surf through your pages. This information tells you about the content of your site and how visitors use it.

Your traffic statistics are an indicator of website performance. When applied in this sense, site stats can be used very effectively to make updates. They can tell you what aspects of your site are popular, and what aspects visitors don't like.

If your website generates its revenue from advertising, effective measurement of visitors to your site is crucial. The price you can realistically charge people to advertise on your site will be determined by how many visitors you get.

Web analytics

Web analytics, also known as page tagging or tracking, involves adding a tracking code to each page of your website, which collects user data. This can then be analysed to produce reports about how users are interacting with your site. There are basically two types of analytics tools you can use: free ones and more advanced web analytics.

Free ones such as Google Analytics (www.google.com/analytics) and Yahoo!'s Index Tools (http://web.analytics.yahoo.com/) offer analytics around statistics such as number of visits and sales your website has achieved over a set period of time. More advanced web analytics providers will tailor analytics to your site and can identify and analyse a greater number of metrics, such as the user journey (how a customer arrives at your site, what they do when they are there and where they go next) and how long it takes from the time they arrived to when they made a purchase. Companies such as Omniture (www.omniture.com) and WebTrends (www.webtrends.com) provide these services.

In my experience

In the early days when money was limited, we managed a Google account for a year, and used free tools from Google. Make the most of free tools.

Company: Glasses Direct
Owner-manager: Jamie Murray Wells

The more bespoke and tailored your web analytics, the more you can understand about your site users. Using web analytics involves collecting and analysing data from a range of sources and the more sophisticated tools on the market offer increased insight into who is using a website and why. If you make use of free tools such as Google Analytics, it's likely you'll be doing web analytics in-house. If you outsource web analytics to an agency, ensure you get regular reports with updates on traffic.

Affiliate marketing

There's only so much you can do to promote your website and attract new customers, so you could consider affiliate marketing to boost your sales. Affiliate marketing involves you paying other sites (known as publishers) based on results for displaying your ads. You'll pay nothing to display an ad on another site but as soon as someone clicks through or it results in a sale, you'll pay. It can be a cost-effective way of attracting new customers and generating sales. The amount varies depending on how it is calculated. You can agree to pay a fixed amount per sale (known as cost per sale), a fixed amount per lead or enquiry, or a percentage of sale (this is common for those sites that sell a variety of products).

The amount of commission you choose for each type of payment will depend on how much you expect to make from a sale and how many leads you can expect to convert into sales – having a certain number of leads is all well and good but they will count for nothing unless you can get sales from them.

There are different ways to run an affiliate marketing campaign. You could choose to work directly with other sites or publishers, which means you'll be responsible for making payments and tracking the number of clicks and sales generated, or you could opt to join an affiliate network. These are companies that will manage your affiliate marketing campaign on your behalf. There are a number of affiliate marketing providers available.

Startups Tips

Regardless of the network you choose, ensure that you communicate with them on a regular basis.

213

From the experts

Company: **moneysupermarket.com**
Owner-manager: **Simon Nixon**

Affiliate marketing can be a cost-effective way of sharing risk, and we used it effectively when we launched moneysupermarket.com. We worked with all the big portals – we had the content, they had the traffic. We still work with many different affiliates today.

How affiliate marketing works in practice

- A consumer visits an affiliate's website, which can be a shopping portal or other retail website, where an ad or link to your website, service or product is displayed.
- The customer clicks on this ad and is taken to your site to complete the purchase.
- The sale is completed online. Software records data such as what was purchased, when and for how much. You then pay a commission to the affiliate for the sale that has been generated.

Startups checklist

- Always submit your website to the major search engines so they are aware of your site.
- Natural search is a long-term strategy so you will need to invest time and effort in this.
- The majority of businesses use a combination of natural and paid search.
- Use search engine optimisation to improve the volume of traffic to your site.
- Aim for keywords that are often searched for but which are not too competitive.
- If you can afford it try using an agency to manage your search engine marketing needs.
- Monitor the traffic to your website to allow you to make effective updates.
- Make the most of free tools such as Google Analytics or Yahoo!'s Index Tools.
- Affiliate marketing can be a cost-effective way of generating sales.

 CHAPTER 5.3

Social media: Blogging, online communities and apps

Think social media and the sites Facebook, Twitter and Flickr would most likely spring to most people's minds. Social media is the term used when online technology is used to help people share content, swap views and give their opinions. It can come in many shapes and forms, including text, images (including photos and links to videos) and audio content such as podcasts. In the last two years, social media has become one of the fastest growing mediums of internet marketing and the influence it has on how people think about and react to brands cannot be ignored by anyone who is serious about starting an online business.

The boom in online video and social marketing has contributed a 10% increase in online advertising spend during the first half of 2010, according to figures from the Internet Advertising Bureau, while Sage Pay's *E-Business Benchmark Report*, shows that when social media is being used well, it can heavily influence purchasing behaviour, by building trusted relationships and subsequently loyal customers.

In this chapter we'll look at the following:

→ How to make the most of blogging

→ The rise of online communities

→ Adding applications and what they can do for your business

→ Mobile apps.

How to make the most of blogging

Blogging has been around for some time now and initially used to refer to people's online journals or their personal experiences published on the web ('web logs' hence the term 'blog'), which were updated on a regular basis. More recently, however, blogs have proven to be incredibly powerful marketing tools, becoming another way to reach your customers and to find out what your customers think about you.

Blogs can therefore be a great way to develop your site, by promoting it in the eyes of your customers, your industry and the press. They are also useful for getting your content onto other people's sites and it's a great way to stay in touch with your customers. More importantly, though, blogs can help to attract more visitors to your website and help to get your site noticed by the search engines and attempt to achieve higher rankings.

 In my experience

A presence on social networking sites is critical for helping to market and grow your business.

Company: Wahanda.com
Owner-manager: Lopo Champalimaud

So how do you get started? To familiarise yourself with blogs and how they work, start by searching for, reading and commenting on blogs that relate to your chosen online business industry. A good place to start is Technorati (http://technorati.com), a blog search engine and directory, which offers real-time information on blogs across a whole variety of sectors. You can get a good feel for style and topic and the type of comments that generate interest. Once you are familiar with blogs, you can think about starting your own. It's important to remember, however, that anything related to social media has to add value to your community or target audience, otherwise it will be more than likely ignored or talked about in a negative way. So don't rush into creating a blog just because there seem to be so many of them out there as there could be other applications that are better suited to promoting your business.

If on the other hand you enjoy writing and have some sort of message to communicate to your target audience, then there's no reason why you can't start blogging. There are millions of blogs in existence and they work because they have a following among a niche audience so it's essential to identify a target audience, decide what you want to say and write it in an engaging and concise way. Blogs, if done successfully, can engender trust as well as adding a personal touch to your business. You'll need to be confident expressing your opinion – while blogs are good at building communities of like-minded people, they generally feature 'one voice' or a small group of people, with the aim of getting a reaction from like-minded people. If you want to start a conversation with a group of people consider starting a forum (see below for more on this).

It also helps if you aren't shy of a bit of publicity. By blogging, you put yourself in the public spotlight, as effectively you are asking people to analyse your business and to comment on it. And once your blog is online, it can be incredibly hard to remove. You might be able to delete the posting from your website, but by this time, it might have been picked up and published on numerous places online.

As with anything published online, keep your blog to a manageable length. The point of blogs is to start an online conversation or to offer your target audience snippets of information that are interesting and which add value. You'll also need to invest time and effort in writing and updating them, however, so consider if you can do this on a regular basis – blogging once a month is not likely to get customers coming back for more but a few each month will keep the content fresh and relevant. On the plus side, blog software (available from the likes of www.blogger.com, www.typepad.com and www.wordpress.com) is easy to use.

 In my experience

When it comes to blogging, you have to be absolutely honest. With social media, people can pick up on absolutely everything. If there is something negative about your business, it's important to get it out there quickly before anyone else. Don't think you can manage the monster – the monster will manage you.

Company: Naked Wines

Owner-manager: Rowan Gormley

Online communities

It's not enough to get customers to visit your site once. You've got to get them to keep coming back and build a loyal community of users. But how do you remind them that you're there?

The rapid rise of social networking sites such as Facebook, MySpace and Twitter has made it easier for online businesses to gain publicity, which adds up to increased traffic and potentially bigger sales. Glasses Direct, for example, actively drives word of mouth referrals using a variety of marketing mechanisms from social web features to member-get-member incentives.

> **Startups Tips**
> Online communities will expose your site to customers time and time again, as well as increasing levels of interactivity and time spent on the site. All of this will boost your traffic figures. For example, moneysupermarket.com offers a variety of online forums.

You could choose to create a branded page on sites such as Facebook, MySpace or Twitter, create videos on YouTube (see below for further details) or you could opt to build an online community on your site, which will give you more control overall, using formats such as chat rooms, forums and blogs. Customers can use Twitter to tell a company (or anyone else) that they've had a great – or disappointing – experience with your business, offer product ideas, and learn about great offers. For example, when electronics buyers look for good deals, the Dell Outlet Twitter account helps them save money with exclusive coupons.

According to Twitter, one of its key benefits is that it gives you the chance to communicate casually with customers on their terms, creating friendly relationships along the way – tough for corporations to do in most other media. With Twitter, you 'follow' people and people 'follow' you. Choose a user name and password, fill out your profile and then you are ready to write postings, known as tweets, which are limited to 140 characters or less. This limit will help to ensure you get your point across succinctly but it can be incredibly frustrating to get your point across in such a short space so spend plenty of time practising first. Above all, remember the point of social media is to add value. Some people tweet all day about nothing but their business – take a step back and put yourself into your readers' shoes. Is this something you would want to read about? By all means post a few tweets about your business but consider what value added content you could provide. This could vary from a series of tips related to your industry, to a book you've read, for example.

By using tools such as bulletin boards, newsgroups, social networking sites and scheduled online chats, you can develop a community of users who return to your site even when they aren't ready to buy something. Each time they return, they are exposed to your new products or special offers and in turn give you increased traffic numbers to boast to your advertisers about.

In my experience

The critical thing is not to think of Facebook and Twitter like direct mail – they are not about building sales. They are about people following you and your business and therefore you have to provide content that is engaging

Company: Naked Wines.
Owner–manager: Rowan Gormley

and that people will want to come back to time and time again. If you want to build a community and get something out of it, you have to put something in.

How social media can help your business

Getting to grips with Facebook

Facebook has taken steps to actively encourage businesses to use their service, by offering initiatives such as Facebook adverts and fan and community pages. Businesses can set up a company profile or groups and message boards where customers can converge to discuss with one another the service they have received.

Keeping content interesting and relevant is crucial to any social media page, and Facebook is no exception. To attract and retain followers or fans, you need to offer exciting content that stands out from the crowd. Consider different forms of content, such as video, audio, pictures or blogs that would most appeal to your target audience. Facebook can also be used as a market research tool, through which companies can poll their fans and measure their reaction to new ideas before applying them to the business.

Once your page or group is set up, think about who you want to attract. Start off small by inviting friends and current customers, who will then invite their friends and so on. Social media is an extremely viral form of communication, so don't expect to have thousands of fans overnight. Discounts and other offers exclusive to Facebook fans or group members can be a great way to generate more followers.

Making the most of YouTube

YouTube is the world's most popular video hosting website. This free-to-use site has approximately 24 hours of video content uploaded every minute, and its mass market audience means it's an ideal marketing channel for small businesses.

In order to maximise YouTube's marketing potential businesses must think creatively. With millions of videos to choose from, it's easy to get lost in the crowd. Therefore, think about what exactly you want your content to portray and the message you are sending out to viewers, because this will reflect on how your brand is perceived.

There are a number of features on YouTube that can help build brand awareness. Businesses can share and embed videos on websites or blogs, or even their pages on other social media sites. Videos can be rated by viewers, and can also be commented upon, all of which may have a positive effect on the brand – so long as the feedback is positive.

Twitter tips

Twitter can be used by companies in a variety of ways. Recruitment and customer services are two examples of how small firms are using Twitter, as well as the obvious tweeting of company news or industry insights. What many businesses fail to do is to retweet and reply to other peoples' tweets, and consequently they are missing an opportunity to build community and influence around their brand. Businesses must be there to engage with their audience when they discuss their products or services and give them the chance to converge with the people behind the brand. This also provides a channel by which businesses can educate customers about their products, and promote themselves further.

With Twitter, it is even more important that businesses are available to engage with their customers because it is an immediate channel. It is quick and easy for businesses to set up alerts to inform them when people have mentioned their brand, thus allowing them to connect with that person on a more intimate level. Whether they are complimented or complained about, businesses ought to be on top of any discussion about their brand.

In my experience

Online forums have been crucial to our business as a way of reaching out to suppliers and to get recommendations from customers.

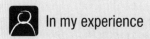

Company: Naked Wines
Owner–manager: Rowan Gormley

Adding applications

Running an online business involves carrying out periodic reviews of your website, checking that links are working and that the copy you have is still current. While carrying out a review, you might also decide that certain applications are worth adding, either to enhance your offering, to increase levels of interaction on your site or because you think it would benefit your customers. And with the high level of broadband penetration available today, the majority of people will be able to download and view multimedia content.

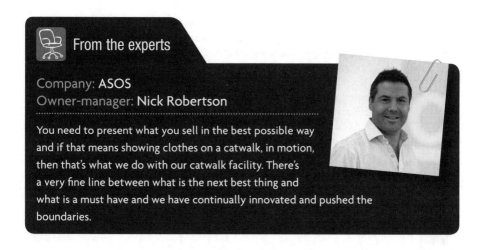

From the experts

Company: **ASOS**
Owner-manager: **Nick Robertson**

You need to present what you sell in the best possible way and if that means showing clothes on a catwalk, in motion, then that's what we do with our catwalk facility. There's a very fine line between what is the next best thing and what is a must have and we have continually innovated and pushed the boundaries.

It might be tempting to use the latest graphics and animations if this is what your competitors are doing, but ensure you put your customers' needs first. Technology changes fast – what is possible now wasn't just a few years ago and it can be tempting to invest in the latest web applications without much thought as to why you are doing this. Jamie Murray Wells of Glasses Direct, for example, says that many of his site's current applications would not have been possible just a few years ago, but they have all been developed with a benefit to the end customer in mind. One of these is a virtual mirror with advanced facial technology to enable customers to upload photos of themselves or use examples of faces to try glasses on.

The key is to choose technology that answers a customer's needs, rather than technology for technology's sake. Technology changes at a fast pace and people are certainly getting used to richer browsing experiences, but their needs won't be adapting at the same pace as technology is changing. Applications you can use include online videos, podcasts, RSS feeds and widgets.

Online video

You don't need to be a genius with a camera to use online videos, nor do you need to have first-class editing skills. What is important is to produce videos that are both engaging and entertaining for your target audience and which say something meaningful about your business. You could choose to host the videos on your site, or follow the lead of many other online businesses and post your videos on YouTube and direct people to the site. Chocolate retailer Hotel Chocolat, which has a presence on the web, high street and through mail order, posted videos on YouTube showing the company's co-founder, Angus Thirlwell, explaining why the business bought a cocoa plantation and showing the process of making chocolate from bean to bar.

Posting a video on YouTube is free, but you will need to sign up to a YouTube membership to do this. Any videos you post will remain live until you choose to remove them, or they may be taken down by YouTube if you violate any of their terms of use (go to www.youtube.com/t/community_guidelines for more information).

 In my experience

Video is an area we are only starting to explore at Wahanda but I think it will become increasingly important as consumers become used to a richer online experience.

Company: Wahanda.com
Owner–manager: Lopo Champalimaud

Using videos will help to make your site more interactive and will put a 'face' to it. Depending on the type of online business you are running, you can use videos to showcase your products, for interviews or to explain the background to your business in more detail. Using online video normally involves using Flash technology which the majority of browsers now support, so video files on your website should be visible to your customers. Video files, however, can take up a lot of bandwidth – every time a customer clicks on the video, they'll use up some of this bandwidth, so check with your web host to see how much bandwidth is allocated in your contract, or you may need to pay extra if you exceed your limits. You'll also need to ensure that any videos you use are of high quality otherwise it is likely to put people off as well as looking unprofessional.

Podcasts

An increasing number of people are downloading podcasts – digital media files (audio or video) which are stored and played on a computer – and you can use these to both market your website and increase levels of interactivity with your customer base. You can create podcasts to promote new products or new content on your site and depending on the type of business you launch, you could demo a product or deliver a tutorial via podcast. Decide on a format and length – many podcasts range from 60 seconds to 30 minutes so work out exactly how much time you can devote to them and how many you are thinking of doing in, say, a six-month period. You may decide on a five minute podcast once a month, but to film, record and edit this could take you several hours and doing this once a month will soon add up.

Equipment-wise, you will need a computer, microphone and recording software. Don't skimp on the quality of the microphone as your podcast needs to come across clearly to your listeners and sound quality is key. One of the most popular voice recording software programs available is Audacity, and it's also free to use (http://audacity.sourceforge.net/). It enables you to record and edit sounds and can be used across most operating systems, including Mac OS X and Microsoft Windows. Once you've recorded your podcast, you'll need to convert it to an MP3 file and upload it to your website.

RSS feeds

RSS (really simple syndication or rich site summary, depending on who you talk to) feeds enable you to deliver newsletters and messages direct to your subscribers' desktops, instead of doing this by email, for example. It's a method of distributing links to content in your website that you would like others to use, as if you were syndicating content. You can alert customers who have opted in to receive messages from you about new content added to your site so it can be a powerful way to stay in touch with your customer base. It's basically a text-based headline with a link and a short summary attached; this is what a subscriber sees. If your customers/subscribers want to read more, they can click on the link and be taken to your site. If your content is interesting enough, other people may add it to their website, increasing your exposure.

Widgets

These are embeddable chunks of code that can be implemented into any HTML coded site, basically small boxes that you can place on websites. They can hold a variety of content, from games to audio files and you click on them to activate them, interacting with a website in the process. Websites are increasing their use of widgets to simplify and enhance the internet user's experience. Buttons, drop-down menus, and basically any other element located on a web page that is able to be manipulated by the user to perform a function is considered a widget.

Startups Tips
There are a wealth of web applications available to use so think carefully about the ones that would bring the most benefit to you, your business and your customers before making your choice.

Mobile apps

A mobile app is like a software programme for smartphones (think iPhone, BlackBerry and phones that run on Google's Android system). They are feature-rich and include maps, games and guides and also enable people to access social media sites. They allow you to customise a phone to your particular needs.

You will often have come across the app in its desktop form. For example, TweetDeck is a near identical version of Twitter, so you can use this in the same way, responding to customers, promoting news and introducing offers.

There are some very good reasons you might want to use mobile apps to promote your business – they are all the rage at the moment and can help to build loyalty among your potential customer base. Businesses that use apps as a marketing strategy range from corporate giants like Nike right down to small-scale start-ups.

Developing apps can be expensive though, so before deciding whether this is the right move for you, take a long hard look at your customers and their tech habits: if there aren't enough smartphone users in your target market or customer base, you should think twice about using mobile apps. Having said that, an app can always be used to reach out to new customers and some companies have used rather quirky apps for brand extension or as part of a marketing programme. If you do it right, your brand marketing app can go viral. A prime example of this is Carling's iPint, which used the iPhone's accelerometer to allow customers to virtually 'drink' a pint.

The uptake of apps among consumers is only set to grow as more and more people upgrade their everyday feature phone to a smartphone, but bear in mind that apps only work on the phone for which they were created, such as iPhone apps or Android apps, so if you're looking to target a specific market demographic, such as iPhone users, then it makes sense to design an app with that user and phone in mind.

 In my experience

We believe that mobile apps are becoming increasingly important and will undoubtedly be an important aspect of everyone's media strategy.

Company: Wahanda.com
Owner-manager: Lopo Champalimaud

Startups checklist

- To make the most of social media: It has to add something of value to your customer base.
- You need to commit a certain amount of time to blogs in order to update them and keep them topical: Consider whether you can devote the time needed.
- With applications, it might be tempting to use the latest graphics and animations if this is what your competitors are doing, but ensure you put your customers' needs first.
- Don't get carried away by the next wave of technology: Consider whether it is something that can actively benefit your business.
- The key is to choose technology that answers a customer's needs, rather than technology for technology's sake.

 **CHAPTER 6**

eBay: What it's all about

If you've bought or sold something online before, the chances are it was through eBay. The online auction site is something of a retail phenomenon and arguably one of the most successful companies of the dot com era. Set up in 1995 in the US by Pierre Omidyar, the site is now established in 39 markets (including partnerships and investments). eBay.co.uk has over 14 million users and there are more than 10 million items for sale on the site at any one time so it's easy to see why so many people choose to set up an eBay business. According to the site, a mobile phone is sold every minute and a car every four minutes. Its three biggest markets are the US, the UK and Germany.

Reputation is the key to surviving on eBay but once you become a 'Power Seller' the opportunities are endless. Setting up an eBay store is something which many sellers use as a way to have their own store front without having to set up their own website.

In this chapter we'll cover:

‒› Quick guide to eBay
‒› How to sell
‒› Getting stock
‒› Managing your reputation
‒› Payment options
‒› Opening an eBay shop.

Quick guide to eBay

Opportunities offered by eBay are far and wide – it's not just a place where you can get rid of clutter or sell unwanted Christmas gifts and bric-a-brac items – it gives you the chance to turn an interest or hobby into a business, incurring relatively low costs and using secure transactions. It has allowed millions of people to start their own online businesses when they previously would not have considered it and tap into an international customer base. For many others, an eBay business is generating healthy second incomes and for some, sourcing and selling items on eBay for a profit is a full-time job. Another advantage of an eBay business is that you shouldn't be too tangled up in red tape – the site is user-friendly and accessible and there are tools available such as a customised website and credit card merchant that can do all the hard work for you.

eBay: Opportunities are far and wide

You can sell just about anything on eBay – if you've ever wondered whether someone would have a use for an item that you no longer need, then you've got a good chance of finding such a person on eBay. Of course, there are some items that are not allowed to be sold on the site (see below), so ensure you check out the list of restricted items before proceeding. eBay promises tough action against those breaking the rules and you could find yourself barred if you persistently flout the code of conduct. Admittedly, there are also some fairly wacky items for sale that constantly make the headlines, such as the housewife who put herself up for sale for £25,000, but there are also plenty of thriving businesses taking advantage of what eBay has to offer.

Items eBay considers unacceptable for auction

- Aeroplane tickets
- Alcohol
- Animals and wildlife products
- Catalogue and URL sales
- Counterfeit currency and stamps
- Counterfeit and trademarked items
- Credit cards
- Drugs and drug paraphernalia
- Embargoed items and prohibited countries
- Encouraging illegal activity
- Firearms and ammunition
- Fireworks
- Football tickets
- Franking machines
- Government IDs, licences and uniforms
- Human parts and remains
- Lockpicking devices
- Lottery tickets
- Mailing lists and personal information
- Multi-level marketing, pyramid, matrix and trading schemes
- Offensive material
- Prescription drugs and materials
- Recalled items
- Satellite, digital and cable TV decoders
- Shares and securities
- Stolen items
- Surveillance equipment
- Tobacco and tobacco products
- Train tickets
- Travel vouchers
- Unlocking software
- Used cosmetics

Obviously most UK small firms wouldn't consider selling human remains for example, but it's worth going through this list as selling agreements on items such as football and aeroplane tickets are strictly controlled. Other items such as food and batteries are in a grey area for eBay, which describes them as 'questionable'.

While eBay may be a ready-made business model to tap into, you stand to make real money from the site so you'll need to comply with all the legal rules that apply to any other online business. You'll need to register with HM Revenue Customs within three months of starting up and profit on your business will be subject to income tax. Those eBay sellers who are not paying their share are likely to be under increasing scrutiny from the taxman so ensure you keep records of all your transactions.

Whether you are looking to sell personal items on eBay or run a full eBay-based business, this guide provides the information you need to get started on eBay and become an eBay success story. In this chapter, we'll look at how to use eBay to your advantage, how to open an eBay shop and we offer information and advice on the most common problems encountered with eBay and how to overcome them.

How to use eBay to your advantage

Researching how and what to sell

The first rule of thumb is to understand how eBay works – an eBay business should be approached like any other e-commerce venture you are considering. Do the necessary research first, as there are many different selling formats. You can sell auction-style, where you receive bids and sell to the highest bidder in a fixed length of time, sell at a fixed price so buyers can purchase items immediately without any bids, sell through a reserve auction, where you specify the minimum bid that needs to be reached or a multiple-item auction, where you can sell more than one identical item at the same time. Selling using classified ads has recently been introduced – there is no bidding in this case, so you should put the advertised price of your item, service or property as the price that you would like to receive for it, and not the starting price as you would in an auction-style listing.

Once you've chosen a selling format, you need to decide what to sell. One of the most important things to consider is finding a niche that few other people are competing in. You might think this is easier said than done, given the number of businesses trading on eBay, so the trick is to spend some time checking out both eBay and other similar websites. eBay has a section which will tell you what are currently the most popular searches, what items are being watched the most and the largest shops. Here is an example of what to look for.

Identify items that are niche, those that sell like hotcakes and those that everyone else is selling. While you'll be primarily interested in the selling side of the site, it's a good idea to consider the experience from the customer point of view. It's not uncommon to find that some of eBay's most successful sellers started off as buyers. If you haven't already

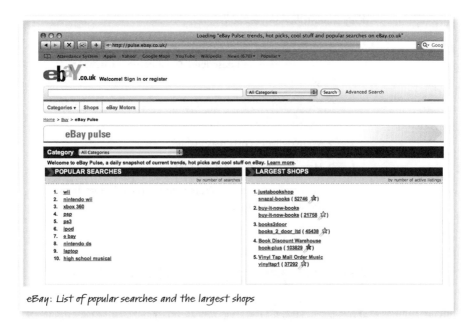

eBay: List of popular searches and the largest shops

bought from eBay then consider doing so – it will help to put you in your potential customers' shoes.

The process will give you an idea of how the system works, what buyers are looking for and any problems you may come up against. Make a note of your experience in the following areas, assessing any problems you may have encountered and what solutions you would come up with if you were the seller.

Successful eBay businesses

RochfordTyres has been selling car wheels and alloys on eBay since 2003. It initially trialled the site in a bid to shift around £60,000 worth of stock and was surprised by the amount of interest and sales generated. It says that upping the stakes is easier if you have the ability to buy cheaply and that's where the wholesale leads that the business had worked hard to build over the years became so valuable.

Parkers of Bolton has been selling bicycles on eBay and says that sites such as eBay provide a market where smaller businesses can compete with the big boys. It says that eBay's level playing field is encouraging because it means that any seller can reach millions of buyers. It says that you just need to get under the skin of eBay to make it work.

eBay research: Ask yourself

→ How was the customer service you experienced?

→ Was the item well described: Did it come across as genuine?

→ Were there any pictures of the product and what was the benefit of this?

→ Were delivery costs reasonable?

→ How easy was the final transaction?

→ Was it easy to communicate with the buyer? What areas would you improve?

→ Was the eBay shop well designed?

Advantages of using eBay

Making a profit on the items you buy and then sell is the very essence of starting an eBay business. There is no sure-fire way to make a profit, but by sourcing goods at a low price and selling them at the going rate, with prompt delivery, you should begin building up your takings. There is certainly no shortage of people out there looking to buy and while the UK has emerged from the recession, many people are still taking a cautious approach to their finances and are still likely to be more price sensitive, actively seeking out models such as eBay.

As any financial risk to your eBay enterprise is small, you can experiment with the goods you are putting online. If you have, for example, amassed a collection of vintage clothes, designer shoes and handbags, you could consider making this an eBay business. Vary the prices to see what the market rate is and then stick to it. Check out what your competition is doing whenever possible, as they may be undercutting you. With so many eBay businesses in the UK, the chances are that someone else is doing what you are doing.

By their very nature, auctions are unpredictable, but they are the only way to 'test the water' and see what kind of demand there is for your stock. When you are posting your first few products, set a low price and see how many bids you get and how much the price rises. Remember, though, there is no guaranteed way of making a profit on the site.

There are plenty of online resources too that you can refer to for more tips and hints on selling through eBay:

⇢ Discussion boards on eBay, including feedback forums and blogs: http://community.ebay.co.uk

⇢ News and blogs: www.tamebay.com

⇢ Forum for online retailers, including eBay sellers: http://thenetsellers.com.

Start selling

Simply choose a name and password and you're in. To begin selling on eBay, register and then create a seller's account (which is free), providing credit or debit card details and bank account information for verification purposes. All new sellers must offer PayPal as a payment option (see p.137 for more on this).

To start selling you follow the clear instructions giving details of the item you are selling and selecting the relevant subsection. You can also upload a picture from a digital camera, or one from the web, to illustrate your product. Buyers like to see what they may be spending their money on, so including a picture can enhance sale prospects.

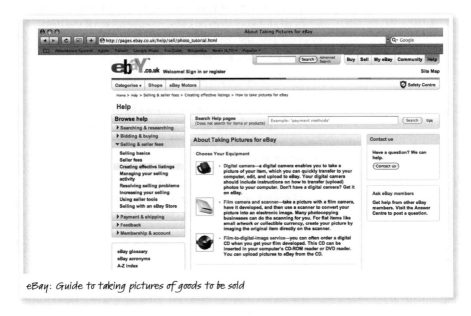

eBay: Guide to taking pictures of goods to be sold

The next steps are creating a business account, and setting up an online shop. To start trading under your business name, set up a business account when you register with eBay. All you need in order to do this is a UK address, to receive a confirmation letter through the post, and bank account details to set up a direct debit.

If you enter your VAT registration number when you create this account, then you won't pay any VAT on seller fees. (If you don't have a VAT registration number, register with HM Revenue & Customs. See p.248 on details on how to do this.)

What it costs to sell on eBay

It costs between 10p and £1.30 to list an item on eBay, depending on the opening value or reserve price of the item, although fees are different for specific products, such as mobile phones with contracts. The site takes a slice of the selling fee once an item is sold, depending on how much the item is worth.

The fees you will be charged are directly related to the listing and sale of your item and the majority of fees are paid only when you sell the item. These include:

- ⟿ Insertion Fee: A non-refundable fee charged to your account when you list your item on eBay; you pay it even if the item does not sell. The level of this fee depends on the starting price of your item and varies by category.

- ⟿ Optional Feature Fee: These features, such as Buy It Now and Featured First (appearing as one of the listings on the first page of search results in the Featured Items section), can help enhance your listing, making it more attractive to buyers and increasing bids. The fee is dependent on the type of feature you use.

- ⟿ Final Value Fee: Depending on what you successfully sell your item for, eBay will charge a small percentage of the final value in fees. This is only charged if the item sells.

Getting stock

If there's one thing that sellers will never reveal, it's where they get their stock from. One of your biggest challenges when setting up an eBay business is likely to be finding plenty of low cost products you can sell at a profit. Many older items are sourced from markets and charity shops, whereas newer items tend to originate from wholesalers, manufacturers and liquidators.

The most obvious and efficient way to accumulate products is to buy them in bulk from wholesalers. Finding a wholesaler that will supply you with cut-price stock can be a challenge, but if you shop around you will be able to find bargains. Remember that you make money on eBay when you buy your stock, rather than when you sell it, so it pays to drive a hard bargain. If you strike an agreement with a wholesaler, you should be able to get a constant supply of warehouse stock for your new business but never rely on one supplier only – it's like putting all your eggs into one basket. If they let you down, you'll have to turn elsewhere to source products.

Above all, when sourcing stock, keep in mind the margins you expect to make – any effort you put into sourcing stock, such as time and money, needs to be justified by the profit you expect to make. There's little point in selling many items if you are only able to make the smallest of profits or just about break even – it might be wiser to concentrate on selling a few items, but those which command higher prices and therefore better margins.

Reputation is key

The anonymous nature of online businesses is such that reputation and trust are key to building repeat business and encouraging customers to come back time and again. Having an eBay business is no different. As a seller, your reputation is the most valuable asset you have and it will depend on a number of factors, such as how long you have been a member of the site and more importantly, your feedback score. The system enables members to rate sellers by leaving positive, negative or neutral comments.

The more positive feedback you gain, the better the prospects will be for your business. The ratings you receive and leave for others reveals a lot about what you are like as a seller, and it's an area that any potential customers will focus on before parting with their money.

As with any business, issues likely to affect your reputation include effective customer communication, ensuring the buyer has had a positive experience, dealing with any problems swiftly, developing clear and concise terms of sale and knowing how to handle those awkward customers who never seem satisfied.

There are a number of precautions you can take to ensure your reputation is as enhanced as possible. It pays to do the research thoroughly and to be sure of your answers before you list any items for sale. There's nothing worse than withdrawing or changing your terms once a transaction has been completed as it will do little to instil confidence in your abilities to run an eBay business. The following areas are important when considering how to build and enhance your reputation.

'About me' page

This page, as eBay describes, enables you to tell the world about yourself and your interests. You can use it to display items you are selling and to describe your hobbies or profession. It's a simple enough process and it's free and easy to create so there's every reason to take advantage. To get started, enter your page content, add pictures if you want and select a page layout. You can preview before submitting the page to be published and can update information on this page as and when necessary.

Sales descriptions

Preparing items for sale on eBay is no different to any other e-commerce business – you'll need to come up with a concise description of the goods, take pictures where possible and combine these to create an online catalogue. Of course, as eBay is an auction site, you don't need to specify a fixed price, but can suggest one at which the bidding should start. For help with descriptions, have a look at how other people have described their items. Essentially, you should be looking to keep any descriptions you use concise and informative, with a heading that engages a buyer and attracts their attention.

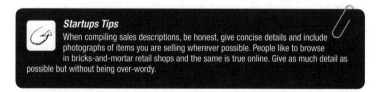

Startups Tips

When compiling sales descriptions, be honest, give concise details and include photographs of items you are selling wherever possible. People like to browse in bricks-and-mortar retail shops and the same is true online. Give as much detail as possible but without being over-wordy.

Terms of sale

There are no hard and fast rules when it comes to setting out your terms of sale, but these should be clearly and concisely communicated and be visible to the buyer. Ensure that you are comfortable with any terms of sale you have listed. Ask yourself the following: how quickly are you expecting payment, what type of payments are you willing to accept and are you prepared to send goods abroad? How quickly can you expect to get the goods to the buyer – the faster you ship, the happier the buyer will be and you are likely to generate repeat business. It's important to promise what you commit to – if you have problems with shipping, for example, inform your customer as soon as possible and offer them an alternative arrangement.

Be clear with payment options

Everyone seems to know someone who has encountered problems with receiving payments after selling an item on eBay. This could range from all contact with the buyer coming to a sudden end, cheques bouncing, or the buyer insisting on paying in ways that eBay strongly advises against, such as cash. eBay provides protection to sellers but familiarise yourself with their guidelines. If problems arise at time of payment, you are under no obligation to send the item to the winning bidder but instead can relist it. To ease problems with payment, it's to your advantage to accept different forms of payment.

Guide to payment options on eBay

- eBay requires all sellers to offer payments through PayPal, a system that allows people to pay with a debit or credit card, bank account or balance in an account, without sharing any financial details with the seller.
- Listings in some categories are exempt from PayPal, including cars, caravans, boats and property.
- You can also offer buyers the option of paying directly with a credit card online or by phone, if you have a merchant credit card processing account or use a third-party credit card processor.
- Don't be tempted to accept cash in the post, even if the buyer insists. Cash should only be used for transactions carried out face-to-face.

Pay attention to packing and shipping

Your job is not done when an auction ends – you have to get the item safely and quickly to the highest bidder or buyer. Goods that arrive damaged or badly packed are hardly a good selling point. Ensuring that items are packed in such a way as to minimise damage will reassure buyers – you might even consider adding a note to tell them of any similar items you have recently listed or are going to list in the near future. This might encourage them to actively seek you out next time they want to buy.

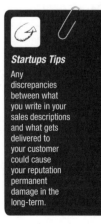

Startups Tips

Any discrepancies between what you write in your sales descriptions and what gets delivered to your customer could cause your reputation permanent damage in the long-term.

eBay language

You'll come across many different sorts of terms when researching an eBay business, everything from an affiliate to a PowerSeller. Check out our list of the key terms to be aware of and what they mean.

Affiliate: Driving traffic from your site to eBay's site that results in a sign up or purchase.

PowerSeller: Business sellers who are consistently offering excellent service and professionalism. The PowerSeller programme is designed to help sellers grow their eBay business and to reward those upholding the highest service standards.

Turbo Lister: A free software program that helps you create professional-looking item listings in bulk on your computer and upload them to sell at eBay. It's suited to medium to high volume sellers.

Verified Rights Owner (VeRO) programme: Enables rights owners to report listings that infringe on their rights (such as copyright, trademark, patent).

Opening an eBay shop

The simplicity of setting up an eBay business is a big attraction for many people. You don't really need anything other than a computer, an internet connection and storage space for your goods. You could take this one step further by opening an eBay shop, a feature from eBay offering you the opportunity to showcase your listings in a customisable eBay shop front – it's basically just like having your own website, in return for a monthly subscription that starts from £14.99.

You post items for sale at fixed prices and can keep stock listed for 30, 60, 90 or an unlimited number of days at a time. There are three different types of eBay shop: basic, featured and anchor. According to eBay, 75% of sellers say that opening an eBay shop increased their sales. Impressive as this figure is, opening an eBay shop is not for everyone as there are certain criteria you need to fulfil.

To open a shop you must be a registered eBay user with a seller's account. You'll also need to meet the following requirements, depending on the type of shop you set up.

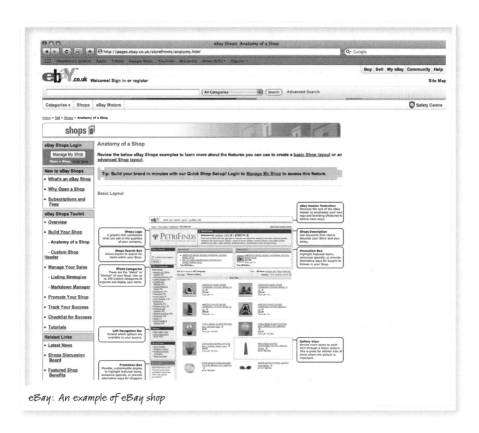

eBay: An example of eBay shop

Basic Shop:

    → Minimum feedback score of 10

    → Must be PayPal verified.

Featured Shop:

    → Must be a registered business seller on eBay

    → Must be PayPal verified

    → Must maintain a 12-month average detailed seller ratings score of 4.4 or above in each of the four areas.

Anchor Shop:

    → Must be a registered business seller on eBay

    → Must be PayPal verified

    → Must maintain a 12-month average detailed seller ratings score of 4.6 or above.

eBay shops: There are a variety of tools to increase buyer interest.

According to eBay, the shop is most suited to those people who have already acquired considerable experience with the site, in terms of listing volume and sales generated. There are a variety of ways you can increase buyer interest and sales, using tools such as promotion boxes, where you can highlight special offers and post email newsletters. The Listing Frame tool enables you to add your shop categories, search box and category navigation to all of your item pages in one click, while with the Custom Shop Header you can choose from four templates to promote and highlight featured items.

Becoming a PowerSeller

As mentioned previously, PowerSellers are business sellers consistently offering excellent service and professionalism. The PowerSeller programme is designed to help sellers grow their eBay business and to reward those upholding the highest service standards. PowerSellers are those who have achieved and maintained a 98% positive feedback rating and a solid sales performance record. To qualify, you'll need to have carried out a minimum of 100 transactions to UK and eBay.ie buyers per 12 months and achieved a minimum sales volume of £2,000 per 12 months (based on sales to UK and IE buyers).

It doesn't cost anything to become a PowerSeller, although the process is reviewed on a monthly basis to ensure that people qualify to maintain their status. There are numerous benefits to be gained. You are eligible to receive substantial discounts on final value fees in return for providing a good service to customers, measured through eBay's detailed seller ratings. You can also use the PowerSeller icon next to your user ID, so buyers are aware of your status. There are five levels to aspire to: bronze, silver, gold, platinum and titanium (the lowest being bronze, the highest titanium). All offer personal phone support, fast priority email support and a range of final value discounts. A personal account manager is assigned to gold, platinum and titanium members only.

There are certain tools you can use to help improve your sales and your chances of being rated as a PowerSeller. Software such as Turbo Lister and Selling Manager Pro can help you to create professional listings, automate your process and track sales, while eBay's Picture Services can enable you to present your items in the best possible way. Consider setting up an eBay shop as this will give your goods more exposure and will encourage repeat buyers to find your listings easily (see previous section on opening an eBay shop).

Frequent eBay problems and how to overcome them

Setting up an eBay business can be a relatively pain-free process but once you are up and running, there are a number of issues over which you need to exercise caution. Many of these can be applicable to any internet business and the more familiar you are with these problems, the better equipped you will be to deal with them.

Be aware of fraudulent emails

One of the biggest threats to the security of your eBay account and your identity is fraudulent email and websites, called 'spoof email' and 'spoof websites'. Like many other internet sites, eBay has been the subject of spoof emails so it's important to recognise any warning signs that someone is trying to access your personal and account information.

Both spoof emails and websites are used to get personal and account information. A spoof email pretending to be from eBay typically contains a link that takes you to a fake website that requests that you sign in and submit personal and account information.

Dealing with fraudulent payments

Make sure that the payment has been received and confirmed before you despatch any items. eBay recommends that if the buyer uses a credit card, contact the card issuers and verify that the name on the card matches both the postage and contact information.

When a buyer does not pay

Try to communicate directly with the buyer to resolve the situation. eBay guidelines stipulate that if seven days have passed since a buyer won your item and you have not received payment, you should contact the buyer to assess the situation. If this fails to work, you can open a case at eBay's Resolution Centre, which helps create a dialogue between you and the buyer and tracks your case for you.

Startups checklist

- To build up your experience of the site, start off by selling something you know about or are familiar with.
- Do some thorough research, both on eBay as well as on other sites to get an idea of what level to pitch your product.
- When researching the competition, try to identify any unique selling points related to your goods.
- Build up positive feedback. This is the bedrock of eBay and will set you apart as a reliable seller. Excellent customer service is key here; if you say you will do something, honour this.
- Monitor the competition. Don't just do the occasional research at the beginning – it's something you need to do on a regular basis, as your competitors will be checking you out too.
- Start small and then look to build the business depending on demand for certain products, the experience you have had or what you notice the competition is doing.
- Don't spend huge amounts of money on stock until you have gauged levels of interest and demand.
- Be as upfront and open with potential buyers as possible. Hidden costs and misleading product descriptions will alienate your customers. Trust is vital for building an eBay business.

 # CHAPTER 7

Keeping customers

The saying goes that a customer who has a bad experience is likely to tell at least 10 people about it, whereas one that has a good experience will only tell one other person. No matter what kind of business you are running, you need to keep your customers and keep them happy or they will go elsewhere. And when you consider that it costs six to 10 times more to acquire a customer than to retain one, it makes sense to invest in a retention programme.

In this chapter we'll look at:

→ Building customer confidence
→ Implementing an online database
→ Email newsletters
→ Special offers
→ Inviting feedback.

Building customer confidence

Your business won't survive if your customers don't trust you, but building customer confidence online can be a challenging proposition. The anonymity of the web means that many customers will look to purchase goods or services from the big boys – brands they can trust and which perhaps also have a high-street operation. For a start-up business this can be a hard proposition to match.

 In my experience

We had a customer-oriented approach right from the beginning, which was very important as the web can be quite anonymous. We needed to make it more transparent.

Company: *Glasses Direct*
Owner-manager: *Jamie Murray Wells*

The reality is that online businesses come and go so building a reputation is the key to gaining customer trust and encouraging people to visit the site again. Besides ensuring your contact details, privacy statement and customer helplines are clearly displayed on your website, there are a number of other steps you can take to gain your customers' trust.

Don't promise what you can't deliver. The days of 28-day delivery are long gone – when shopping on the web, people expect instant gratification. If you say you can deliver next day, in three days or in seven days, ensure

 From the experts

Company: **ASOS**
Owner-manager: **Nick Robertson**

If you know an order is not going to go through, you need to let the customer know. We've had lorries breaking down on the M1, for instance. There's no point in driving traffic to your site if you are going to disappoint your customers. You can't fail in this area on the internet.

you stick to this. There's nothing worse than letting customers down when it comes to the fulfilment side of things – they will almost certainly go elsewhere. Of course, much as you can promise, you can't foresee any problems that may occur logistically or technically, so it's equally important to communicate with your customers as soon as you suspect there may be a problem with their order and see what solution you can come up with.

Keep your website content updated and refreshed – there's nothing worse than a customer logging back on weeks after a visit and seeing the same content on the same page or seeing news stories that are months old. It will make them think twice about whether you are still trading and they'll be reluctant to buy from you again. If you are struggling to provide updated content, get your customers to do this for you. Encourage them to post recommendations or reviews to your site (depending of course on what you are selling or what services you are offering) and you can then incorporate this into the copy on your website.

Make it easy for customers to contact you. They may be experiencing technical difficulties, have a query about stock or want to know about delivery times. Whatever the issue, it's imperative your contact details are correct, that your customers can reach you and that you respond accordingly.

Startups Tips

If you want to build trust in your customers, try not to let them down and if any unforeseen circumstances threaten deliveries or stock levels, communicate this to them as soon as possible. Consider issues from their perspective and go the extra mile to exceed their expectations.

Implementing an online database

In order to keep customers coming back, you'll want to stay in regular contact with them, which means creating and using an online database of customer details. In Chapter 3, we looked at your legal obligations when it comes to maintaining and using a database of customers. In order to do this, you have to persuade customers to part with their details in the first place.

There are many ways of collecting information from visitors to your website and many of them can be used regardless of the level of your technical skills. Remember that before you collect any data, ensure your site has robust security, by investing in an SSL certificate, for example (see Chapter 4.2, p.127 for more on SSL certificates and encryption).

Email alerts and newsletters

Wahanda email newsletter

One of the easiest ways to communicate with your customers initially and then stay in touch with them and to inform them of updates to your site content, new stock and services, and seasonal offers is to use email alerts or more detailed newsletters. According to Sage's *E-Business Benchmark Report*, emails and newsletters ranked high as one of the most important ways of communicating with potential customers, with 30% of respondents choosing this. Of those surveyed, 79% with above average conversion rates used email newsletters, versus 70% of those with average or below average conversion. You could also include links to vouchers and 'recommend a friend links' to boost retention rates and gain a few new customers at the same time. Wahanda, for example, sends its subscribers an email newsletter packed with news and tips and new subscribers get a discount code as a special gift.

Moneysupermarket.com, meanwhile, sends email alerts which keep its users up to date on the latest best buys, with articles from a team of experts about the best and worst products on the market. In addition, when it identifies a money-saving deal, it notifies users by email.

In my experience

If there is one piece of advice I would give to any business in any area, it would be to make sure they are building their customer email database and have the ability to communicate with them.

Company: Wahanda.com
Owner-manager: Lopo Champalimaud

You might not have the time or the skills to devote to writing a regular newsletter, but consider sending smaller email alerts every few weeks with some information about your business that will not involve any extra work, such as drawing their attention to other parts of your site or reaffirming your product base. At the very least, it will remind customers that you are still in business and encourage them to click through the links to visit your site.

When it comes to the content of your newsletters, put yourself in your customers' shoes. Ask yourself what kind of information they would be interested in and what might encourage them to click through to your site. If you don't have the time or the ability to write newsletters, you could consider employing someone on a freelance basis to write them or depending on the type of industry you are in, you could seek permission to reproduce content from other (non-competitive) websites either by putting the content direct into the newsletter or embedding links.

What to include

In terms of the structure, you'll need to keep copy short – no one likes to read lengthy copy on the web or have to scroll down endless pages, so employ the same style for your newsletters. The subject line will have to strike a balance between being concise and enticing enough for people to click on. Avoid using words such as 'hello', and 'free' or monetary signs as these are all likely to trigger spam filters. If you need inspiration have a look at your inbox and make a list of the emails you are tempted to open and those that you would delete without a second thought. It's also a good idea to test a small segment of your customer database before you send a mass email out; that way you can test just exactly what percentage of customers were enticed enough to open the email (known as open rates).

From the experts

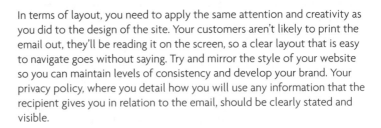

Company: **moneysupermarket.com**
Owner-manager: **Simon Nixon**

We encourage people to sign up to personalised email
alerts with news covering aspects of the industry the
business is focused on, such as finance and travel. If you
bombard people with crap, your open rates will reduce
dramatically. You should aim for an open rate of 15%–20%, anything less
than that and the quality and content of your emails are not good enough.

In terms of layout, you need to apply the same attention and creativity as
you did to the design of the site. Your customers aren't likely to print the
email out, they'll be reading it on the screen, so a clear layout that is easy
to navigate goes without saying. Try and mirror the style of your website
so you can maintain levels of consistency and develop your brand. Your
privacy policy, where you detail how you will use any information that the
recipient gives you in relation to the email, should be clearly stated and
visible.

Adding a personal touch to the email, addressing recipients by their
first names, for example, will attract more attention than a simple 'Dear
Sir' or 'Dear Madam'. Text should be clear and easy to read and you
should consider offering the newsletter in both text and HTML format
depending on customer preferences, and because some software and
web-based email accounts (such as Hotmail) block images by default.
Use images wisely but sparingly – if you use too many, the newsletter
may not display properly or may take too long to download. Include a
link at the top of your email newsletter which says something along the
lines of 'If you are having trouble viewing this newsletter, click here to
see it on the web' or 'Show content' with a link to the email newsletter
online.

Check that all the links used in the newsletter are correct and click
through to the right page. Above all, an email alert or newsletter should
not be used as a sales vehicle, but as a way of engaging with your
customers and increasing their levels of loyalty.

Email etiquette

There are certain guidelines to follow when it comes to sending email newsletters – fall foul of these and you are likely to alienate customers rather than encourage repeat purchases.

Unsolicited email (spam) clogs up people's inboxes and is against the law. Regulations require that you get individuals to opt in before sending them marketing emails, unless they have already shown interest in products or services similar to the ones in your alert or newsletter.

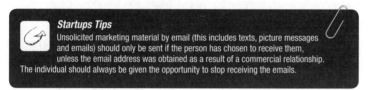

Startups Tips
Unsolicited marketing material by email (this includes texts, picture messages and emails) should only be sent if the person has chosen to receive them, unless the email address was obtained as a result of a commercial relationship. The individual should always be given the opportunity to stop receiving the emails.

People may also have decided they don't want to receive communications via email from any business (known as opt-out), by signing up to the Email Preference Service. Check out the *Guide to the Privacy and Electronic Communications Regulations* at the Information Commissioner's website (www.ico.gov.uk) and see the information below.

Email newsletters: What you should be aware of

Electronic mail marketing messages should not be sent to individuals without their permission unless all these following criteria are met:

- The marketer has obtained your details through a sale or negotiations for a sale
- The messages are about similar products or services offered by the sender
- You were given an opportunity to refuse the marketing when your details were collected and, if you did not refuse, you were given a simple way to opt out in every future communication. The regulations do not cover electronic mail marketing messages sent to businesses.

Autoresponders

These are used to acknowledge receipt of customers' questions relating to technical support or stock query for example. You can either choose to install an autoresponder on your server or subscribe to an autoresponder service that is hosted on another server – your web host would normally offer you an autoresponder service too.

Special offers

One of the tried and tested ways of keeping customers is to offer them something more than they would normally expect. Exceed their expectations. Develop ways to reward your customers for repeat purchases. Ensure that any rewards or special offers are in line with what your business can afford – it makes little sense to come up with special offers that are not within your budget. Cost-effective rewards include vouchers offering a 10% discount for example, or money off dependent on spending a certain amount, gift certificates for recommending a friend, free shipping and money off future purchases. You can include special offers and discounts in email newsletters and on the site.

For a longer-term approach, you could consider developing a customer loyalty programme, which will call for investment upfront. Price is not the primary reason most people stay loyal to brands, rather it is the experience they gain from interacting with your business and making a purchase. Before setting up a loyalty scheme, consider the resources you currently have available in-house. Are they able to support a loyalty scheme? You'll also need to assess how many customers you have on your database, how they behave and your budget.

Inviting feedback

Starbucks: Inviting feedback via the web

Dell: Inviting feedback via the web

One of the keys to customer retention is the ability to listen to your customer base, inviting comments and feedback and responding to these in a positive manner. Coffee giant Starbucks, for example, launched a website in 2008 to encourage customers to give feedback and suggest ideas on how it can improve its service. Customers shared their ideas and voted on the feedback of others. Computer manufacturer Dell, which has suffered its share of negative customer feedback in recent years, launched IdeaStorm, a website enabling customers to share their experiences and ideas directly with the company and their peers.

While gaining customer feedback is a simple enough process, many small businesses lack the time or the resources necessary to do this, by running questionnaires for example and then not collating the answers, much less following up on anything learned from the process. Many view feedback as a cost of doing business rather than an opportunity.

From the experts

Company: moneysupermarket.com
Owner-manager: Simon Nixon

We invite comments from our user-base and encourage people to go to our forums online. It's a key way to engage with people and to keep them coming back. It's more cost-effective to retain existing customers than to acquire new ones.

Get feedback even when a customer is not happy with the service or goods they have received. The quickest way to alienate any customer is to ask for input and then ignore it. Many small businesses make the mistake of ignoring such feedback or sweeping it under the carpet but the speed at which a complaint can be dealt with will signal to your customers that you care, regardless of whether their responses are positive or negative. Continued analysis of feedback can help you to identify any areas of weakness and to improve on them, upping your levels of customer service.

Make it as obvious and as easy as possible for people to get in touch with you – as your business exists in a virtual environment they can't physically pop in to return goods or voice a grievance. Put an 'About us' section indicating who to complain to. Collecting customer feedback and analysing it is even more valuable in a challenging economic environment as you are likely to be cutting back spending in other areas and looking to make more money from your existing assets. Set aside some space on your website for forums, where users can interact with each other and post advice and recommendations.

Startups Tips
Set up a method for collecting and responding to customer feedback. This could be in the form of a general online questionnaire that you send out in the first six months of business for example, or you could encourage customers to give you feedback after a purchase, assessing areas such as ease of use of site and delivery. You could then use these on your website.

FAQs

FAQs or frequently asked questions are a resource that many customers will look at when browsing a particular site. Many websites devote more than one page to frequently asked questions that will provide information regarding your business operations. If you're tempted to do quite a few (and this really depends on the type of business you are running), consider grouping all the questions together into categories at the top of the page, enabling consumers to scan and browse the answer, before clicking onto a link. No one wants to read pages and pages of FAQs and grouping the questions together means that customers can access the areas they need to quickly.

You'll also need to pay attention to what goes into FAQs – both in terms of content and style. Ask your friends and family to come up with potential scenarios based around your site that you can then answer. The latter need to be concise but informative and should be written in a clear and engaging style as FAQs can help to boost levels of interaction with customers further. In terms of presentation, have a look at other websites for inspiration and for ideas on how not to do it. As a rule of thumb, FAQs should be clearly presented and you should have information on how people can send questions clearly displayed on the site.

Startups Tips

Check out your favourite sites and have a look at their FAQ sections for advice and inspiration. The key is to keep these concise and informative.

Startups checklist

- Complaints shouldn't be viewed as negative: Encourage as much feedback as possible and if there are complaints, look at ways of solving them. This will encourage your customers to spread the word about your customer service so they become advocates.
- Deal with customer complaints and queries as quickly as possible: As the old saying goes, a customer who has a bad experience is likely to tell 10 other people.
- Email newsletters need to be concise as well as engaging: Ensure you measure open rates so you can decide whether you need to change tactics.
- Try giving customers special offers: It's easier to retain loyal customers than find new ones.
- Check with your web host provider to see whether autoresponders are part of the package.
- FAQs need to be concise and to the point: Otherwise you risk alienating customers. Check out other websites to see how these are displayed.

8

KEEPING SHIPSHAPE

 **CHAPTER 8.1**

Running and adapting the business

Your site has gone live. The launch party is over. Your staff are trained and traffic is slowly but surely building up. You're the master of your own destiny sitting pretty, picking the hours you want to work.

This is the point where anyone who's already progressed beyond this point breaks into a knowing chuckle because, as you'll soon find out, going live is only half the battle. Maintaining the business and managing yourself, your staff and your time is the real challenge. This is the time when you should be monitoring your website and its content closely to make sure there are no glitches.

In this chapter we'll cover:

→ Post-launch: What to consider
→ Technology issues
→ Adapting your website
→ New trends
→ Updating content
→ How to manage yourself
→ When to take advice
→ Managing staff
→ Work-life balance
→ Staff costs/benefits.

Post-launch: What to consider

Don't panic. You should prepare for your first few weeks to be fairly slow so don't freak out when they are. It's always going to take a while for word to get out and it will take weeks, even months for your site to be well optimised enough to attract visitors. In turn, don't bury your head in the sand either, and use the time wisely. A slow start is not necessarily a bad thing, as it can give you a chance to hone your operation. A slower start allows you to perfect your model, test your ideas and assess what works.

As your reputation in the area builds, so too should your customer base. You should have accounted for a gradual increase in trade in your business plan anyway. The key to surviving the first few months is doing everything you can to keep the cash flowing in, while keeping overheads low. Too many online businesses actually get more than enough customers to their site and convert these into sales, but suffer because their overheads are disproportionately high.

If you are running an online retail business, from the first month's trading adjust your stock levels so you're not carrying more than you need to. Don't cut back your product range, just buy what you can best predict you're likely to sell and keep as much cash as you can in the pot. Similarly don't go employing staff until you absolutely need them and if you do, take people on a casual basis first explaining a permanent role will follow as soon as you can afford and justify it.

Technology concerns

You might have a fantastic range of products that literally fly off your homepage and dedicated customer service, but in the world of online business, your site is only as good as the company that hosts it. If there is a problem with your web hosting company, there'll be a problem with your site – which could range from pages that are slow to load, to those that don't load at all, to a site that is unavailable most of the time. All of this will result in lost customers and sales, not to mention the damage it does to your reputation. In Chapter 4 (see p.114) we highlighted the importance of ensuring that your web host provider can accommodate your bandwidth needs. It's reassuring to see that traffic to your site reaches unexpected peaks, but it's a different story if your web host cannot support this growth. In the first six months of business, monitor traffic levels carefully and see if you can predict when further spikes will occur, so you can plan in advance if you need increased bandwidth.

Taking advantage of free time

While trade is slower this may be a good opportunity to bring in some of your marketing skills. Think about the different kinds of special offers you can introduce to try to boost trade. Avoid emblazoning your site with the word 'sale' as this can portray desperation more than invitation, but don't be scared to use calls to action on your homepage such as 'introductory offer', 'just launched', 'browse our great selection of . . .'.

The Establishing your presence chapter (p.175) gives you more detail on this but it's something to consider during your early stages of trading. You should also look to stagger PR throughout the first six months. If you've come up with five great PR stories, don't use them all for the launch, but rather keep in regular contact with journalists. If you've had a great month, press release it, if you've had a celebrity visitor advertise it; keep thinking how you can make the news and stay fresh in people's minds. This could form the content for any email newsletters or email alerts, encouraging people to come back to the site.

If you've any budget for marketing, overcoming the lull that inevitably follows the highs of a launch month is the time to spend it. It's actually much better to spend money on advertising after a month or so because by then people might have heard of your business, logged on and are more influenced to browse – that's a far more likely scenario than reacting to an advert for an online shop you've never heard of before.

More than anything, stay calm but focused. Measure everything. Record everything. You should know the unit sales of every product, the number of hits to your website, what you're making most mark-up on and not just how many sales each member of staff is making, but how cost-effective they are for you. Resist outlandish, wholesale changes and stick to your identity and business plan, but carry out subtle experiments with website lay-out, and perhaps even products and measure the impact.

Startups Tips

Stagger potential publicity over the first few months post-launch. It will mean people keep on talking about your business and will give you time to develop some relevant news for your customer base.

Startups Tips

The first six months should teach you about your business and your customers – like any other relationship, you'll need to get to know one another and if you don't work at it, nothing will improve.

New ideas/trends

One of the most common reasons any website either fails to take off or sees trade drop is because it takes its eye off the ball. The internet moves like the wind so all that work you did researching the products your customers want and expect can never stop. Indeed, if you researched it and then spent three months creating and designing the site, it was probably out of date the minute your website went live.

It's more of a concern for some sectors than others. If you're in the fashion or electrical market, anything longer than a three-month cycle is archaic.

You should always have a line of classic bestsellers but you need to stay in touch with the latest trends.

Buy the magazines your customers buy, know what and who they aspire to, visit the competition and work harder than them to find new suppliers and never miss a trade fair. You should be just as passionate and knowledgeable about the area or niche you're operating in as your customers are — in fact, you, your staff and your website should be the experts in that area that the customers turn to for advice and guidance.

In my experience

Like fashion, a website soon looks dated. Who are you most likely to purchase from: a smartly dressed fashion conscious young lady or a long-haired bearded hippy wearing loons and a tie-dyed t-shirt?

Company: Country Products

Owner–manager: Mark Leather

Adapting your business

When you're getting your website set up and everything is brand new, it's easy to forget that all may not run smoothly. Being able to make changes and ongoing support are an important element of your website plans and something you should consider from the get-go.

While your first few months in business should be a constant learning process, there is a point where you need to stop, take stock and ask if the website is ever going to work without some wholesale changes.

If you've been tweaking, experimenting and measuring the impact of different approaches you'll be in a far better position to make the decision than if you've sat on your hands hoping that miraculously your site will soon receive thousands of hits. Just because you've pumped your life savings into a business, given up the safety of a salary and spent months developing your site, it can then be massively difficult to accept it's not going quite as well as you'd hoped.

Unfortunately, though, there are no assurances in business no matter how much planning and preparation you put in and the biggest celebrity entrepreneurs who sit on TV telling others how to do it have all had their flops – and will again.

The most important thing is to be open-minded and prepare yourself in advance so if you do have to make some pretty drastic changes it won't come as a big shock – and if you don't want to lose face you can tell everyone that it was part of the plan all along!

Assessing what works

The key is to look at the business basics and get to the bottom of the problem. Go back to your business plan and hold it up to your website. Is it a true reflection of the plan? If it is, then you need to look for what's going wrong. Usually it'll either be that you're not getting enough hits to your site, that your customers are not buying your products or using your services, or, if they are, that your pricing or supply line is wrong.

If, when you compare your site to the one in your business plan you see something different, then you could have found your answer. Is it true to the USPs and identity you outlined? Did you get lost or sidetracked from the original vision somewhere? Are you differentiating yourself enough and communicating the right messages as you'd originally intended? If you're not, then start reversing those problems and get back on track.

If you still can't work out where the problem lies, look at your finances because that's certainly where the problem will be hidden. Remember, it doesn't matter how many customers you have or how much you love your website if it's losing money. Money doesn't have to be your motivation for running an online business, but profit is your oxygen and you need to be striving for it in every buying and selling transaction.

Look at your suppliers. Can you source cheaper elsewhere? Can you buy better quality for the same price that would encourage more sales? Have you got any big overheads eating into your profit? If you have, be hard. Lose them. Yes, that includes people. Many, many entrepreneurs say that their biggest regret is trying to grow their business too quickly, getting in a mess and having to lay people off to save it. However, many of them did it, survived as a consequence and went on to employ multiples of the people they upset by letting them go.

Startups Tips

Concentrate on the core business. If you're making big changes to your site and the business, update your business plan, then you'll have something to refer back to if you're still haemorrhaging money in a month's time.

Tweaking your site

Wholesale changes to your website are not something to be taken lightly but making small changes to your website is something you should be prepared to do on a regular basis, as it's essential to both attract new customers and retain existing ones. Just as a shop changes its window display, you'll need to do the same with your homepage. Returning visitors will see new, fresh content that will encourage them to explore the site further, and you might want to appeal to new ones by adding testimonials to your site or replacing images to attract their attention.

Bear in mind the future development of your site and consider the kind of upgrades and new technologies you may require. If you want to add sub-sites at a later date for instance, you need to know whether this will be possible. Ask your provider what kind of costs you can expect in the future.

Revisit your website and make note of all the areas you think should be tweaked or which could benefit from a more substantial change; that is a list of changes which you 'need to have' and those changes which would be 'nice to have'. You should also do a thorough check to spot any errors or broken links. Of course, the bigger the change, the more time, effort and money it will cost, so only consider making a major change if you think it is strictly necessary; for example, the navigation could be made clearer or you need to insert a site map to help people find their way around the site. Carry out a thorough audit and organise any notes you have made into those areas that can wait and those that need immediate attention.

What to check for

Check links on a regular basis – the more your site develops the greater the number of links you are likely to have, so it makes sense to check a certain amount at set intervals, otherwise you could find yourself overwhelmed. Make sure you remove 'dead links' (which click through to nothing) and links that are out of date, as these are areas that most frustrate consumers. Scan the content for any typos or formatting errors and to ensure that images are displaying properly. It's equally important to check that any ads you are hosting on your site are still live and that any affiliate deals you have in place are actually working. Load the site onto different browsers too to ensure that it displays properly.

Don't introduce changes just because you've noticed your competitors have added some features – you need to put your customers' needs first at all times. Having already built up a reputation, the last thing you want to do is to radically change your site – it will only result in confusing your customers and potentially sending them elsewhere. While new internet technologies are launched on a regular basis and it may seem tempting to try them out, remember that your customers may not be adopting these technologies at the same rate as they are being released and used.

Web content management systems

If you commissioned a web designer, you may have factored in access to a web content management system (CMS), which is basically a maintenance tool for creating, editing, searching and publishing HTML content on your business website. A CMS is particularly suited to those websites that have a substantial number of pages and where the contents need to be changed on a regular basis. Even if you have no knowledge of programming or mark up languages, these web applications should allow you to create and manage online content – everything from images and audio files to video and electronic documents – with relative ease. A good CMS will allow you to edit content easily; manage your workflow; and extend your site's functionality to scale as you grow.

If you opted for a custom-built site, and don't have access to a CMS, scalability depends on the people who built the site for you. You'll probably have to go back to that person or that company and have them upgrade it for you.

Updating content

New content on your website will not only encourage existing customers to come back but it will also stand you in good stead with search engines. They love new content and if you update your website regularly, you'll stand a better chance of achieving a higher ranking among search engines, not to mention increasing the number of visits to your site.

There are many ways to introduce updated content without incurring too much time, effort, resources or expense on your part. Consider writing a blog to promote your products or to give a view on your chosen sector. Sites such as http://wordpress.org offer free blogging software, enabling

Startups Tips

Carry out a website review soon after launch. Check that all aspects of the site are working and use this opportunity to assess if any of the content or tools need tweaking.

Startups Tips

Aim to update your website content at least once every few weeks. You should ideally aim to refresh content once a week.

you to get a blog up and running in a matter of minutes (see Chapter 5.3: Developing your site, p.215, for more information on blogging). Refresh your list of frequently answered questions (FAQs) as often as is possible and reasonable – new customers will often click on this section first to find out more about your business.

News and views

Creating a news section on your site will enable you to promote product launches, changes to your website, new staff hires – anything, in fact, that you feel would interest your customers and add value to your business. News stories don't have to be as detailed as press releases as they are not intended to be sent to the media but are being used more to promote your products and refresh website content, so you could try to write these yourself.

Archive your old newsletters. In Chapter 7 (p.246) we discussed the importance of email newsletters and how to write them to create the maximum impact. Make sure you keep a record of all the newsletters you create and send out. These can then be uploaded to the site.

Statistics related to your business are also a quick and easy way of adding new content to the site. Depending on the type of business you are running, you could highlight the products that have sold the most for a particular month, or include general statistics related to your sector.

If you feel that your writing skills won't be up to scratch, then you could employ a freelance journalist or copywriter to help and draw up a schedule of when updates need to be done by, such as by a particular day once a month.

Is your website easy to use?

Have you ever been to a website because you know there is something you want, but even after numerous clicks, you simply can't find it? Most people's reaction would be to go elsewhere – if this happened to your business, you would potentially be losing out on sales. Website usability assesses how easy it is for users to find their way around the website, search for items and click on those pages and offers that you want them to click on.

With your website, you are aiming to build something that is easy to understand, navigate and use. If your customers can find what they need, then this results in sales, subscriptions, and everything else the website is intended to achieve. In theory, this seems like second nature, in reality, usability is an area many websites struggle with and lack of ease of use is one of the main reasons your customers will go elsewhere.

Usability includes areas such as links, content and navigation. When you carry out periodic reviews of the website, and each time you add any new content, ensure you click on the links to test that they take you to where you want to go. Carry out user testing among your friends and family and ask them to rate how easy it has been to find the content and features they want.

When updating content:

- Check your spelling and grammar: The fewer mistakes the better
- Keep your paragraphs brief: Blocks of text are not search engine friendly
- Lists (either bullet point or numbered) are quick ways to add new content and will stand out
- Sentences should not be too long.

How to manage yourself

The minute you employ another person you go from being a humble online business owner to a boss, a manager and the point from which authority and company culture flows. Some people react by becoming too authoritarian, others try too hard not to change and end up losing respect. To run a motivated, disciplined workforce you'll need to strike a balance between the two and lead by example.

Taking advice

We covered the value of taking advice from others in Chapter 1 (p.26), but it's important to remember this is not something you should forget about once you're up and running. Mentors and established entrepreneurs can have something to offer your business even if it's a decade old. Networking should be an ongoing process and, don't rule out general free business networking events. As the owner of an online business, you mustn't think that only other online businesses can offer useful advice or guidance.

Identifying your strengths and weaknesses

If you want to maintain a successful business, you have to dedicate just as much time to your own self-development as to your business.

In my experience

The challenge for the online entrepreneur is that you need to be quite rounded. When you have limited resources, you want it all in one.

Company: *Glasses Direct*
Owner–manager: *Jamie Murray Wells*

It can be hard to measure your own personal development when you're your own boss. If you employ someone with more online or technical experience than you and see them following certain processes, swallow your pride and ask them about it.

If you can't afford an army of experts then take advantage of the help available to you. Contact your local Regional Development Agency (www.englandsrdas.com), or visit a Business Link (www.businesslink.gov. uk) adviser. The industry moves fast. What's in vogue for an internet retail business one month may seem passé half a year down the line. You need to keep up to date with the latest online trends.

 In my experience

It depends on the nature of your business but if you are a technology-driven business like ours, then you need to have technical staff as part of the team from the start. You need to build technology into the DNA of your business and that starts on day one. Of course, having a technology team doesn't mean you can't still use off-the shelf technology to support your initiatives.

Company: *Wahanda.com*
Owner–manager: *Lopo Champalimaud*

Motivating yourself

The start-up process is incredibly demanding both physically and psychologically. After all that hard work you clearly need to slow down the pace slightly, but you can't sit back and hope the business will run itself. In the same way you might set targets for staff, and KPIs (key performance indicators) to measure performance and flag training and resource needs, you need to do the same for yourself.

Time management

With so many hats to wear in your role as online business owner, managing your time effectively is absolutely essential from a very early stage. This is particularly important for those running an online business, where there are no set working hours and your company is effectively operating every day of the year.

The most important aspect of time management is to list and prioritise everything you need to do, so you recognise the difference between what's important and what's urgent.

 In my experience

If you looked at any of the online businesses out there, such as Facebook, Yahoo! and YouTube, I don't think you need relevant online experience. You need a sense of pragmatism and determination – the online model lets you do things faster and has a wide reach and you have to put yourself in the minds of your customers.

Company: Glasses Direct
Owner-manager: Jamie Murray Wells

Running an online business will involve various 'to do' lists. This will include your long-term goals such as growing turnover, and your monthly goals, which could be introducing a new product range. And of course there'll be daily and weekly objectives as well.

Here are a few tips for prioritising workloads:

→ List all the tasks you need to do, and then prioritise them in order of what is most urgent and important.

→ Don't underestimate the amount of time interruptions can steal from your schedule. When allocating time for a particular task, build in room for disruptions.

➜ Break large tasks up into manageable chunks. It's tempting to run lots of little errands instead of getting stuck in to a big important job.

Holidays and work–life balance

The temptation to carry on working even while on holiday can prove too strong for some. However, you will have worked incredibly hard to get the venture up and running and may feel in desperate need of a break by this point.

The main thing to remember is that you need to achieve a balance between working hard to make sure the business thrives during its early days, and making sure you don't burn out yourself.

If you do decide to take a break then test the waters first. Handing over the reins for a weekend while you're still close at hand, perhaps even just at home, is the next step. You can test if things are capable of running smoothly in your absence while still being nearby if any real problems arise.

Managing staff

No matter who you're managing you need to clearly outline and put down in writing what their role is, make it clear what you expect from them and demonstrate how their performance will be measured. You then need to ensure you set clear lines of communication, to flag and deal with any problems.

The best bosses are fair. They're firm but they listen and they apply the same rules to themselves as they do to staff. You should lead by example in every respect.

Despite this, there should always be a separation between you and the people that work for you. There's nothing stopping you getting on with your employees and even becoming friends, but keep a professional distance.

Staff training and courses

The online business environment moves at a fast pace, so it's vital that you provide staff with access to training and courses, particularly in areas such as online marketing and security. New techniques and technologies are being developed in these areas all the time and it's important for you and your staff to have at least some knowledge of what is out there, even if you aren't likely to implement it for some time. There are plenty of courses, most of which can be done in a day or less, which teach the fundamentals in any online skill.

Dealing with staffing problems

Online businesses move at a rapid pace and some people who joined in the early days of the business may not have the appropriate skills as the business grows. Unless you're extremely lucky, or only hire friends and family to work in the shop, it's likely you'll have to confront some of the following problems.

Bad service and laziness

You have to provide a friendly and helpful service and provide a positive shopping experience for every customer every single minute of every single hour you're open, every single day of the year.

For an internet business, this can be a challenging problem as all of the contact you and your staff will have with customers will be on a remote basis, so you will have to work harder to create a professional and welcoming atmosphere. Good customer service is something you can't relent on and you should never tolerate a slip in standards, no matter how frustrating or downright awkward the customer. It doesn't matter if the customer is right or wrong if they go away and tell 20 people your online business is rubbish.

When recruiting look for natural enthusiasm and people skills, it's generally something you can't teach, unlike other skills.

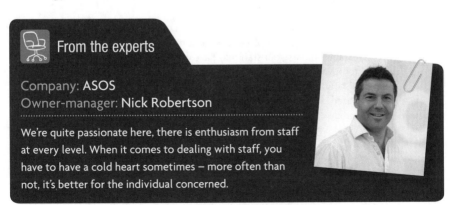

From the experts

Company: ASOS
Owner-manager: Nick Robertson

We're quite passionate here, there is enthusiasm from staff at every level. When it comes to dealing with staff, you have to have a cold heart sometimes – more often than not, it's better for the individual concerned.

Discrimination

We've already touched on the issue of discrimination during Chapter 4.5 – Hiring staff (p.165) but it's important to note that this is something you must constantly bear in mind. To summarise, you must consider the following legislation in the day to day running of your online business or you could find yourself in serious hot water.

Legislation outlawing age discrimination came into force in 2006. It includes every member of staff that works for you, both young and old. Employers must have age positive practices. This means you can't recruit, train, promote or retire people on the basis of age unless it can be objectively justified. Many people over 50 want to work but are prevented from doing so by ageist practices. But remember, the recent legislation doesn't just concern older people; it covers young and old alike throughout their working lives.

Skills, experience and the ability to do the job are what's important, not someone's age. The same applies when it comes to discriminating on the grounds of race, sex or disability. It's your responsibility to make sure that not only do you treat all your staff equally, but that discrimination does not take place between other members of the team.

Staff handbook and benefits

While you need to make sure every member of staff has the appropriate training in health and safety, some of the other expectations of employee policy can be detailed in a staff handbook. Here you can list your expectations of all staff and your work policies. That way if a problem ever arises you can refer back to the handbook as an explanation of why you may be taking disciplinary action. You should also use the handbook as a way of flagging up staff benefits.

Thinking about the extra perks that can make your online business stand out as a great place to work compared to the many other establishments your staff may have experienced can reduce your staff turnover. You can offer a range of benefits, including exclusive online discounts and incentivising staff with individual and team commissions based on a percentage of sales for the website per day and on a monthly basis.

Startups checklist

- Don't panic if things start slowly: Use this time to hone your operation, such as ensuring your web hosting company is working properly.
- Stagger your PR efforts throughout your first six months: Now is a good time to focus on your marketing campaign.
- Make sure you keep monitoring new ideas and trends: The internet is a fast moving market so you need to keep up.
- Carry out a thorough audit of your site: Make a list of changes that are 'need to have' and those that are 'nice to have'.
- Introducing new content doesn't have to put a strain on your resources or time: Look at your existing resources and see how you can best use them.
- Your site links should be checked on a regular basis: Or you could find yourself overwhelmed as your site grows.
- Ensure your content is easy to read at all times: Make it as search engine friendly as possible.

CHAPTER 8.2

Finances when you're up and running

Running an online business is what you set out to do and without doubt that's where your energies are best served. As you've had to do throughout this whole process, you'll also need to put time aside for the financial aspect of running a business. After all, that's what allows you to run the company.

You'll already have familiarised yourself with projections, forecasts and basic costings during the planning stage, but the reality of running any business is that you need a firm grip on the numbers at all times. In order to do this successfully you'll need to become familiar with the different types of financial records you should use, such as profit and loss sheets, and learn how to always be aware of your financial status by keeping on top of your cashflow and payments. It may be helpful to hire an accountant at this stage to help you through, or to invest in some accounting software.

In this chapter we'll cover:

→ Accounts
→ Balance sheets
→ Profit and loss (P&L) sheets
→ Cashflow forecasting
→ VAT
→ Day to day finances
→ Managing payments
→ Hiring an accountant
→ Paying your staff.

Accounts

Running a business involves meticulous record-keeping, some of which you are obliged to do, and some of which simply helps you run your business more efficiently. Your accounts can be separated into two main categories – financial and management.

Financial record-keeping

If your business is incorporated, ie a limited company, you are required by law to put together a set of financial records every year and file them with Companies House. Unincorporated businesses are not required to do this; however, they must still keep thorough accounting records to be used alongside their annual tax returns. You are obligated to keep a minimum of the last six years' worth of accounts for HMRC to call upon at any time.

There are detailed guidelines for how to prepare financial accounts on the Companies House website at www.companieshouse.gov.uk, but you will generally have to include the following:

- ⇢ Balance sheet
- ⇢ Profit and loss account
- ⇢ Cashflow statement.

Management record-keeping

Your management accounts are the records you must keep in order to run your business well. This is where you'll cover everything, from how many units of stock are bought and sold, to the payroll data for your staff. You simply cannot run your online business efficiently without up-to-date and methodical records. You also need to take the necessary steps to ensure this information is stored safely and backed up.

What records do you need to keep when running an online business? Your accounting records will be split into daily, weekly, monthly and annual figures, all of which are important. Efficient records will allow you to identify the strong and weak areas of your business and therefore take appropriate action in your day-to-day management and long-term planning.

Records you should keep to have an accurate reflection of your online business' financial health include:

- All sales transactions broken down by date and product
- Stock levels: Daily, weekly and monthly
- Receipts for credit card transactions
- Invoices from suppliers and service providers
- Any licences you require
- Property and lease documentation
- Staff shifts and wages
- Employee tax details
- Cost of other overheads including site maintenance and development.

It's important to note this is not a complete list, and you will need to add to it depending on the type of online business you run.

Financial records

Balance sheets

Essentially, reading a balance sheet is like checking your bank balance – it simply tells you what the business owes or owns at any particular time. But unlike your bank balance it doesn't just give you a number, it also tells you what makes up that number. In essence the first part is everything your business owns, its assets. The second part is everything you owe, the liabilities.

The balance sheet has a debit entry and a credit entry for everything, so the total value of the assets is always the same value as the total of the liabilities.

An example balance sheet is shown at the back of this book (see p.295) but here's a more detailed explanation of all the sections of a balance sheet.

Fixed assets: This is typically anything that you count as an asset of the business but not something that you are likely to sell as part of your daily business. They can be tangible and intangible, so include any premises, website domain names, trademarks, equipment such as computers or furniture that you use for the business.

Current assets: Anything that you sell.

Debtors: Anyone that owes you money should be included in here. If you offer accounts or sell to clients who settle monthly, then include sums owed in this column.

Current liabilities: Anything that you owe that is payable within one year. In our list we have included creditors – which might include your suppliers as you will typically pay them in around 30 days – and the overdraft as this is probably repayable on demand.

Net current assets: This is simply the sum of your current assets and liabilities, both of which are likely to be under one year in lifespan. This is quite a useful figure to calculate as it will show whether you could pay all your debts if you collected all the sums due to you.

Total assets less current liabilities: Unlike the last number you can include all the long-term assets like property in this number.

Equity: Any money that is invested in the business, for example your savings if you used those to set up the business initially.

Profit and loss (P&L) sheet

Put simply, a profit and loss sheet details your business' transactions, subtracting the total outgoings from the total income to give you a reading of how much, if any, profit you have made.

> **Startups Tips**
> A profit and loss sheet, unlike a balance sheet, displays the financial health of your company for a period of time – a month, a quarter or a year. A balance sheet only represents your finances at a particular moment in time.

If your business is incorporated, you are required by law to produce a P&L sheet for each financial year. If your business is not trading as a limited company you don't have to produce one, but the information you give to HMRC to work out your tax bill will amount to the same thing anyway. Even if you're not required to produce one, the P&L sheet is useful to show owners and investors (not shareholders, as if you're not required to produce the P&L sheet it must mean that you're not a company — ie that there are no shareholders) how the business is doing at a glance.

You can find an example P&L sheet for a shop on p.67.

Cashflow statement

A cashflow statement shows your online business' incoming and outgoing money, enabling you to assess how much money you have at your disposal at any one time. Poor cashflow is one of the main reasons that businesses fail. Some businesses can be profitable on paper, earning more than their outgoings, but if the cash isn't in the bank to buy stock and to pay staff you'll soon find yourself in trouble.

Your first few months are the time you're most likely to run into difficulties with cashflow. A lot more money will have been spent by you – on equipment, initial stock, web design, staff – than the first few customers will pay you for their purchases, so on paper you'll be cashflow negative. There are certain things businesses can do to increase their cashflow and the most obvious is to ask their customers to pay them quicker. Online businesses can't really do that but here are a few things you can do to improve cashflow:

- → Lease rather than buy the really expensive equipment you need. You'll then pay a monthly or annual charge rather than having to splash out all at once upfront.

- → Order less stock. Don't order too many of the items that will sit in your stockroom for months before interest grows.

- → Make sure you forecast your cashflow as accurately as you can. That way you can plan ahead for slower revenue periods and make sure you still have enough cash in the bank to cover your outgoings.

Good cashflow forecasting isn't just important for your own business management. You may be required to provide this kind of detail if you need a loan from the bank during your first few months of trading. The forecast will allow you to identify the amount and origin of cash coming into your business and the amount and destination of cash being paid out during any given period of time.

Sage Pay's tips on managing cashflow

Knowing how much money you have coming in and going out helps you make informed decisions about your business. Investing in software is a great way to ensure you have that information when you need it.

Keeping all your financial and business contact information in one place helps you keep things organised. And when you store that information electronically, it's easier to keep it up to date, and you run less risk of losing it.

Accounting software places key information at your fingertips. For example, instead of having to calculate how much money your business has made and how much you owe, software packages such as Sage Instant Accounts and Sage 50 Accounts can show you that information at a glance via an easy-to-read dashboard.

Integrated systems

The same applies to understanding your customers, as the software helps you identify those who have paid and those who have not. Most good accounting software will also enable you to integrate with Microsoft Outlook so you'll be reminded to do things like follow up a sales call, quotation or chase payment.

Another way to encourage cashflow is to use electronic payments, by credit or debit card or BACS (see p.131), reducing the time you have to spend banking your cash. If you're accepting payments over the phone or online, the fastest and most effective way to reconcile payments is to use systems that are integrated. For speedy and accurate results, an accounts package that integrates in some way with your payment gateway and shopping cart, for example, is worthwhile. That way you can limit the risk of human error and spend more time developing your core business.

Finally, using accounting software can also make sure you calculate VAT and tax correctly when submitting returns to HMRC, and avoid potentially costly fines. With accounts packages like Sage Instant Accounts and Sage 50 Accounts, you have the added advantage of making these payments online, leaving you more time to do your tax returns.

www.sagepay.com

Generally you'll produce a forecast for a quarter or year in advance, but during the early stages of trading you might want to do this more frequently, such as a month in advance. When compiling a cashflow forecast it's really important that you don't overestimate your incoming cash.

> **Startups Tips**
> It's much easier to get an accurate reflection of your outgoings as you will know what these are at this stage. However, you won't yet have a really accurate estimate of how many customers you'll have each month, so err on the side of caution to be safe and keep your incoming cash estimates low.

There is an example of a cashflow forecast sheet on p.296.

VAT

VAT or value added tax applies to the majority of transactions involving the sale of goods or services. Once your business reaches a certain level of turnover, currently £70,000 per year, you are legally obliged to register for VAT. You will then have to apply VAT to what you sell and keep records of your incomings and outgoings in order to pay the correct amount of VAT to HMRC.

If your turnover is under £67,000, you can voluntarily register for VAT, which can result in a number of cashflow advantages.

↝ If you sell zero-rated items and buy standard-rated items you would receive a VAT refund from HMRC.

↝ If you have not yet sold anything or don't sell anything during a VAT accounting period, you can still claim VAT back on your purchases.

↝ You have the use of the VAT your customers pay you before you have to pay it to HMRC.

Startups Tips
To register for VAT go to the VAT Online Registration Service on the HMRC website.

There are three rates of VAT:

1. The standard rate: 20%

2. The reduced rate: 5%

3. The zero rate: 0%

It's really important you register for VAT in good time because otherwise you will liable for all VAT due from the time that you should have been registered. In other words you have to pay HMRC the right amount of VAT even if you didn't charge your customers for it. You could also be liable to pay a fine for delaying your registration. How much you'll be fined is dependent on how late you registered, but fines start at £50.

The average time for processing VAT applications is about one month; however, it can take up to six months if HMRC feels it needs to carry out extra checks on the application. You must account for and pay VAT between applying for your registration and receiving your actual VAT number, but you are also allowed to reclaim any VAT you have paid suppliers on your purchases during this period. To do this you need to keep accurate records of any invoices where your suppliers have charged you VAT.

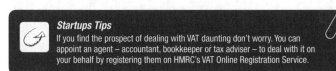

Startups Tips
If you find the prospect of dealing with VAT daunting don't worry. You can appoint an agent – accountant, bookkeeper or tax adviser – to deal with it on your behalf by registering them on HMRC's VAT Online Registration Service.

Price changes

The cost of your outgoings will change, sometimes on a weekly basis. The price of products and the cost of energy are variable and may go up and down frequently. While customers accept inflation as a fact of life, they'll start to cry foul play if your products have jumped in price every time they visit your site. Consequently, you need to find a balance between covering your own costs and maintaining reasonable prices for your customers.

One way of doing this is to set yourself a variable acceptable mark-up. For example, calculate what the lowest possible mark-up for an acceptable return is (for example 60%) then the highest mark-up you can reasonably expect to charge (for example 70%). This gives you some leeway for price changes for your own costings without leaving you out of pocket for not passing the cost on to your customers. However, when your own costs go up so much that it's no longer possible to make at least the 60% mark-up, that's when you'll need to change your prices.

Accountants

Even some of the most mathematically-minded entrepreneurs will tell you a good accountant can be worth their weight in gold. You're running an online business first and foremost and as stated at the beginning of the chapter that's where your passion should remain, not getting bogged down with invoices, PAYE slips and credit notes. Handing that responsibility over to an accountant or someone who completely manages your books can free up your time to spend on planning, development and working on your grand designs for your business.

Choosing an accountant

When you're just starting out, your accountant can act as one of your most valued business advisers so you need to make sure you employ one that you trust. There are many ways to find a good accountant and one of the best methods is through a recommendation. Ask friends and contacts if they would recommend their accountant. Also ask businesses around you if they go to someone locally.

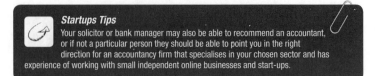

Startups Tips
Your solicitor or bank manager may also be able to recommend an accountant, or if not a particular person they should be able to point you in the right direction for an accountancy firm that specialises in your chosen sector and has experience of working with small independent online businesses and start-ups.

When seeking recommendations, make sure you ask people what they used their accountant for as you might not need the same kind of service. Ask what in particular they recommend about them and what their weak points are if they have any. Most importantly it is advisable to choose someone who is a member of one of the main professional accounting bodies. There is no legislation to stop anyone setting up as an accountant so asking for member accountants in your area will ensure you are getting someone fully qualified.

These are the main accounting organisations in the UK.

Association of Chartered Certified Accountants
Tel: 020 7059 5000
www.acca.org.uk

Institute of Chartered Accountants, Scotland
Tel: 0131 347 0100
www.icas.org.uk

Institute of Chartered Accountants, England and Wales
Tel: 020 7920 8100
www.icaew.co.uk

Remember you're likely to be working closely with your accountant and if you don't get on at a basic level, your professional relationship may be more difficult than it needs to be. If you find someone you think you like ask if you can speak to their other clients. This is like asking for references and will be a real test of the calibre of the firm or individual accountant. If they are confident that their service has impressed, they shouldn't have a problem referring you to a few people.

Accounting software

If you decide you're going to manage the books yourself you'll want to get yourself some accountancy software. Whoever's job it is, yours or an accountant's, the person balancing the books, chasing invoices, managing suppliers and paying staff doesn't need to be worrying about the latest technology and it's probably the last thing on their mind. However, buying an accountancy software package can slash the amount of time and effort you put into managing your finances.

When choosing a package consider the following before you buy:

- Value for money: What services do you get for your cash?
- Level of support: Does the package include a free helpline you can call for technical or set-up support?
- Is the software industry specific?
- Does it integrate easily with HMRC's online filing system? This can save you a lot of time when it comes to filing your returns.

Paying your staff

Online businesses often have a lot of casual and temporary staff to cope with seasonal demands at busy times such as Christmas and Easter, for example, and it can be tempting to just pay them cash at the end of each week or shift. However, it's your responsibility as an employer to make sure the payment of your staff is all above board and both they and your business are making the appropriate tax and National Insurance contributions.

PAYE

PAYE (Pay As You Earn) is HMRC's system for collecting income tax and National Insurance at the source of payment – ie before the employee receives it. It's your responsibility to make sure you know how much to deduct from your staff in terms of their personal tax requirements. You must send the deducted amounts to HMRC by the 19th of every month (or the 22nd if you make electronic payments). However, if monthly payments are under £1,500 you can do this on a quarterly basis. From 6 April 2010, HMRC introduced a new penalty regime, whereby penalties may be incurred if PAYE payments are received late.

You have three choices when it comes to organising PAYE. You can either keep written accounts and calculate tax and National Insurance deductions yourself, buy specialised software to help calculate it for you, or outsource the whole operation.

PAYE is applied to all payments your employees receive when working for you. This includes:

→ Wages

→ Overtime

--> Tips

--> Bonuses

--> Statutory sick pay

--> Statutory maternity/paternity/adoption pay

--> Any lump sums including redundancy payments.

Once again, a quick visit to the HMRC website will allow you to register your business for PAYE. You should have already done this before employing your first member of staff, but if you haven't done so already, give the New Employer Hotline a call on 0845 60 70 143 and order a New Employer Starter Pack. This will talk you through the basics of registering.

Staff records

There are three main types of documentation to give your staff so they have a record of what they've earned and how much income tax and National Insurance they've paid. These are:

--> Wage slips: This shows how much they've earned and how it has been calculated

--> P60 form: This shows the tax deducted during the whole tax year. You can order this from HMRC by calling the Employer Orderline on 0845 7646 646

--> P45: You only need to give your employees this when they stop working for you. It will contain their individual tax code which they need to pass on to their new employer.

Outsourcing payroll

Many businesses decide to outsource their payroll duties so they don't have to calculate tax and National Insurance deductions themselves. This will obviously be an added expense for your business but can save you a lot of time and money in the long-run. By outsourcing your payroll you get rid of one of the biggest administrative headaches of running a small business.

If you have an accountant, they should be able to provide you with advice on outsourcing your payroll, and may even be able to do it for you. As with any service, shop around for the best deal as much as time permits.

Before you decide on an outsourced payroll provider, make sure you consider the following:

- Are they used to dealing with online businesses?
- Do they supply monthly or weekly pay slips? (You may find weekly slips are more suited for casual staff.)
- How much will they charge for setting up your payroll system?
- What are the ongoing fees?
- How easy is it to add extra members of staff to the account?
- Is the software they use approved by HMRC?

Startups checklist

- Keep accurate staff records and ensure these are as up to date as possible.
- You are likely to run into cashflow problems in your first few months, so ask for help if necessary.
- Keep an eye on your prices and adjust them according to your outgoings.
- Make sure you register for VAT in good time to avoid HMRC delay fines.
- Don't try to manage it all yourself if you don't have the time or skills. Hire an accountant if you need one.
- Consider outsourcing your payroll but carry out the appropriate checks before handing the process over to a third party.

CHAPTER 9

Where next?

As the internet is a market in continual development, maintaining and developing your site is the real challenge you will face. It requires constant attention, careful planning and a willingness to adapt. You may need to make changes quite soon after launch depending on customer feedback and your sales figures, or you may decide to set aside time at defined points in the year where you carry out a thorough dissection of your site and consider what is and what is not working.

It goes without saying that you'll need to keep up to date with the latest trends, continue to optimise your website and perhaps look at ways of diversifying the business. You'll also need to retain a flexible outlook, adapting your business plan if necessary, revisiting your marketing plans, assessing the quality and competitiveness of your product or service and growing your business to the next level.

In this chapter we'll cover:

→ Diversifying
→ Monitoring the competition
→ Growing your business.

Diversifying

One way to expand and develop your business is to diversify into new areas. It might be that you decide to widen your offering by selling complementary items, or branch out into new areas altogether. Not only can this offer you multiple streams of income, but you might also be able to use it to overcome seasonal voids.

Any kind of diversification away from your core business is likely to carry some risk as you'll be directing funds and your energies elsewhere. As such you shouldn't look to diversify too early. Many businesses have damaged a profitable and thriving business model by investing in a new range of goods or expanding into other sectors that don't work.

From the experts

Company: **moneysupermarket.com**
Owner-manager: **Simon Nixon**

Our goal was to become the number one price comparison site, and not just for money matters. We looked at other areas to launch into. We established an insurance price comparison site as it was close to the original idea of finance, then we went into travel and home services and we have recently launched a shopping comparison site.

If you do diversify into selling other goods, be careful not to dilute your identity or the USPs that make your business unique. For instance, if your online business has established itself by selling premium, organic goods, don't try to cash in by selling cheaper, non-organic products as well. You might gain a few extra visitors to your site but you stand to lose your differentiation as a stand out destination for your original target customer.

Diversifying – you've basically got three options:

→ Find new products or expand your range for existing customers

→ Find new customers for existing products

→ Find new products for new markets.

Finding new products for new markets is the riskiest strategy as you will be venturing somewhat into the unknown and will have to carry out careful research and assess demand – much as when you were starting an online business in the first place. The thought of adding a new revenue stream to a business gives some entrepreneurs a boost and reminds them of the time when they were starting up. But as you have done it before, it's worth reminding yourself of what that entailed and where you made mistakes. It could also put a strain on your time and your resources, although you won't need to put all the administrative and back end operations in place. And remember too that the online environment is fast-paced and can change rapidly – what might be popular today might not be tomorrow – so it's important to keep an open mind when assessing the likely present and future success of your existing business model.

You'll also need to consider the effect diversification will have on your reputation. You've worked hard to build a brand and a name for yourself so you need to ensure that new business interests do not impact negatively on your established reputation – you may be keen to attract a new customer base but you could end up alienating your existing one.

 In my experience

Running two businesses is not two times as hard, it is two to the power of two. Invest that energy into you core business, or get out of it.

Company: Naked Wines
Owner–manager: Rowan Gormley

 Startups Tips
It's not advisable to consider diversification until your core business is stable and profitable. If you're still struggling to win orders and build a sales time for the core product, there is a real danger that diversification could mean taking your eye off the ball.

Monitoring the competition

When you run an internet business, the world is your oyster as far as customers are concerned, with a global audience to tap into. Customer potential may be huge but so too is the competition. Online customers are very savvy when it comes to using the internet to find competitively priced products and services – after all, it only takes them a few clicks to browse, compare and buy. So it's important to keep a close eye on the competition and to monitor their sites carefully. Check out whether they have lowered or raised their prices, if they are running any sales or promotions or if they have expanded their product offering.

From the experts

Company: moneysupermarket.com
Owner-manager: Simon Nixon

It's critical to monitor the competition and to see how their performance compares to yours but don't copy them. We build new products and services with customer insight – we ask our users what they think and design offerings on the back of this.

Take a look at your prices to see if this is an area where you can beat the competition. Ensure you're not just selling at a price people can afford, but a price that's high enough to make your profit. Anyone can trick themselves into thinking they're doing a rich trade if they're pulling in the crowds by simply undercutting the competition. It's a perfectly acceptable strategy, of course, but only if you can do it and still make a profit. It's what the 'experts' mean when they say 'turnover is vanity, profit is sanity'.

If you're keen to offer discounted prices to beat the competition and incentivise customers, you need to claw that profit back elsewhere. Most retailers have some items, often referred to as 'loss leaders', that they use to pull in trade. Don't take this too literally, loss leaders should be sold at cost price, never at a loss. Look to do it with core items or where there's little margin to be made anyway.

If you can't compete on price, consider what else you can offer to incentivise customers, such as a gift with every purchase or free delivery on items over a certain price. Assess your customer service and look at ways you can improve this – your customers are likely to appreciate excellent service over cheaper prices.

In my experience

Don't think you have to always monitor the competition – it's just as important that you do a great job yourself.

Company: Naked Wines
Owner–manager: Rowan Gormley

Growing and improving your business

If you have survived the start-up phase and successfully launched your business then well done. But the hard work doesn't stop there and you may be wondering how to take your business to the next level and grow it beyond its current status. There are numerous options available to help you improve your business, but much will depend on the type of business you have, and how much money, time and effort you are willing to put in. You'll need to ensure you continue to generate healthy sales for the business too.

You could consider taking on staff, or if you have done so already, recruiting additional ones, which could free up your time if you want to look at branching out into other areas and diversifying your product offering. Revisit your supplier contracts and assess your current deals and find out whether you can get a better deal elsewhere. Getting quality, affordable stock is essential in making your business profitable and you'll find that most of your suppliers will be happy to negotiate over prices. Even though the UK is technically out of a recession, business can still be hard to come by. Another option for growing your business is to merge

Startups Tips

Keep a close eye on the competition and if you can't compete with them on price for example, look at other areas you can improve on. Customer service on the web can be just as important as price.

 From the experts

Company: **LinkedIn**
Owner-manager: **Reid Hoffman**

When you turn a company profitable you've gone from a company whose days are numbered to a company whose days can be infinite.

or acquire another online business. This could potentially widen your customer and your product base, as well as giving you access to new or different technology that could help improve your overall business.

Above all, ensure you keep the cash flowing. Debt is not necessarily a bad thing for small firms attempting to grow, but it is essential that you keep up with repayments or you risk putting your business at risk. Try to negotiate repayments so that you can pay in instalments at a time that suits you best and revisit all your service agreements to date to see whether there are any areas where you can reduce costs.

Startups checklist

- Any kind of diversification away from your core business is likely to carry some risk.
- Consider if you can compete on areas other than price.
- Getting quality, affordable stock is key to making your business profitable.
- To grow your business, you could consider merging or acquiring another one.
- Ensure you keep the cash flowing as debts will put your business at risk.

Appendix

SWOT analysis table

Strengths	Weaknesses
• Why should you succeed? • What do you do well? • Why do customers say they enjoy doing business with you? • What distinct advantages does your company offer? • What are your USPs?	• What could be improved about the business? • Is the market strong enough? • Do you have enough/good enough staff on board? • Are your management skills up to scratch? • Do you have enough finance to make it work? • What stumbling blocks do you continue to encounter? • What does your company do that can be improved? • What should be avoided? • What do your competitors do better than you?
S	**W**
O	**T**
Opportunities	**Threats**
• Where are the openings for your business? • Has the market significantly changed recently? • What customer needs are not being met by your competitors?	• What is your competition doing that could take business away from you or stunt your company's growth? • How might your competition react to any moves you make? • What trends in the market do you see that could wipe you out or make your business obsolete? • Might technology changes threaten your products or services? Or your job? • Do you have a stable relationship with suppliers or partners?

Market analysis example for an online lingerie business

Competitors	Number of years established	Price bracket (eg average cost of an underwear set)	Their strengths	Their weaknesses	Your USPs/What you offer the market
High street retailers/with or without internet presence	20	£15	Recognised brand, well established, opportunity to try on pieces	For those without internet presence, limited by choice and opening hours	Sizes that can't be found on the high street
Specialist mail order	15	£12	Wide choice of items	Impersonal service	Ability to look at different colours online and use a 'virtual model' to try on pieces
Other online lingerie business	3	£25	Unusual designs, not found on the high street, easy to find sizes	Prices are high	Aim to offer more unusual pieces but at a more favourable price

Financial budget plan

Startup costs	Estimated cost
Business registration fees	
Initial stock	
Down payments on equipment	
Website design fees	
Technology infrastructure	
Utility set-up fees	
Operating costs	
Your salary	
Rent or mortgage payments	
Telecommunications	
Utilities	
Stock	
Storage	
Shipping /Distribution	
Promotion	
Loan payments	
Office supplies	
Maintenance	
Professional services (such as accountancy fees)	
Website maintenance	

Balance sheet example

	£
Fixed assets	
Intangible assets	1,500
Tangible assets	25,000
Investments	500
	27,000
Current assets	
Cash in hand and at bank	5,500
Stock	7,000
Debtors	8,000
	20,500
Creditors: Amounts falling due within one year	
Bank loans and overdrafts	1,500
Trade creditors	3,000
Other creditors including tax and social security	1,000
	5,500
Net current assets	15,000
Total assets less current liabilities	42,000
Creditors: amounts falling due after more than one year	
Bank loan	2,000
Net assets	40,000
Capital and reserves	
Called up share capital	35,000
Profit and loss account	5,000
Shareholders' funds	

Cashflow forecast

	Month 1	Month 2	Month 3	Month 4	Month 5	Month 6	Month 7	Month 8	Month 9	Month 10	Month 11	Month 12	YTD
Receipts													
Debtors	8,297	8,572	6,798	7,569	7,719	8,071	7,765	7,175	6,179	7,637	5,978	7,173	88,933
Cash	276	421	1,403	1,386	874	835	1,142	1,607	1,946	818	2,036	918	13,662
TOTAL RECEIPTS	**8,573**	**8,993**	**8,201**	**8,955**	**8,593**	**8,906**	**8,907**	**8,782**	**8,125**	**8,455**	**8,014**	**8,091**	**102,595**
Payments													
Purchases	1,687	1,967	2,173	2,469	2,284	2,982	2,642	2,381	2,974	3,129	2,367	2,894	29,949
Rent	2,160	-	-	2,160	-	-	2,160	-	-	2,160	-	-	8,640
Rates ft utilities	528	528	528	528	528	528	528	528	528	528	528	528	6,336
Telephone	-	-	509	-	-	521	-	-	539	-	-	517	2,086
Wages ft Salaries	2,750	2,750	2,750	2,750	2,750	2,750	2,750	2,750	2,750	2,750	2,750	2,750	33,000
PAYE	1,018	1,018	1,018	1,018	1,018	1,018	1,018	1,018	1,018	1,018	1,018	1,018	12,216
VAT	102	-	-	47	-	-	156	-	-	174	-	-	479
TOTAL Payments	**8,245**	**6,263**	**6,978**	**8,972**	**6,580**	**7,799**	**9,254**	**6,677**	**7,809**	**9,759**	**6,663**	**7,707**	**92,706**
NET OPERATING CASH FLOW	**328**	**2,730**	**1,223**	**(17)**	**2,013**	**1,107**	**(347)**	**2,105**	**316**	**(1,304)**	**1,351**	**384**	**9,889**
Fixed Asset purchases	539				1,299				3,675				5,513
Loan repayments													-
Net cash inflow/(outflow)	**(211)**	**2,730**	**1,223**	**(17)**	**714**	**1,107**	**(347)**	**2,105**	**(3,359)**	**(1,304)**	**1,351**	**384**	**4,376**
OPENING BANK BALANCE	1,628	1,417	4,147	5,370	5,353	6,067	7,174	6,827	8,932	5,573	4,269	5,620	1,628
CLOSING BANK BALANCE	1,417	4,147	5,370	5,353	6,067	7,174	6,827	8,932	5,573	4,269	5,620	6,004	6,004

Web analytics report sample for online lingerie business

Visitor profile	Last visited	Average visit duration	Visits	Repeat rate
Viewed special offers	January 20, 2011 at 12.43pm	2 minutes and 40 seconds	7,890	23%
Registered for newsletter	January 20, 2011 at 5.15pm	1 minute and 10 seconds	550	25%
Clicked through promotion on home page	January 25, 2011 at 9.05am	50 seconds	6,789	37%
Purchased online	January 27, 2011 at 11.50pm	6 minutes and 10 seconds	290	35%

Index

V

VAT *152–53*, *278–79*
Virus protection *126*

W

Web analytics *211–13*, *297*
Web design *117–23*

Web hosting *(see hosts)*
Wholesalers *156–57*, *234–35*
Widgets *223*

Y

Yahoo! *205*, *211*, *212*
YouTube *103*, *219–20*, *221–22*

startups

build a better business

Every year we help 1 million start-up and small business owners

ONLINE >

"You'd be mad not to look at this site if you want to start a business"

The Times

10,000 pages of trusted, expert business advice

FORUM >

Join our lively community to support all your start-up efforts

startups.co.uk/forum

Over **37,000** members

AWARDS >

Celebrating the UK's best start-up businesses

startupsawards.co.uk

16 categories championing true talent

---

www.startups.co.uk There's no better place to start than Startups